THE PRACTITIONER'S GUIDE TO DATA QUALITY IMPROVEMENT

Morgan Kaufmann OMG Press

Morgan Kaufmann Publishers and the Object Management Group™ (OMG) have joined forces to publish a line of books addressing business and technical topics related to OMG's large suite of software standards.

OMG is an international, open membership, not-for-profit computer industry consortium that was founded in 1989. The OMG creates standards for software used in government and corporate environments to enable interoperability and to forge common development environments that encourage the adoption and evolution of new technology. OMG members and its board of directors consist of representatives from a majority of the organizations that shape enterprise and Internet computing today.

OMG's modeling standards, including the Unified Modeling Language™ (UML®) and Model Driven Architecture® (MDA), enable powerful visual design, execution and maintenance of software, and other processes—for example, IT Systems Modeling and Business Process Management. The middleware standards and profiles of the Object Management Group are based on the Common Object Request Broker Architecture® (CORBA) and support a wide variety of industries.

More information about OMG can be found at *http://www.omg.org/*.

Morgan Kaufmann OMG Press Titles

Real-Life MDA: Solving Business Problems with Model Driven Architecture
Michael Guttman and John Parodi

Systems Engineering with SysML/UML: Modeling, Analysis, Design
Tim Weilkiens

Building the Agile Enterprise: With SOA, BPM and MBM
Fred Cummins

Business Modeling: A Practical Guide to Realizing Business Value
Dave Bridgeland and Ron Zahavi

Architecture Driven Modernization: A Series of Industry Case Studies
Bill Ulrich

Information Systems Transformation: Architecture-Driven Modernization Case Studies
Bill Ulrich and Philip H. Newcomb

THE PRACTITIONER'S GUIDE TO DATA QUALITY IMPROVEMENT

DAVID LOSHIN

AMSTERDAM • BOSTON • HEIDELBERG • LONDON
NEW YORK • OXFORD • PARIS • SAN DIEGO
SAN FRANCISCO • SINGAPORE • SYDNEY • TOKYO

Morgan Kaufmann Publishers is an imprint of Elsevier

Acquiring Editor: Jenifer Niles
Development Editor: David Bevans
Project Manager: Julie Ochs and Laura Smith
Designer: Kristen Davis

Morgan Kaufmann is an imprint of Elsevier
30 Corporate Drive, Suite 400, Burlington, MA 01803, USA

Notices
Knowledge and best practice in this field are constantly changing. As new research and
experience broaden our understanding, changes in research methods or professional
practices, may become necessary. Practitioners and researchers must always rely on their
own experience and knowledge in evaluating and using any information or methods
described herein. In using such information or methods they should be mindful of their own
safety and the safety of others, including parties for whom they have a professional
responsibility.

To the fullest extent of the law, neither the Publisher nor the authors, contributors, or editors,
assume any liability for any injury and/or damage to persons or property as a matter of
products liability, negligence or otherwise, or from any use or operation of any methods,
products, instructions, or ideas contained in the material herein.

Library of Congress Cataloging-in-Publication Data
Application submitted

British Library Cataloguing-in-Publication Data
A catalogue record for this book is available from the British Library.

ISBN: 978-0-12-373717-5

Printed in the United States of America
10 11 12 13 14   10 9 8 7 6 5 4 3 2 1

For information on all MK publications visit our website at www.mkp.com

CONTENTS

FOREWORD

In my job, I work with a very large number of organizations interested in making progress on minimizing or even completely removing their data quality issues. The diversity of their circumstances is amazing – organizations of different sizes, industries, and structures, all with burning data quality issues that impact their businesses in a variety of different ways and in various business functions and processes. Even the manner in which they plan to attack these issues, from the approach to building a business case to the tactics of data quality issue resolution, are all over the map.

But the one thing that all of these organizations have in common is their desire for practical, easily implemented, and immediately effective approaches to making progress on their issues. In effect, they are asking "how?" How to get started. How to scope. How to engage the right people. How to benchmark the current state of data quality. And most importantly, how to generate business value from their efforts. They want practical and effective tactics that they can readily apply.

I also read a lot of books on the topic of data quality improvement. Many people write about this discipline in the abstract. Much of that writing is highly theoretical or even academic in nature. It's great if you want to understand the high-level principles and the philosophy of how data quality can be optimized in a perfect world. But of course we don't live in a perfect world, and therefore we need practical approaches that can be directly translated into effective action in our organizations – action that will get our data quality improvement initiatives off on the right foot and generate immediate business value.

In this book, David Loshin has done a great job of delivering such practical approaches. He covers the fundamental building blocks of a solid data quality improvement program, with a focus on organizational approaches, key processes, and the role of technology. From my point of view, that is exactly the right sequence of priorities that organizations need to adopt. First, get the right people involved and ensure they have the right skills (organization). Next, give those people prescribed and repeatable activities to execute (process). And then support them with tools when and where it makes sense (technology). And of increasing importance is the role that data quality improvement plays in critical related initiatives, such as data governance, master data management, and broader enterprise information management.

Being a practitioner's guide, the content is presented in terminology that is readily understood by both business and IT professionals, and with concrete examples and advice that readers will be able to map to their own situations. This is key – data quality improvement is not the domain of IT alone, and it requires strong leadership and engagement by the business. Organizations that are brand new to the discipline need these fundamentals to guide their early efforts. Organizations with extensive experience tackling data quality issues will also benefit from these principles as they tune up and broaden the scope of their efforts.

Data quality improvement is a great discipline to be working in – especially now, when data is increasingly viewed as the most critical of assets. Achieving success is also incredibly hard. It takes passion, focus, and a whole lot of persistence. It also requires a solid grasp of the fundamentals and an ability to harness effective tactics. Apply the insights in this book and you'll be well on the way to having the most important weapons in hand. Best wishes for success in your ongoing data quality improvement efforts.

Ted Friedman
Vice-President and Distinguished Analyst
Gartner Inc.

PREFACE

Having worked as a data quality practitioner for the past 15 years, I have noticed a significant change in the ways that we can approach data quality management. Data quality is rapidly transitioning from an industry dominated by simplistic approaches to name and address cleansing to one that more closely mirrors a business productivity management environment. The growing recognition that high quality data more efficiently fuels the achievement of business objectives implies that the need to develop an enterprise data quality program.

But in order to build this program, one needs more than name and address cleansing tools. Instead, one needs the basic policies, processes, and maturity that contribute to the management and governance framework for maintaining measurably high-quality data. This book is intended to provide the fundamentals for developing the enterprise data quality program, and is intended to guide both the manager and the practitioner in establishing operational data quality control throughout an organization, with particular focus on:

- The ability to build a business case for instituting a data quality program;
- The assessment of levels of data quality maturity;
- The guidelines and techniques for evaluating data quality and identifying metrics related to the achievement of business objectives;
- The techniques for measuring, reporting, and taking action based on these metrics; and
- The policies and processes used in exploiting data quality tools and technologies for data quality improvement.

Data Quality Knowledge Transfer

In order to transfer the knowledge that our company has accumulated over the years, I am assembling this book to help those individuals tasked with roles in areas such as data quality, data governance, master data management, customer data integration, as well as a host of other data management roles succeed in these types of activities:

- Building a business case for establishing a data quality program

- Developing a strategy for enterprise data quality management, data governance, and data stewardship
- Developing an implementation plan
- Assigning roles and responsibilities
- Developing policies and procedures for data quality assessment, data quality metrics, and ongoing monitoring and reporting
- Using data quality tools and technology
- Building a data standards management program
- Monitoring data quality and performance trends

Why You Should Still Buy "Enterprise Knowledge Management – The Data Quality Approach"

Although my 2001 book "Enterprise Knowledge Management – The Data Quality Approach" (EKM) provided valuable insight into the mechanics of business rule-based data quality management, that book focused largely on the technical aspects of data quality, with a smaller concentration on the business and organizational aspects of data quality management. In the years since EKM's publication there have been new developments and interests in data quality management whose treatments would not just complement the material in EKM, but also present new material to a much wider audience comprised of both a business and technical bent.

When EKM was written in 1999-2000, the use of data profiling tools was limited to early adopters, and although we provided insight into the technology in EKM, we did not refer to it using its now commonly accepted name. At that time, many data quality initiatives were triggered by reaction to negative data quality events. Today there is a great desire for a business model that justifies an investment in a data quality program to help assess current gaps and provide a framework for targeting performance improvements.

In the late 1990s and early 2000s, data quality was seen as a "patch" to correct flawed data warehouse implementations. Today, data quality and data governance are more tightly integrated across both analytical and operational applications and the lines of business those applications serve. The value of standardized data definition and a process for reaching consensus in defining common business terms has emerged as one of the most important factors in information management; though

EKM did not have a large section on this notion, this Practitioner's Guide will discuss this topic in great detail.

However, EKM has had a long shelf life, especially because it was intended to provide a broad overview of the *data quality technology.* **And even though some of the topics are covered very similarly in this Practitioner's Guide, it is intended to be a companion to rather than replacement for EKM.**

Why You Should Buy "Master Data Management"

I actually started writing this Practitioner's Guide in 2006. So why did it take so long to finish? Well, in the middle of writing this book it occurred to me that you guys were looking for a good guidebook about master data management (MDM), a topic that has been growing in importance since around 2005. I stopped working on this book and quickly put my thoughts together on MDM and turned them into a book called "Master Data Management," which was published in 2008. That book picks up where this book's chapter 19 ends, and if MDM is in your future, it would be worth getting a copy of that book also.

Putting My Money Where My Mouth Is

More to the point: in the 10 years that have elapsed since EKM was published, I have devoted myself to helping organizations strategically improve organization information quality. My prior experiences in failed data management activities drove me to quit my last "real job" (as I like to say) and start my own consulting practice to prove that there are better ways to make data quality happen. My company, Knowledge Integrity, Inc. (www.knowledge-integrity.com), was developed to help organizations form successful information quality, data governance, and master data management programs. As a way of distinguishing my effort from other consulting companies, I also instituted a few important corporate rules about the way we would do business:

1. Our mission would be to develop and popularize methods for enterprise data quality improvement. As opposed to the craze for patenting technology, methods, and processes, we would openly publish our ideas so as to benefit anyone willing to invest the time and energy to internalize the ideas we were promoting.

2. We would encourage clients to adopt our methods within their success patterns. It is a challenge (and perhaps in a way, insulting) to walk into an organization and tell people who have done their jobs successfully that they need to drop what they are doing and change every aspect of the way they work. We believe that every organization has its own methods for success, and our job is to craft a way to integrate performance-based information quality management into the existing organizational success structure.

3. We would not establish ourselves as permanent fixtures. We believe that information quality management is a core competency that should be managed within the organization, and our goal for each engagement is to establish the fundamental aspects of the program, transfer technology to internal resources, and then be on our way. I often say that if we do our job right, we work ourselves out of a contract.

4. We are not "selling a product," we are engaged in solving customer problems. We are less concerned about rigid compliance to a trademarked methodology than we are about making sure that the customer's core issues are resolved, and if that means adapting our methods to the organization's, that is the most appropriate way to get things done. I also like to say that we are successful when the client comes up with our ideas.

5. Effective communication is the key to changing management. Articulating how good information management techniques enhance organizational effectiveness and performance is the first step in engaging business clients and ensuring their support and sponsorship. We would invest part of every engagement in establishing a strong business case accompanied by collateral information that can be socialized within and across the enterprise.

With these rules in mind, our first effort was to consolidate our ideas for semantic, rule-oriented data quality management in a book, "Enterprise Knowledge Management – The Data Quality Approach," which was published in 2001 by Morgan Kaufmann. I have been told by a number of readers that the book is critical in their development of a data quality management program, and the new technical ideas proposed for rule-based data quality monitoring have, in the intervening years, been integrated into all of the major data quality vendor product suites.

Over the subsequent years, we have developed a graduate level course on data quality for New York University and multiple day-courses for The Data Warehousing Institute (www.tdwi.org);

presented numerous sessions at conferences and chapter meetings for DAMA (the Data Management Association); provided columns for Robert Seiner's Data Administration Newsletter (www.tdan.com), monthly columns for DM Review (www.information-management.com), and a downloadable course on data quality from BetterManagement (www.bettermanagement.com); and hosted an expert channel and monthly newsletter at the BeyeNETWORK (www.b-eye-network.com).

We are frequently asked by vendors across the spectrum to provide analysis and thought leadership in many areas of data management. We have consulted in the public sector for federal, state, and other global government agencies. We have guided data quality management and data governance in a number of industries, including financial services, health care, manufacturing, oil and mining services, insurance, and social services.

Since we started the company, the awareness of the value of information quality management has been revealed to be one of the most important topics that senior management faces. In practices that have emerged involving the exploitation of enterprise data, such as Enterprise Resource Planning (ERP), Supply Chain Management (SCM), and Customer Relationship Management (CRM), there is a need for a consolidated view of high quality representations of every critical instance of a business concept. Increased regulatory oversight, increased need for information exchange, business performance management, and the value of service-oriented architecture are driving a greater focus on performance-oriented management of enterprise data with respect to accessibility, consistency, currency, freshness, and usability of a common information asset.

Overview of the Book

This book contains three parts:
- Part 1 (chapters 1-5) focuses on the organizational aspects of data quality: understanding the impacts of poor data quality, aspects of a data quality program, organizational preparedness and maturity, the place of enterprise data quality among other enterprise initiatives, developing a business case, blueprint, and roadmap, and socializing data quality improvement as a valuable contributor to competitive advantage. The chapters are:
  - 1: Impacts of Poor Data Quality
  - 2: The Organizational Information Quality Program
  - 3: Data Quality Maturity

- 4: Integration with Complementary Initiatives
- 5: Preparation, Planning, and the Information Quality Road Map
- Part 2 (chapters 6-13) looks at implementing the core processes of a data quality program: metrics and data quality performance improvement, data governance, defining dimensions of data quality, data requirements analysis, data standards, metadata management, data quality assessment, remediation, and data quality service level agreements. The chapters are:
  - 6: Metrics and Performance Improvement
  - 7: Data Governance and Performance Management
  - 8: Dimensions of Data Quality
  - 9: Data Requirements Analysis
  - 10: Data Standards, Metadata, and Business Rules
  - 11: Data Quality Assessment
  - 12: Data Quality Remediation and Improvement
  - 13: Inspection, Monitoring, and Tracking
- Part 3 (chapters 14-19) looks at the types of tools, techniques, algorithms, and other technologies are employed to support the data quality processes described in part 2. This includes data profiling, parsing and standardization, identity resolution, auditing and monitoring, data enhancement, and master data management. The chapters are::
  - 14: Data Profiling
  - 15: Parsing and Standardization
  - 16: Entity Identity Resolution
  - 17: Auditing, Monitoring, and Tracking
  - 18: Data Enhancement
  - 19: Master Data Management

Finally, the last chapter (20: Bringing It All Together) reviews the concepts discussed throughout the book and can be used as a handy quick guide for the data quality practitioner.

Contact Me

While my intention is to provide a guidebook that the data quality practitioner can use to assemble the data quality program from start to finish, there are situations where some expert advice helps get the ball rolling. The practices and approaches described in this book are abstracted from numerous real client engagements, and our broad experience may be able to jump-start your mission for data quality improvement. In the spirit of openness, I am always happy to answer questions, provide some additional details, and hear feedback about the approaches that

I have put in this book and that Knowledge Integrity has employed successfully with our clients since 1999.

We are always looking for opportunities to help organizations establish the business case for data quality and help get them started on the road to data quality management, so I mean that. I really want to hear from you.

I can be reached via my email address, loshin@knowledge-integrity.com, through Knowledge Integrity's company website, www.knowledge-integrity.com, via www.davidloshin.info, or through the website I have set up for this book, www.dataqualitybook.com.

ACKNOWLEDGMENTS

What is presented in this book is a culmination of years of experience in projects and programs associated with master data management tools, techniques, processes, and people. A number of people were key contributors to the development of this book, and I take this opportunity to thank them for their support:

First of all, my wonderful wife Jill deserves the most credit for perseverance and for her encouragement in completing the book. I also must thank my children, Kira, Jonah, Brianna, Gabriella, and Emma for their help as well.

Richard Ordowich, one of the principal consultants from Knowledge Integrity, has contributed a significant number of ideas to furthering the creation of a data quality management program, and for a number of years has acted as both a springboard and a critic.

Critical parts of this book were inspired by works that I was commissioned to assemble for vendors in the data quality and master data management spaces, such as DataFlux, Informatica, IBM, Initiate Systems, Microsoft, and Pitney Bowes Business Insight. Additional invaluable sources include material presented through my expert channel at www.b-eye-network.com and at conferences hosted by Wilshire Conferences, DebTech International, The Data Warehousing Institute, and MDM-DQ University and vendor-hosted webinars and live events.

Folks at Dataflux provided significant input during the process: Tony Fisher, Katie Fabiszak, Daniel Teachey, James Goodfellow, and Dan Soceanu.

Ted Friedman from Gartner has always provided feedback and ideas about the data quality industry and how management processes and best practices supplement tools.

Marty Moseley, Chief Technology Officer at Initiate Systems has provided some insights over the years on data governance and master data management.

My involvement with the folks at the Business Intelligence Network (www.b-eye-network.com), especially Ron Powell, Shawn Rogers, Jean Schauer, and Mary Jo Nott (to name only a few) has provided me with a platform to develop material relevant to this book.

Special thanks to Tony Shaw at Wilshire Conferences, presenters of the annual DAMA/Meta-Data and Data Governance conferences, The Data Warehousing Institute, and Davida Berger at DebTech International for allowing me to develop and teach courses supporting the concepts in this book. And very special thanks to our clients, such as Greg Wibben, who provided us with an environment for demonstrating the value of the processes in this book.

Thanks to the list of Elsevier editors for this book, including Diane Cerra, Greg Chalson, and Rick Adams.

ABOUT THE AUTHOR

David Loshin is President of Knowledge Integrity, Inc., a company specializing in data management consulting. The author of numerous books on performance computing and data management, including *Master Data Management* (2008), and *Business Intelligence – The Savvy Manager's Guide* (2003), and creator of courses and tutorials on all facets of data management best practices, David is often looked to for thought leadership in the information management industry.

BUSINESS IMPACTS OF POOR DATA QUALITY

Most organizations today depend on the use of data in two general ways. Standard business processes use data for executing transactions, as well as supporting operational activities. Business analysts review data captured as a result of day-to-day operations through reports and analysis engines as a way of identifying new opportunities for efficiency or growth. In other words, data is used to both *run* and *improve* the ways that organizations achieve their business objectives. If that is true, then there must be processes in place to ensure that data is of sufficient quality to meet the business needs. Therefore, it is of great value to any enterprise risk management program to incorporate a program that includes processes for assessing, measuring, reporting, reacting to, and controlling the risks associated with poor data quality.

Flaws in any process are bound to introduce risks to successfully achieving the objectives that drive your organization's daily activities. If the flaws are introduced in a typical manufacturing process that takes raw input and generates a single output, the risks of significant impact might be mitigated by closely controlling the quality of the process, overseeing the activities from end to end, and making sure that any imperfections can be identified as early as possible. Information, however, is an asset that is generated through numerous processes, with multiple feeds of raw data that are combined, processed, and fed out to multiple customers both inside and outside your organization. Because data is of a much more dynamic nature, created and used across the different operational and analytical applications, there are additional challenges in establishing ways to assess the risks related to data failures as well as ways to monitor conformance to business user expectations.

This uncovers a deeper question: to what extent does the introduction of flawed data impact the way that your organization does business? While it is probably easy to point to specific *examples* of where unexpected data led to business problems, there is bound to be real evidence of hard impacts that can be directly associated with poor quality data. Anecdotes are strong motivators in that they raise awareness of data quality as an issue, but our intention is to develop a performance management framework that helps to identify, isolate, measure, and improve the value of data within the environment. The problem is that the magnitude and challenge of correlating business impacts with data failures appear to be too large to be able to manage – thus the reliance on anecdotes to justify an investment in good data management practices.

But we can compare the job of characterizing the impacts of poor data quality to eating an elephant: it seems pretty big, but if we can carve it down into small enough chunks, it can be done one bite at a time. To be able to communicate the value of data quality improvement, it is necessary to be able to characterize the loss of value that is attributable to poor data quality.

This requires some exploration into assembling the business case, namely:
- Reviewing the types of risks relating to the use of information,
- Considering ways to specify data quality expectations,
- Developing processes and tools for clarifying what data quality means,
- Defining data validity constraints,
- Measuring data quality, and
- Reporting and tracking data issues,

all contributing to performance management reporting using a data quality scorecard, to support the objectives of instituting data governance and data quality control.

Many business issues can be tied, usually directly, to a situation where data quality is below user expectations. Given some basic understanding of data use, information value, and the ways that information value degrades when data does not meet quality expectations, we can explore different categories of business impacts attributable to poor information quality, and discuss ways to facilitate identification and classification of cost impacts related to poor data quality. In this chapter we look at the types of risks that are attributable to poor data quality as well as an approach to correlating business impacts to data flaws.

1.1 Information Value and Data Quality Improvement

Is information an organizational asset? Certainly, if all a company does is accumulate and store data, there is some cost associated with the ongoing management of that data – the costs of storage, maintenance, office space, support staff, and so on – and this could show up on the balance sheet as a liability. Though it is unlikely that any corporation lists its data as a line item as either an asset or a liability on its balance sheet, there is no doubt that, because of a significant dependence on data to both run and improve the business, senior managers at most organizations certainly rely on their data as much as any other asset.

We can view data as an asset, since data can be used to provide benefits to the company, it is controlled by the organization, it is the result of a sequence of transactions (either as the result of internal data creation internally or external data acquisition), it incurs costs for acquisition and management, and it is used to create value. Data is not treated as an asset, though; for example, there is no depreciation schedule for purchased data.

On the other hand, the dependence of automated operational systems on data for processing clearly shows how data is used to create value. Transaction systems that manage the daily operations enable "business as usual." And when analytic systems are used for reporting, performance management, and discovery of new business opportunities, the value of that information is shown yet again. But it can be a challenge to assign a direct monetary value to any specific data value. For example, while a computing system may expect to see a complete record to be processed, a transaction may still be complete even in the absence of some of the data elements. Does this imply that those data elements have no value? Of course not, otherwise there would not have been an expectation for those elements to be populated in the first place.

There are different ways of looking at information value. The simplest approaches consider the cost of acquisition (i.e., the data is worth what we paid for it) or its market value (i.e., what someone is willing to pay for it). But in an environment where data is created, stored, processed, exchanged, shared, aggregated, and reused, perhaps the best approach for understanding information value is its *utility* – the expected value to be derived from the information.

That value can grow as a function of different aspects of the business, ranging from strictly operational to strategic. Sales transactions are necessary to complete the sales process, and therefore part of your sales revenues are related to the data used to process the transaction. Daily performance reports are used to identify and eliminate high-cost, low-productivity activities, and therefore the money saved is related to the data that composed the report. Streamlined processing systems that expect high-quality data can process many transactions without human intervention, and as the volume of processed transactions increases, the cost per transaction decreases, which represents yet another utility value for data.

All of these examples introduce an interesting point – while it may be difficult in most instances to directly assign a monetary value to a piece of data, it is possible to explore how the utility value changes when the data does not meet business client expectations. In other words, it is possible to analyze how data is being used for achieving business objectives, and how the achievement of those goals is impeded when flawed data is introduced into the environment. To do this, we must consider:

- What the business expectations are for data quality,
- How business can be impacted by poor data quality, and
- How to correlate business impacts to specific data quality issues.

1.2 Business Expectations and Data Quality

There is a common expectation that objective data quality improvement necessarily implies business value, giving the impetus for the topic often to appear as one of the top concerns of senior managers. Unfortunately, the limited awareness and understanding of what data quality improvement can truly imply often drives technical approaches that don't always translate into improving the business. For example, the concept of data quality often drives "golden copy," "single source of truth," or "data mastering" projects. This approach, though, does not take into account the fact that data quality is *subjective,* and relies on how data flaws are related to negative business impacts within your own organization.

Objective data quality metrics (such as number of invalid values or percentage of missing data elements) may not necessarily be tied to your business's performance, and this in turn raises some interesting questions:

- How do you distinguish high-impact from low-impact data quality issues?
- How do you isolate the source of the introduction of data flaws to fix the process instead of correcting the data?
- How do you correlate business value with source data quality?
- What is the best way to employ data quality best practices to address these questions?

This challenge can be characterized by a fundamental distinction between data quality expectations and business expectations. Data quality expectations are expressed as rules measuring aspects of the validity *of data values:*

- What data is missing or unusable?
- Which data values are in conflict?
- Which records are duplicated?
- What linkages are missing?

Alternatively, business expectations are expressed as rules measuring performance, productivity, and efficiency of *processes,* asking questions like*:*

- How has throughput decreased because of errors?
- What percentage of time is spent in reworking failed processes?
- What is the loss in value of transactions that failed because of missing data?
- How quickly can we respond to business opportunities?

To determine the true value added by data quality programs, conformance to business expectations (and the corresponding business value) should be measured in relation to its component data quality rules. We do this by identifying how the business impacts of poor data quality can be measured as well as how they relate to their root causes, then assess the costs to eliminate the root causes. Characterizing both the business impacts and the data quality problems provides a framework for developing a business case.

1.3 Qualifying Impacts

Data issues may occur within different business processes. The approach to analyze the degree to which poor data quality impedes business success should involve detailing business impacts, categorizing those impacts, and then prioritizing the issues in relation to the severity of the impacts.

Although data analysts typically are not trained in business analysis, a simplified approach allows one to classify the business impacts associated with data errors within a classification scheme. This categorization is intended to support the data quality analysis process and help in differentiating between data issues that have serious business ramifications and those that are benign. This classification scheme is a simple taxonomy listing primary categories for evaluating either the negative impacts related to data errors, or the potential opportunities for improvement resulting from improved data quality:

- Financial impacts, such as increased operating costs, decreased revenues, missed opportunities, reduction or delays in cash flow, or increased penalties, fines, or other charges
- Confidence and satisfaction-based impacts, such as customer, employee, or supplier satisfaction, as well as general market satisfaction, decreased organizational trust, low confidence in forecasting, inconsistent operational and management reporting, and delayed or improper decisions
- Productivity impacts, such as increased workloads, decreased throughput, increased processing time, or decreased end-product quality
- Risk and compliance impacts associated with credit assessment, investment risks, competitive risk, capital investment and/or development, fraud, and leakage, and compliance with government regulations, industry expectations, or self-imposed policies (such as privacy policies)

Even though individuals tend to concentrate on what amounts to financial impact, risk, compliance, and productivity are also often compromised by the introduction of data quality issues. For example, in the financial service industry, there is particularly sensitivity to compliance:

- Anti–money laundering aspects of the Bank Secrecy Act and the USA PATRIOT Act have mandated that private organizations take steps to identify and prevent money laundering activities that could be used in financing terrorist activities.
- Section 302 of the Sarbanes–Oxley Act mandates that the principal executive officer or officers and the principal financial officer or officers certify the accuracy and correctness of financial reports.
- Basel II Accords provide guidelines for defining regulations as well as guiding the quantification of operational and credit risk as a way to determine the amount of capital financial institutions are required to maintain as a guard against those risks.

- The Gramm–Leach–Bliley Act mandates that financial institutions are obligated to "respect the privacy of its customers and to protect the security and confidentiality of those customers' nonpublic personal information."
- Credit risk assessment requires accurate documentation to evaluate an individual's or organization's abilities to repay loans.
- System development risks associated with capital investment in deploying new application systems emerge when moving those systems into production is delayed because of lack of trust in the application's underlying data assets.

Although the sources of these areas of risk differ, one similarity becomes clear: not only do these mandate the use or presentation of high quality information, they also require means of demonstrating the adequacy of internal controls overseeing that quality. Organizations must be able to assess, measure, and control the quality of data as well as have the means for external auditors to verify those observations. Ultimately, the objective is to maximize the value of the information based on reducing the negative impacts associated with each set of potential problems. In turn, determining when and where poor information quality affects one or more of the variables that contribute to these categories becomes the core task of developing a business justification for data quality improvement.

1.4 Some Examples

The general approach to correlating business impacts to data quality issues is not new. Here are some interesting examples showing a variety of situations in which data flaws contributed to serious risks and impacts.

1.4.1 Credit Risk

Managing credit risk is an important task in any business, particularly with respect to supplier management and spend analysis. A 2002 survey on credit risk data performed by PricewaterhouseCoopers suggested that a significant percentage of the top banks were deficient in credit risk data management. Areas of particular concern included counterparty data repositories, counterparty hierarchy data, common counterparty identifiers, and consistent data standards [1].

[1] R.J. Inserro, Credit Risk Data Challenges Underlying the New Basel Capital Accord, The RMA Journal (April 2002), accessible at http://www.pwc.com/tr/eng/about/svcs/abas/frm/creditrisk/articles/pwc_baselcreditdata-rma.pdf.

1.4.2 Fraudulent Disbursements

In an example in which data is deliberately introduced or modified, the Association of Certified Fraud Examiners noted in their 2006 Report to the Nation [2] a number of different methods that employees use to generate fraudulent payments. As a by-product of employees introducing incorrect or invalid data, there is an increase in improper disbursements, and the report provides details about the costs associated with these fraudulent payments.

1.4.3 Payroll Overpayments

Attempting to link business impacts to data quality issues is not a new idea, as can be seen by the way the U.S. Department of Defense (DoD) categorized business impacts in their "Guidelines on Data Quality" in 1997. The DoD looked at four specific areas: prevention, appraisal, internal failure, and external failure, and then sought to correlate impacts and their relative costs in relation to the types of data errors that occurred. By looking at the types of data errors, it was suggested that it would be reasonable to assess the value improvement that could be gained by correcting problems as opposed to costs incurred by ignoring them, and then determine the next steps. By iteratively refining the types of costs (e.g., direct versus indirect costs), analysts could get a better idea about prioritizing remediation tasks. For example, the report documents how poor data quality impacts specific business processes: ". . . the inability to match payroll records to the official employment record can cost millions in payroll overpayments to deserters, prisoners, and 'ghost' soldiers. In addition, the inability to correlate purchase orders to invoices is a major problem in unmatched disbursements" [3].

1.4.4 Underbilling and Revenue Assurance

NTL, a cable operator in the United Kingdom, sought to apply data quality techniques in order to improve efficiency of an operator's network and found that invalid data was responsible for discrepancies between services provided and services invoiced.

[2] 2006 ACFE Report to the Nation on Occupational Fraud and Abuse, accessible at http://www.acfe.com/documents/2006-rttn.pdf.

[3] DoD Guidelines on Data Quality Management, U.S. Dept. of Defense, 1997, accessible via http://www.tricare.mil/ocfo/_docs/DoDGuidelinesOnDataQualityManagement.pdf.

The result was an exposure of wasted, "unknown" capacity as well as underbilling. In turn, they were able to achieve a return on investment – the data quality improvement program was essentially self-funded by analyzing "revenue assurance to detect underbilling. For example, ... results indicated leakage of just over 3 percent of total revenue" [4].

1.4.5 Insurance Exposure

A 2008 survey prepared by consulting company Ernst & Young attempted to bring to light the importance of data quality specifically within the insurance industry. The report noted that "shortcomings in exposure data quality are common," and that "not many insurers are doing enough to correct these shortcomings." The report called out some specific types of data flaws, including missing or inaccurate values associated with insured values, locations, building class, and occupancy class, as well as additional characteristics [5].

1.4.6 Development Risk

Often, business applications that do not meet expectations are scheduled for renovation or replacement. However, if the root cause of the application failure is due to inherent data issues, leading to organizational mistrust, updating the application will not eliminate the source of missed expectations. We have seen a common pattern in which a financial investment in hardware, software, and resources for software development has been made to renovate business application systems, yet the deployment of those systems is delayed (or perhaps even canceled) because of organizational mistrust of the underlying data. We call this a development risk, since the cost and the potential value of the new application cannot be actualized until the data issues have been resolved.

1.4.7 Integration Risks

When attempting to assemble a comprehensive "system of record," or a master data management program, it is important to be able to integrate data from across many different systems.

[4] B. Herbert, Data Quality Management – A Key to Operator Profitability, Billing and OSS World (March 2006), accessible at http://www.billingworld.com/articles/feature/ Data-Quality-Management-A-Key-to-Operator.html.
[5] Ernst & Young, Raising the Bar on Catastrophe Data, 2008, accessible via http:// www.acordlondon.org/Documents/Ernst_Young_Catastrophe_Exposure_Data_Quality_ Survey.pdf.

Errors and flaws in the data impact the consolidation process when they are left unaddressed and will require additional (and unusually unexpected) effort for remediation before integration.

1.4.8 Health Risks

In the health care world, there can be serious health risks associated with incorrect data. An obvious severe example is the 2003 case of heart transplant patient Jesica Santillan, where inaccurate information regarding blood typing resulted in a botched heart–lung transplant, which not only led to the girl's death, but also prevented other critically ill patients from receiving needed donated organs. Although there may be disagreements about the number of critical events that are attributable to medical errors, discrepancies related to incorrect or invalid information are often identifiable as the root cause.

1.4.9 Policy Management Risks

More often, information policies expressed through external channels introduce constraints. For example, privacy, security, and limitation of use are introduced within governmental dictates, at the national; state or provincial; and county, municipal, or jurisdictional (e.g., courts) levels. As an example of privacy risk, in the Health Insurance Portability and Accountability Act of 1996 (HIPAA), the regulatory aspect underscores health insurers' ethical responsibility to ensure patient privacy. Properly capturing and managing data related to with whom an individual's health information may be shared impact many aspects of that person's life, ranging from protection against physical abuse to employment discrimination, among others.

1.4.10 Fraud Risks

Exposure to operational fraud may be masqueraded throughout your applications when fraudulent behavior is performed to exploit information failures within the system. The lack of quality of ensuring unique identification of individuals, orders, and so on, enables unscrupulous characters to run roughshod over your business. The challenge many institutions are facing can be illustrated by a simple example: a few years ago a man was able to fool the computer fraud programs at two music-by-mail clubs by using 1630 aliases. He repeatedly exploited the clubs' introductory offers that typically provided a large number of free CDs with the purchase of one CD at the regular price, then resold the discs at a profit.

1.5 More on Impact Classification

Classifying the business impacts helps to identify discrete issues and relate business value to high quality data, so it is valuable to delve deeper and look more closely at each impact category and provide some subcategories and examples. Impacts can be assessed within each subcategory, and the process is to determine a means for quantification as the area of impact is iteratively refined. Ultimately, a scorecard reporting the value of high quality data can be rolled up as a combination of separate measures associated with how specific data flaws prevent the achievement of business goals.

1.5.1 Financial

Financial impacts are associated with missing expectations associated with costs, financial management, and revenues. In Table 1.1, we show some of the subcategories of financial impacts, along with some specific examples.

Table 1.1 Subcategories of Financial Impacts

Subcategory	Examples
Direct operating expenses	Direct labor, materials used for fulfilling contractual obligations, subcontractor costs associated with fulfilling contractual obligations
General overhead	Rent, maintenance, asset purchase, asset utility, licensing, utilities, administrative staff, general procurement
Staff overhead	Staff necessary to run the business, such as clerical, sales management, field supervision, bids and proposals (B&P), recruiting, and training
Fees and charges	Bank fees, service charges, commissions, legal fees, accounting, penalties and fines, bad debt, merger and acquisition costs
Cost of goods sold	Design of products, raw materials, production, cost of inventory, inventory planning, marketing, sales, customer management, advertising, lead generation, promotional events, samples, order replacement, order fulfillment, shipping
Revenue	Customer acquisition, customer retention, churn, missed opportunities
Cash flow	Delayed customer invoicing, missed customer invoicing, ignored overdue customer payments, quick supplier payments, increased interest rates, Earnings Before Interest, Taxes, Depreciation, and Amortization (EBITDA)
Depreciation	Property market value, inventory markdown
Capitalization	Value of equity
Leakage	Collections, fraud, commissions, interorganizational settlement

1.5.2 Confidence and Satisfaction

Confidence and satisfaction impacts are linked to missing expectations associated with meeting expectations in the consumer marketplace or satisfying the internal ability to execute against strategy. In Table 1.2, we show some of the subcategories of confidence and satisfaction impacts, along with some specific examples.

1.5.3 Productivity

Productivity impacts are associated with hard measurements of operational efficiency. In Table 1.3, we show some of the subcategories of productivity impacts, along with some specific examples.

Table 1.2 Subcategories for Confidence and Satisfaction

Subcategory	Examples
Forecasting	Predictability of staffing, financial, material requirements, spending vs. budget
Reporting	Timeliness of reports, currency of reports, availability of reports, accuracy, need for reconciliation
Customer satisfaction	Sales costs, retention, purchases per customer, products per customer, sales costs, service costs, time to respond, referrals, new product suggestions
Employee satisfaction	Costs to recruit, hiring, retention, turnover, compensation

Table 1.3 Subcategories of Productivity

Subcategory	Examples
Workloads	Increased need for reconciliation of reports
Throughput	Increased time for data gathering and preparation, reduced time for direct data analysis, delays in delivering information products, lengthened production and manufacturing cycles
Output quality	Mistrusted reports
Supply chain	Out-of-stock products, delivery delays, missed deliveries, duplicate costs for product delivery

Table 1.4 Subcategories of Risk and Compliance Impacts

Subcategory	Examples
Regulatory	Reporting, protection of private information
Industry	Processing standards, exchange standards, operational standards
Safety	Health hazards, occupational hazards
Market	Competitiveness, goodwill, commodity risk, currency risk, equity risk, demand
Financial	Loan default risk, investment depreciation, noncompliance penalties
System	Delays in development, delays in deployment
Credit/underwriting	Credit risk, default, capacity, sufficiency of capitalization
Legal	Legal research, preparation of material

1.5.4 Risk and Compliance

These impacts, with some examples in Table 1.4, are associated with the ways that data issues can increase exposure to various risks, whether they are compliance risks, financial risks, or increased ability to execute in the marketplace.

1.6 Business Impact Analysis

This set of tasks is intended to document the impacts that are attributable to data quality. First, there may already be some existing documentation within an incident reporting system, so determine if there is a logging and tracking system for data quality issues. If there is, review each logged issue to note:

- The business function/role reporting the issue,
- How and at what point in the business process the issue was discovered,
- Who discovered the issue,
- Why this was reported and which business impacts are related to the issue,
- How the issue was remediated, and
- Any business rules or data quality checks recommended.

In addition, or if there is no data quality issue logging and tracking system, subject matter experts and representatives of the business functions should be interviewed to solicit descriptions of business impacts. The discussion with the subject matter expert is centered around "points of pain" and further drill-down to determine whether noted impacts are related to the use of data. An interview may take this form:

1. Open-ended request to describe most critical business application problems
2. For each problem, ask:
   a. What makes this a critical business problem? (assess level of criticality)
   b. What are the business impacts? (help quantify the issue)
   c. How is the business problem related to an application data issue? (establish a relationship with data)
   d. How often does the data issue occur? (both time frame and as a percentage of interactions or transactions, to gauge frequency and probability of occurrence)
   e. When the data issue occurs, how is it identified? (determine if there is an inspection process in place)
   f. How often is the data issue identified before the business impact is incurred? (determine if there is an existing data stewardship and data issue remediation process)
   g. What remediation tasks are performed? (note the effort for remediation)

Specific business impacts can be collected and then collated within the defined impact categories.

1.7 Additional Impact Categories

Of course, the impact categories listed in this chapter are by no means inclusive. Because every industry is different, every business is different, and every organization is different, there may be many ways that poor data quality affects operations or achieving goals. It is important, though, to understand not just what the impact categories are, but how they relate to different business activities, since this will help in both aggregating impacts and communicating those impacts to the right people in the organization.

There are no great secrets to the process of identifying your organization's impact categories. Bear in mind that the process is to look at how data is being used for achieving business objectives, and how the achievement of those goals is impeded when flawed data is introduced into the environment. Business goals typically revolve around maximizing the way that the organization's customers are served, and that suggests a process such as this:

1. Enumerate the products and services that the organization provides.
2. For each product or service, evaluate what data is being used as input and how the output is employed.
3. For each product or service, determine the top three to five data objects that are critical to successful operation.
4. For the most important data items, consider what kinds of errors can be introduced into the system.
5. For each introduced error, review how the introduction of the error affects the ability to provide optimal value.

Applying this process should expose data quality impacts that are related specifically to your business. Here are some examples:

- Incomplete insurance claim forms not only introduce additional staff resources needed to collect the right amount of information, missing diagnostic codes ultimately lead to inaccurate actuarial computations, which may be used to incorrectly set provider rates.
- Inaccurate contact information used in locating debtors may delay the time to initiate income withholding, reducing overall collections.
- Poor identity management results in conflicts over how sales commissions are distributed, which in turn reduces the amount of time the sales staff spends making sales.
- Improperly documented mechanical components are viewed as nonworking; proper documentation allows them to be put back into operation.
- Inaccurate inventory allows commodity components to depreciate when the application systems are not aware of the correct numbers of available items.

1.8 Impact Taxonomies and Iterative Refinement

Although this book presents four high-level impact classifications, these are not necessarily inclusive. If within your organization there are additional high-level classes with their own impact categories, it is desirable to document the new class and the categories that belong to that class. Alternatively, the categories provided in this chapter may still be at too gross a level, requiring further segmentation.

Take an iterative approach – use this chapter's impact categorization scheme as a model that can be tweaked and modified. Classify the impacts into a taxonomic hierarchy that shows how small impacts will roll up at different levels, and ultimately feed into a data quality scorecard.

1.9 Summary: Translating Impact into Performance

The objectives of designing an impact hierarchy are twofold. First, our original intention of determining how poor data quality impacts our business processes is a much more manageable task when it can be broken up into small analytic pieces. But more interestingly, the categorical hierarchy of impact areas will naturally map to our future performance reporting structure for gauging improvement. As we identify where poor data quality impacts the business, we will also be identifying where data quality improvement will enhance the business. This provides a solid framework for quantifying measurable performance metrics that will eventually be used to craft key data quality performance indicators, and we will continue to explore the manifestation of these ideas in chapter 6, "Metrics and Performance Improvement."

THE ORGANIZATIONAL DATA QUALITY PROGRAM

Once it has been determined that poor data quality does have a negative impact on the ways the business operates, it will be necessary to plan the approach for assembling a data quality management program and instituting the practices that will lead to improvement. That plan must consider:

- The processes that need to be instituted,
- The participants that will execute those processes and their roles and responsibilities, and
- The tools that will be used to support the processes.

In other words, instituting a practical data quality management program involves people, process, and technology to succeed. This chapter will provide an overview of these items. The discussion begins with an overview of the data quality improvement cycle, followed by an overview of data quality processes. The stakeholders and participant roles are then reviewed. Last, we look at tools and techniques that support the data quality processes.

2.1 The Virtuous Cycle of Data Quality

As opposed to the tasks in a vicious cycle, when executing the tasks in a virtuous cycle the data quality practitioner provides positive feedback that leads to overall improvement in the quality of organizational information across the board. Each time we cycle through our virtuous cycle, the effects are to increase the value of the ways that an organization's information asset supports the achievement of business objectives.

As shown in Figure 2.1, the virtuous cycle consists of five stages. During the first stage, the practitioner seeks to understand the scope of how poor data quality affects the ways that the business processes are intended to run. This is a combination of top-down and a bottom-up approaches. The top-down activity surveys the business users of the data to document what they do, how they use information, and what their most significant sources of pain are, with respect to data. The bottom-up component employs statistical and data analysis tools and techniques (such as data profiling) to identify potential data anomalies that can be reviewed with subject matter experts.

During the second stage, the data quality analysts synthesize the results of both the top-down and bottom-up activities and concentrate on the data elements that are deemed critical based on the selected business users' needs. In turn, the results of the empirical analysis will provide some types of measures that can be employed to assess the levels of data quality within a particular business context.

Any areas of interest in which the data does not meet the acceptability thresholds are candidates for review, which leads to stage three. During this stage, the data quality issues are

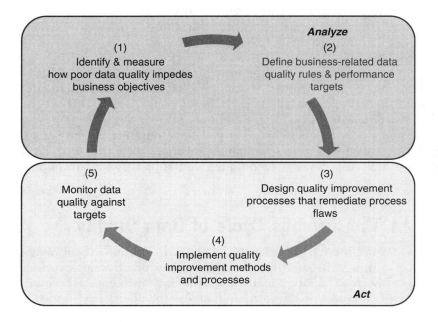

Figure 2.1 The virtuous cycle of data quality.

prioritized based on their severity as well as the feasibility for remediation, a plan for action is developed, and selected solutions are designed.

Once those solutions have been designed, the fourth stage is to actually implement them. The remediation may consist of corrections, inspections, and notifications and may not be limited to installing tools, but may involve training staff members on operational process improvements.

Having identified data quality rules and acceptability thresholds in stage two, and having developed methods for measuring the data against those rules, stage five allows the data quality analysts to review the degree to which the data does or does not meet the levels of acceptability. If there are issues to be researched, the data stewards are notified and a separate resolution process is kicked off. Meanwhile, this brings us to the beginning again, in which a different data set, or a different business process, is selected.

There is an apparent duality in the phasing of these tasks. The first two tasks are analysis tasks used to assess a target data set and figure out if there are any egregious errors that are impacting the business. The third, fourth, and fifth tasks are the action tasks, intended to put together a plan of attack and execute against that plan. Together, these two phases provide a repeatable process for incrementally accumulating metrics for data quality that will contribute to populating a data quality scorecard and a data quality dashboard, as well as driving proactive data quality management. This chapter will provide a survey of the processes that contribute to the execution of the virtuous cycle, consider the roles of the associated stakeholders and participants, and consider how responsibilities and accountabilities are allocated across that landscape.

2.2 Data Quality Processes

To implement the phases of the virtuous cycle, the data quality practitioners must institute a number of processes, as shown in Figure 2.2. The brief description of these processes provided here collectively establishes the context for subsequent sections of the book.

2.2.1 Business Impact Analysis

Chapter 1 discussed the business impacts of poor data quality and provided the starting point for understanding how data quality management fits into the enterprise. This process enables the

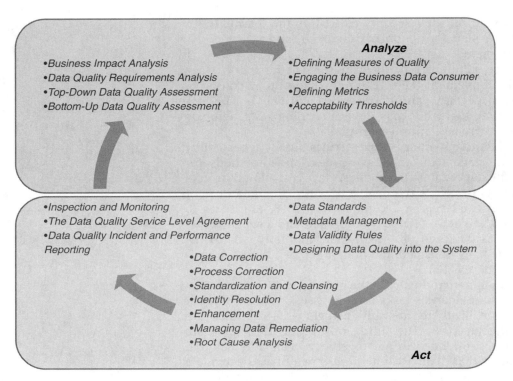

Figure 2.2 Data quality processes aligned with the phases of the virtuous cycle.

data quality analyst to interview business clients to document how selected business processes depend on high quality data.

During this process, the data quality analyst will note any potential data-related issues that increase costs, reduce revenues, impact margins, or introduce inefficiencies or delays in business activities. Any other negative business impacts that are attributable to data that do not meet a specific level of acceptability are also noted. This qualitative review is the first step in understanding whether there are critical pain points and in which parts of the business process these points of pain have greatest impact. As a result, the analyst will scope the business requirements for information for the assessment, narrow the list of data sets that will be examined, and guide the identification of data quality requirements.

2.2.2 Data Quality Requirements Analysis

This process is a top-down identification of data quality expectations. At this point, the analysts will synthesize data quality expectations for consumed data sets based on the business impact analysis. Data sets will be identified and targeted for assessment, and specific dimensions of data quality (see Chapter 8) will be isolated for review. The selected dimensions will be used to list specific measures that will be evaluated in relation to the business impacts.

2.2.3 Bottom-Up Data Quality Assessment

This process performs a bottom-up, empirical approach to identifying potential data issues. Using data profiling and other statistical and analysis techniques, the analysts can identify potential data anomalies, which are noted in preparation for business review.

2.2.4 Top-Down Data Quality Assessment

This process is to review discovered anomalies with business clients within the context of the documented business impacts. During this process, the analysts work with the business subject matter experts to differentiate between relevant and irrelevant issues, prioritize issues based on business impact, and explore different strategies for remediation. In addition, at this point the business users can be solicited to define their data requirements.

2.2.5 Defining Measures of Quality

Correlating business impacts to data issues through defined business rules allows one to represent different measurable aspects of data quality. These measures can be used in characterizing relevance across a set of application domains to support data quality management. The same measures that are used in establishing the baseline of the levels of quality can also be used on an ongoing basis to inspect data quality performance at different stages of business application workflows, enabling monitoring of both line-of-business and enterprise data governance.

2.2.6 Engaging the Business Data Consumer

Once the measures have been defined, the business data consumers can be brought back into the process to validate the measures and evaluate the suitability of the measures in relation to the business impacts.

2.2.7 Defining Metrics

Having identified the dimensions of data quality that are relevant to the business processes and identified the dimensions and the specific measures, the analyst will then define specific reportable metrics that can be presented to the business data stewards. These may be basic metrics composed of directly measured rules, or may be more complex metrics that are composed as weighted averages of collected scores. Other aspects include reporting schemas and methods for drilling into flawed data for root cause analysis.

2.2.8 Acceptability Thresholds

Once we have reviewed methods for inspecting and quantifying data quality dimensions, the next step is to solicit acceptability thresholds from the business users. Scoring below the acceptability threshold indicates that the data does not meet business. The acceptability threshold is the point at which measured noncompliance with user expectations may lead to material business impact. Integrating these thresholds with the methods for measurement completes the construction of the data quality metric.

2.2.9 Data Standards

The absence of a common frame of reference, common business term definitions, and an agreed-to format for exchange makes it difficult for parties to understand each other, and this is acutely true when different business applications need to share information. A data standard is basically an agreement between parties on the definitions of common business terms, the ways those terms are named and represented in data, and a set of rules that may describe how data is stored, exchanged, formatted, or presented. This process describes the policies and procedures for defining rules and reaching agreement about standard data elements.

2.2.10 Metadata Management

Because the use of the data elements and their underlying concepts drive how the business application operate using master data, the enterprise metadata repository effectively becomes the "control center" driving and controlling the business applications. Aside from the need to collect standard technical details regarding the numerous data elements that are potentially available, there is a need to determine

- the business uses of each data element;
- which data element definitions refer to the same concept;
- the applications that refer to manifestations of that concept;
- how each data element and associated concepts are created, read, modified, or retired by different applications;
- the data quality characteristics;
- inspection and monitoring locations within the business process flow;

and how all the uses are tied together. Therefore, a valuable component of an information architecture is an enterprise business metadata management program to facilitate the desired level of standards across the organization.

2.2.11 Data Validity Rules

The assessment process will expose potential anomalies, which are reviewed with the business users to identify data quality measures and, ultimately, data quality metrics. Yet in order to transition away from a reactive approach that remediates data quality issues once they are manifested at the end-user interface, the organization must engineer data controls into the application development process so that data errors can be identified and addressed as they occur.

This process has the data quality practitioners developing data validity assertions that can be specified as rules. When possible, these rules can be integrated into the business processes to validate conformance with expectations at the earliest point possible. Integrating the development and implementation of these controls is discussed in chapter 9.

2.2.12 Inspection and Monitoring

The availability of rules for validating data against defined expectations is the basis for data quality inspection and monitoring. This provides the means for notifying the appropriate people when data quality issues are identified so that any agreed-to remediation tasks can be initiated. Mechanisms for data inspection and monitoring and the corresponding process workflows must be defined for the purposes of inspecting data and ensuring that the data elements, records, and data sets meet downstream requirements.

This process involves defining the data quality inspection routines, which may include both automated and manual processes. Automated processes may include the results of edit checks executed during application processing, data profiling or data analysis automation, data integration tools, or customized processing. Manual inspection may require running queries or reports on data sources or even obtaining samples of data which are then examined. Inspection procedures are defined for each relevant data quality dimension. The inspection methods are customized for each system as appropriate.

2.2.13 The Data Quality Service Level Agreement

A service level agreement is a contract between a service provider and that provider's consumers that specifies the service provider's responsibilities with respect to different measurable aspects of what is being provided, such as availability, performance, response time for problems, and so on. A data quality service level agreement, or DQ SLA, is an agreement that specifies data consumer expectations in terms of data validity rules and levels of acceptability, as well as reasonable expectations for response and remediation when data errors and flaws are identified. DQ SLAs can be expressed for any situation in which a data provider hands off data to a data consumer.

This process is to specify expectations regarding measurable aspects relating to one or more dimensions of data quality (such as accuracy, completeness, consistency, timeliness, etc.), as suggested by other processes already described. The DQ SLA, then, would incorporate a number of specifications regarding conformance to those expectations as well as processes to be executed when those expectations are not met. Reported issues will be prioritized, and the appropriate people in the organization will be notified to take specific actions to resolve issues before any negative business impacts can occur.

2.2.14 Data Quality Incident and Performance Reporting

Supporting the enforcement of a data quality service level agreement requires a set of management processes for the reporting and tracking of data quality issues and corresponding activities. This can be facilitated via a system used to log and track data quality issues. By more formally requiring evaluation and initial diagnosis of emergent data events, encouraging data quality issue tracking system helps staff members be more effective at problem identification and, consequently, problem resolution.

Aside from improving the data quality management process, issue and incident tracking can also provide performance reporting including mean-time-to-resolve issues, frequency of occurrence of issues, types of issues, sources of issues, and common approaches for correcting or eliminating problems. A good issues tracking system will eventually become a reference source of current and historic issues, their statuses, and any factors that may need the actions of others not directly involved in the resolution of the issue.

2.2.15 Designing Data Quality into the System

Incorporating data validation and data quality inspection and reporting into business processes and the corresponding business application suggests that the general system development life cycle (SDLC) needs to be adjusted so that organizational data requirements can be solicited and integrated into the requirements phase of system development. This process looks at business ownership of data and how business process modeling can be used to elaborate on the information needs in addition to functional requirements for business operations. Since downstream users such as business intelligence reporting consumers will depend on the data collected during operational activities, there is a need to formally collect data requirements as part of the SDLC process.

2.2.16 Managing Data Remediation

In addition to a process for reporting and logging data quality incidents, there must be an accompanying mechanism for managing the tasks performed to remedy any critical issues. This means that the catalog of potential issues must be classified and categorized into a hierarchy for reporting, rules for prioritization and remediation must be integrated into the incident management system, and expectations for root cause analysis and recommendations for corrective actions must be defined. In addition, this process will have the team define the rules for determining when issues have not been addressed within a reasonable time frame and what actions are initiated to ensure compliance with the data quality service level agreement.

2.2.17 Root Cause Analysis

If a data control triggers a notification that a data error has occurred, it is up to the data stewards to not just correct the data, but also identify the source of the introduction of the errors into the data. This process describes how data controls can be used to isolate the processing phase in which the error is introduced as well as ways to drill down into the data and the associated application tasks to seek the root cause.

2.2.18 Data Correction

The first type of remedy for flawed data is reactive – directly correcting the data errors. This incorporates governed process for correcting data to meet acceptability thresholds when the source of the errors cannot be fixed. It is important to ensure that corrections are synchronized with all data consumers and that data suppliers are aware of modifications, especially when the data is used in different business contexts. This is especially important when comparing reported data and rolled-up aggregate results to operational systems, because different numbers that have no explanation will lead to extra time spent attempting to reconcile the variant results. In addition, it is necessary to make sure that there are controlled channels for correcting so that any dependent business processes are aware of any modifications.

2.2.19 Process Correction

Although correcting the data addresses the acute need for high quality, the fact that erred data enters the organization usually means that there are flawed processes that need review. Process correction encompasses governed process for evaluating the information production flow, business process workflow, and the determination of how processes can be improved to reduce or eliminate the introduction of errors.

2.2.20 Standardization and Cleansing

This process incorporates working with the data standards and metadata staff to define rules and use tools for standardizing and normalizing data values for the purposes of data cleansing. This is supported by parsing, standardization, and cleansing tools and techniques (see section 2.4).

2.2.21 Identity Resolution

The need to uniquely identify key data concepts within and across different systems means that the tools for entity identity resolution must be synchronized with the operational procedures for record linkage, searching and matching, batch linkage, and data consolidation. See sections 2.4.4 and 2.4.5.

2.2.22 Enhancement

Our last process focuses on enrichment of data through the use of parsing, standardization, and other techniques. Additional data sources can be identified that can be linked to organizational data sets to improve the utility or value of the data. This process involves identifying those data sources, engineering tasks for data integration and appending, and managing the data supplies to ensure that their data meets the organization's data quality expectations. See section 2.4.7.

2.3 Stakeholders and Participants

When considering the importance of managing data quality, one must consider the necessity of engaging potential stakeholders across the enterprise. Each of these roles plays some part in ensuring that the data requirements are solicited, collected, documented, monitored, and observed. In turn, these roles take on certain responsibilities relating to data quality management.

2.3.1 Senior Management

Senior management support is likely to provide the initial motivation for the other staff members to engage in the data quality program. Senior management also plays a special role in ensuring ongoing engagement by the rest of the organization. Adopting a strategic view to oversee and communicate the long-term value of the transition and migration should trump short-term tactical business initiatives. In addition, senior managers should also prepare to adapt as responsibilities and incentives change from focusing on the use of data for success of functional silos to managing data at the enterprise level to achieve corporate-wide success.

2.3.2 Business Clients

Within each area of the business, there are processes whose operations and success rely on predictably high quality data. In general, though, the business clients (or business process owners) are not intricately involved in the underlying technology associated with the application, and are more concerned that there are no glitches or flaws that will interrupt the successful execution of their workflow. Business clients will be satisfied as long as the information used within the existing business applications meets their expectations. Therefore, it is necessary to survey the business clients to understand the way they use data, their levels of tolerance for errors, and how those concerns can be translated into measurable data rules for inspection, monitoring, and reporting.

2.3.3 Application Owners

Within an organization, there is bound to be some degree of data sharing across applications, and consequently shared requirements for managing data quality. For example, customer information collected when rates are quoted and policies are bound will be used at a later point for other business applications such as billing, customer service, claims, and marketing. As with the business owners, the application owners are concerned with ensuring predictable levels of data quality.

Since the successful continued predictable operation of the application relies on the reliability and quality of the corporate data asset, the participation of the application owner is critical. When identifying data requirements in preparation for developing a master data model, it will be necessary to engage the application owner to ensure that operational data quality expectations are documented, cross-referenced, and incorporated into an operational data governance program.

2.3.4 Data Stewards and Data Quality Analysts

A data quality initiative introduces new constraints on the ways that individuals create, access, use, modify, and retire data. To ensure that these constraints are not violated, the data governance and data quality staff must introduce stewardship, ownership, and management policies, as well as the means to monitor these policies.

The value of instituting data quality management becomes apparent to the organization as more lines of business participate in data standards, data quality, and data governance activities, both as data suppliers and as data consumers. Ultimately, this suggests defining information policies that specify the acceptable levels of data quality for shared information and imposing some layer of governance, which may include:

- Incorporating metadata analysis and registration
- Data quality assessment

- Defining data quality expectations and rules
- Monitoring and managing quality of data (as well as monitoring data changes)
- Creating stewardship to oversee automation of data correction and enhancement
- Developing processes to research root causes – and subsequently eliminate sources of flawed data

2.3.5 Metadata Analysts

"Just enough" metadata is key to data quality processes. From the data quality perspective, metadata management informs the processes of modeling data, developing applications, and defining data quality rules. In this environment, metadata incorporates the consolidated view of the data elements and their corresponding definitions, formats, sizes, structures, data domains, patterns, value domains, valid ranges, and so on and provides the appropriate level of detail for impact analysis, extraction and transformation, and data sharing.

2.3.6 System Developers

Aspects of performance and storage change as data is shared, reused, or repackaged for alternate uses. Data created in one application may ultimately be made available to other applications in contexts for which the data was not originally intended. To ensure that the proper levels of quality are met, system developers must be aware of their direct clients' data quality requirements and integrate those requirements with those already established by the upstream data creators. The developers of the upstream systems must also be willing to incorporate enterprise data quality validations into their applications to support downstream data quality requirements.

2.3.7 Operations Staff

Once systems have been established in production, changes in the business environment may create a need for the operations staff to bypass the standard protocols for data access and modification. In fact, this approach to bypassing standard interfaces is institutionalized in some organizations, with metrics associated with the number of times that "fixes" or modifications are applied to data using direct access (e.g., updates via SQL) instead of going through the preferred channels.

Alternatively, desktop applications are employed to supplement existing applications, as an additional way to gather the right amount of information in order to complete a business process. Bypassing standard operating procedures and desktop supplements poses a challenge to a data quality management program, and this situation requires engaging the operations teams with a program for change management to reduce or eliminate modifications that are not managed within defined data governance procedures.

2.4 Data Quality Tools

This section provides an overview of the tools that support the data quality processes, although each will be discussed in much greater detail in part 3 of the book. Throughout this book we will continue to refine how data quality tools and technologies are mapped to the processes described; those tools include:

- Data profiling
- Parsing
- Standardization
- Identity resolution
- Record linkage and merging
- Data cleansing
- Data enhancement
- Data inspection and monitoring

2.4.1 Data Profiling

Data profiling is a set of algorithms for statistically analyzing and assessing the quality of data values within a data set as well as exploring relationships that exist between data elements or across data sets. Data profiling provides the ability to identify data flaws as well as a means to communicate these instances with subject matter experts whose business knowledge can confirm the existences of data problems. A data profiling tool will scan all the values in a column and provide a frequency distribution of that column's values, suggesting the type and potential uses of each column. Cross-column analysis can expose embedded value dependencies, whereas inter-table analysis explores overlapping values sets to identify foreign key relationships between entities. Data profiling can help discover business rules embedded within data sets, which can be used for ongoing inspection and monitoring.

2.4.2 Parsing

Often, data values are expected to conform to expected formats and structures, but slight variations in data values may confuse individuals as well as automated applications. For example, consider these different data values, each of which refers to the same data concept (the political entity known as the state of California): {California, CA, Calif., US-CA, Cal, 06}. Some of these values use characters, another uses digits, and some use punctuation or special characters. For the most part, one might read these and recognize that they all represent the state of California, but automating the process of determining whether these values are accurate or similar requires that the values be parsed into their component segments and then transformed into a standard format. Parsing is used to determine whether a value conforms to recognizable patterns. Pattern-based parsing then enables the automatic recognition and subsequent standardization of meaningful value components, such as the area code and exchange in a telephone number, or the different parts of a person's name.

2.4.3 Standardization

Parsing uses defined patterns, regular expressions, or grammars managed within a rules engine along with table lookups to distinguish between valid and invalid data values. When patterns are recognized, other rules and actions can be triggered to transform the input data into a form that can be more effectively used, either to standardize the representation (presuming a valid representation) or to correct the values (should known errors be identified). To continue our example, each of our values for the state of California {California, CA, Calif., US-CA, Cal, 06} can be standardized to the U.S. Postal Service two-character abbreviation of CA.

2.4.4 Identity Resolution

Because operational systems have grown organically into a suite of enterprise applications, it is not unusual that multiple data instances in different systems will have different ways to refer to the same real-world entity. Alternately, the desire to consolidate and link data about the same business concepts with a high level of confidence might convince someone that a record might not already exist for a real-world entity when in fact it really does. Both of these problems ultimately represent the same core challenge: being able to compare identifying data within a pair of records to determine similarity between that pair or to distinguish the entities represented in those records.

Both of these issues are addressed through a process called identity resolution, in which the degree of similarity between any two records is scored, most often based on weighted approximate matching between a set of attribute values between the two records. If the score is above a specific threshold, the two records are deemed to be a match, and are presented to the end client as most likely to represent the same entity. Identity resolution is used to recognize when only slight variations suggest that different records are connected and where values may be cleansed, or where enough differences between the data suggest that the two records truly represent distinct entities. Since comparing every record against every other record is computationally intensive, many identity resolution tools use advanced algorithms for blocking records that are most likely to contain matches into smaller sets in order to reduce computation time.

2.4.5 Linkage, Merging, and Consolidation of Duplicate Records

Identity resolution provides the foundation of a more sophisticated technique: duplicate record analysis and elimination. Identifying similar records within the same data set probably means that the records are duplicated, and may be subjected to cleansing, elimination, or both. Identifying similar records in different sets may indicate a link across the data sets, which helps facilitate merging of similar records for the purposes of data cleansing as well as supporting a master data management or customer data integration initiative.

Identity resolution leads into the merging and consolidation process to establish the single view of the customer. While some business applications may be able to proceed by looking at a set of records containing information, automating the merging process will select the best data values from those records and allow for the creation of a single "best copy" of the data that can support both operational processes and analytics to improve ways of doing business.

2.4.6 Data Cleansing

After determining that a data value does not conform to end-user expectations, the data analyst can take different approaches to remediation. One approach is to transform the data into a form that meets the level of business user acceptability. Data cleansing builds on the parsing, standardization, and enhancement tools; identity resolution; and record linkage. By parsing the values and triggering off of known error patterns, data cleansing will apply rules to figure out the right data values, correct names or addresses, eliminate extra bits of information, reduce meaningless data, and even merge duplicates.

Although a best practice in data quality is to determine where the source of errors is and to eliminate the root causes of poor data quality, frequently the data quality team does not have the administrative control to effect changes to existing production applications. Therefore, an alternative that may be necessary to ensure high quality data is to cleanse the data directly, and at least provide data that meet a level of suitability for all downstream data consumers, and data cleansing makes this possible.

2.4.7 Data Enhancement

A different approach to data value improvement involves enhancement, in which additional information is appended to existing records. Data enhancement, which builds on parsing, standardization, and record linkage, is a data improvement process that adds information from third-party data sets (such as name standardization, demographic data imports, psychographic data imports, and household list appends). Data enhancement is simplified when the provider has partnered with data aggregators, whose data can be used both as a system of record against which data instances are matched and as a resource for appending. A typical data enhancement activity, address standardization and cleansing, relies on parsing, standardization, and the availability of third-party address information.

There are few industries that do not benefit from the use of additional data sources to append and enhance enterprise information. Whether it means address standardization and correction to reduce delivery costs and improve direct response rates, geodemographic appends that provide insight into customer profiling and segmentation, credit data used to assess and reduce risk, historical information (such as automobile service histories or medical events) to provide greater insight into diagnostic and preventative care, among others, data enhancement is a process that optimizes business decisions within operational and analytic contexts.

2.4.8 Inspection and Monitoring

Because data profiling exposes potential business rules used within and across different business processes, the data analyst can document the rules and confirm their criticality in coordination with the business subject matter experts. These rules essentially describe the end-user data expectations and can be used to measure and monitor the validity of data. Inspection and monitoring of defined data quality rules provide a proactive assessment of compliance with expectations, and the results of these audits can feed data quality metrics populating management dashboards and scorecards.

Inspection and monitoring build on the parsing and data profiling techniques to proactively validate data against a set of defined (or discovered) business rules. This data inspection can notify analysts when data instances do not conform to defined data quality expectations and provide baseline measurements against which ongoing data quality inspections can be compared.

2.5 Summary

Instituting a data quality management program means more than just purchasing data cleansing tools or starting a data governance board. An iterative cycle of assessment, planning, execution, and performance management for data quality requires repeatable processes that join people with the right sets of skills with the most appropriate tools. In the next chapter we will look at a maturity model for data quality management; chapter 4 will show how the technology and processes work together; and chapter 5 guides the development of a business case and a road map for the data quality management program.

DATA QUALITY MATURITY

What does organizational maturity mean in the context of good data management practices? From a holistic standpoint, the differences in organizational maturity for data quality are gauged by the sophistication of the processes in place for managing the identification of flawed data as well as the levels of capability of those tasked with managing data quality. Most organizations are reactive when it comes to resolving issues, meaning that problems are addressed at the time that the impacts have manifested themselves, but long after the failure has occurred. But as the practitioners in the organization gain a more thorough understanding of the methods for identifying the sources for data flaws, they become more proactive in identifying and resolving potential issues before negative business impacts occur.

In chapter 2, we provided an overview of the processes, people, and technology that are part of a data quality program. This chapter explores the concept of a capability/maturity model for data quality management, the life cycle of the data quality program, and how the organization transitions from one that is reactive into one that is proactive in ensuring high quality data.

3.1 The Data Quality Strategy

A strategy encompasses a long-term plan of action designed to achieve a specific objective. This plan provides a way to guide the efforts to ensure that they are contributing to the achievement of stated goals. We can therefore propose that a data quality strategy directs the organization to take the steps that will reduce the business impacts of poor data quality to an acceptable level.

Chapter 1 outlined some of the challenges and benefits of data quality management, whereas chapter 2 provided a more comprehensive introduction to the data quality program. And though there are clear benefits to an organizational data quality management program, the need to coordinate the efforts of different personalities in the organization means that there are bound to be conflicts that will arise among participants as the data quality program evolves. Even though most business applications and business operations depend on data quality, it cannot necessarily be mandated across administrative boundaries. Because of this, the expected benefits of improved information value can only be achieved when all participants willingly contribute to successful data quality management.

Frequently, defined data quality activities largely focus on evaluation and procurement of data quality tools, but won't encompass the management, technical, and operational infrastructure that must be in place to support a generalized conformance to acceptability levels of properly defined and documented expectations. Yet measuring this conformance demonstrates that the effort is succeeding. This suggests that when developing the data quality strategy, consider describing an operational framework for instituting best practices in the context of a level of maturity, and lay out the roadmap to address the challenges and achieve the benefits. Apply industry best practices and combine those with quality disciplines from other industrial domains (e.g., manufacturing, software development, or service industries). Ultimately, the data quality practices and processes should be relevant within your organization, and the approach to building the program should follow the patterns for other successful organizational programs.

It is a formidable challenge to establish the appropriate level of data quality to meet the needs of the diversity of participants, regulatory bodies, policy makers, and information clients when coupled with the different technologies and practices already in place. To address these, a data quality strategy requires governance, policies, practices, technology, and operational solutions that are all-encompassing yet present themselves to all participants as pragmatic and practical. Some things to keep in mind:

- **The Information Lifecycle:** When assembling a data quality strategy, it is necessary to identify the key success objectives for the program, evaluate the variables by which success is measured, establish information quality expectations, develop the governance model for overseeing success, and develop protocols for ensuring that policies and procedures for maintaining high quality data are followed by the participants across the enterprise. Information follows a "life cycle" (e.g., create, distribute, access, update, retire), so it is necessary that the data quality framework provide protocols for measuring the quality of information at the various stages of that life cycle.

- **Performance and maturity:** A data quality framework defines management objectives that are consistent with the key success objectives and the enterprise expectations for quality information, either through integration of services across an enterprise information architecture, or through the collaborative implementation of data governance policies and procedures. Performance associated with data quality expectations can be tied to a data quality maturity model. This maturity model establishes levels of performance and specifies the fundamental best practices needed to achieve each level of performance.
- **Data governance roles and responsibilities:** Also included in your data quality framework should be a model for data governance that outlines various data quality roles for the participants in the enterprise community. This model will provide an organizational structure and the policies and procedures to be followed by the community to ensure high quality data. The governance model defines data ownership and stewardship and describes accountability for the remediation of data quality issues across the various enterprise information systems. If necessary, the model will also define procedures for the data quality certification of participants as well as ongoing auditing of data quality.
- **Meeting expectations:** To achieve assurance of high quality data, the framework should provide for the identification, documentation, and validation of data quality expectations. These expectations can be transformed into data quality rules and metrics used to assess the business impact of poor data quality, develop performance models to gauge severity of data quality issues, track data quality events and issues, and provide ongoing data quality measurement, monitoring, and reporting of conformance with customer expectations.
- **Staff training and education:** To encourage coordination with the efforts to ensure data quality, there is value in educating participants in ways to integrate data quality as an important component of the system development life

cycle. The development of a component model for data quality services will expose the appropriate topics for training materials to facilitate data quality integration.

In addition, these concepts from chapter 2 should also be addressed in the data quality strategy:

- Provide a framework of data quality concepts
- Specify a data governance model to manage the oversight of data quality, incorporating data ownership, stewardship, and accountability for community-wide data quality
- Formalize approaches for identifying, documenting, and validating data quality expectations
- Provide practices to evaluate the business impacts of poor data quality and to develop performance models for issue management and prioritization
- Integrate methods and processes for data quality event tracking, data quality monitoring and measurement, and reporting of conformance with customer expectations
- Formulate a component service model for data quality services that is integrated with the enterprise/community interoperability model

3.2 A Data Quality Framework

Ultimately the practitioner must align the framework for data quality to meet the needs of the organization without overwhelming the individuals who will participate in the program. Casting the observance of data quality expectations within the context of key business performance metrics while minimizing intrusion and extra effort enables the program to gain traction and increase participation. The framework looks at varying degrees of maturity with respect to concepts introduced in the previous chapter, including:

- Defining data quality expectations
- Creating measurement using data quality dimensions
- Defining policies for measured observance of expectations
- Implementing the procedures supporting those policies
- Instituting data governance
- Agreeing to standards
- Acquiring the right technology
- Monitoring performance

3.2.1 Data Quality Expectations

Although the expectations associated with data quality measurements are often explicit, at times many of these expectations are implied or embedded within directives that drive other areas of importance. The data quality framework must address measuring conformance to expectations of data quality as they relate to particular participant needs. The framework must also specify:

- The relevant measures of data quality attributable to all data elements ("dimensions"),
- Metrics for evaluating conformance within each dimension, and
- Processes and services for evaluating conformance within each dimension.

3.2.2 Dimensions of Data Quality

This theme will continue to ring true throughout this book: it is said that one cannot improve something that cannot be measured. In the data quality program, the concept of "dimensions" classifies aspects of data quality expectations and provides measures to evaluate conformance to these measures. These metrics are used to quantify the levels of data quality and will be used to identify the gaps and opportunities for data quality improvement across an information flow. A thorough discussion of data quality dimensions will be presented in chapter 8.

3.2.3 Policies

The complexity of managing the different types of information policies that will be in place at your organization often leads to a limited capability for ensuring policy conformance. Whether the policies are defined internally (security, access), reflected across the customer space (e.g., privacy, sales, and support policies), or are externally imposed (e.g., legislative or regulatory industry standards), the challenge of policy management within the context of an information architecture should not be ignored. Policy management incorporates data quality dependencies among the areas of:

- Data certification (such as certification of trusted data sources or establishing trust with external data consumers),
- Privacy (including maintaining consistency with supporting the privacy framework based on limitations of use, storage, and duration stored),
- Lineage (such as tracking the origin and transference of data),
- Limitation of use (thereby overseeing the limits of the use of your organization's data outside of the enterprise), and
- Single source of truth (such as providing inquiry access through a single reference data index).

3.2.4 Procedures

The data quality procedures describe the operational aspects of a system to validate the existence and effectiveness of key data management activities. In addition, those procedures incorporate inspection to either automatically or (if necessary) manually validate data quality, and include preventative measures for proactive data quality assurance as well as control processes for identifying and providing guidance in eliminating the source of errors. These processes augment the information management activity to focus on:

- Data quality management,
- Standardized data inspection templates,
- Operational data quality,
- Issues tracking and remediation,
- Manual intervention when necessary,
- Integrity of data exchange,
- Contingency planning, and
- Validation.

As part of a set of protocols, service-level agreements may be specified for these activities and be integrated with the set of information policies, and this will be covered in greater detail in chapter 13.

3.2.5 Governance

The definitions and the management of data quality must incorporate the participation, collaboration, and oversight management from all enterprise participants, and to this end, the data quality framework specifies a data governance structure for management and oversight, and a set of data stewardship processes for all participants. Governance is required at various touch points to ensure consistency and conformance to the framework. Chapter 7 provides a model for developing a data quality governance model, with the outline for a data quality charter along with an organization structure, roles, responsibilities, and workflow for activities by the various participants.

3.2.6 Standards

Many industries participate within wider communities of data and information sharing. A data standards program facilitates the definition of and conformance with externally and internally defined standards for information exchange. Common business terms and their definitions are reflected at the information level, and data standards management looks at the data quality issues associated with:

- Data definitions,
- Semantics, and
- Data exchange.

These standards are managed as enterprise metadata, and are discussed in chapter 10.

3.2.7 Technology

To deploy the data quality framework, the participants within the enterprise will be expected to employ tools and technology intended to support the stated data quality protocols and processes, support the level of data quality services (e.g., validation, parsing and standardization, search/locate) via a single reference data set, and validate/verify the conformance of data values and records to explicitly defined data quality expectations. This will incorporate:

- Service component design guidance,
- Data quality technology,
- Business rule–based validation,
- Verification of data accuracy,
- Searching and indexing,
- Data quality issues tracking,
- Data quality performance management, and
- Identity resolution, record matching and linkage, and record splitting and merging when necessary.

3.2.8 Performance Management

Having specified processes for governance and stewardship and identified data quality expectations and ways to determine conformance of data to those expectations, it is necessary to provide a performance management scheme for continuously monitoring enterprise-wide data quality. This includes conforming to data quality expectations, identifying where significant negative impacts are incurred due to poor data quality, tracking relevant issues and providing a means for root cause analysis, and providing a set of services for the assessment of data quality performance. Together, this scheme will support auditing and monitoring that can be reported in a management dashboard characterizing data quality performance, highlighting areas that require special attention, and providing an audit trail for root cause analysis and remediation within the governance model.

3.3 A Data Quality Capability/Maturity Model

To take an approach of performance management for data quality, it is useful to visualize how data quality management dovetails with all organizational information-dependent activities. The challenge is that in many organizations, data management evolves in lockstep with the functional application needs, often as an afterthought. The data analysts starting to look at the organizational value of data as a corporate asset expose gaps showing the disconnect between the functional requirements for a collection of siloed business application and good data management practices. One way to evaluate and then resolve this disconnect is to assess the current level of maturity associated with data quality practices and then visualize a target level of maturity that best meets the organization's needs. In turn, this approach sets this vision as a yardstick by which one organization's maturity can be compared to the way that other organizations work.

This data quality maturity model is patterned after the Capability Maturity Model (CMM) developed by the Software Engineering Institute at Carnegie Mellon University. Capability maturity models are management tools that characterize levels of organizational refinement in addressing design, implementation, manufacturing, problem resolution, and so on. These kinds of models have been applied to many application domains, including software development, programmer development, and project management domains. This data quality maturity model defines five levels of maturity, ranging from an initial level where practices and policies are ad hoc, to the highest in which processes and practices lead to continuous measurement, improvement, and optimization.

3.3.1 Initial

At the initial level, the processes used for data quality assurance are largely ad hoc, with most of the effort expended in reacting to data quality issues. Problems that arise are acute, require immediate attention, and often require significant rollback and rework. The environment is relatively unstable, and as a result it becomes challenging to trace back the sources of the introduction of flawed data and to determine the quick fix. Fixes are onetime, and most likely will not address any long-term improvement in the information or the processes. Success is often correlated to individual heroics in correcting data flaws, not on proven processes for root cause analysis and managed remediation. At this level, there is little or no sharing of information or experiences, and therefore there is limited or no ability to repeat successes.

3.3.2 Repeatable

At the repeatable level, there is some basic organizational management and information sharing, augmented by some process discipline, mostly in recognizing good practices and attempting to replicate them in similar situations, enabling some ability to repeat success. There is an introductory level of governance with limited documentation of processes, plans, standards, and practices. When representatives from the lines of business application understand these good practices and attempt to put them in place, their ability to respond to data failures is more streamlined.

The rate of adoption of data management practices varies across different lines of business. Some considerations of the impacts of poor data quality lead to introductory efforts for business evaluation and identification of gross-level measures. These measures may be for proactive data quality management. Some technology components are in place, but they may not be standardized and their behaviors are not synchronized. A focus on the need for technology eclipses the identification of business needs for tools and the definition of methods for using any acquired tools.

3.3.3 Defined

At the defined level, a structured team of data quality practitioners begin to document good practices, which are:
- An established set of data governance policies,
- Processes for defining data quality expectations,
- Technology components, and
- Processes and services for implementing data quality validation, assurance, and reporting.

Once these are documented and can be made available across the organization, there emerges a degree of consistent use. An enterprise-wide data quality team has scheduled meetings to discuss organizational issues, review methods and technology, and to exchange ideas.

A framework for determining responsibility and accountability for the quality of the organization's information is in place, and accountability is monitored by an organizational governance board with representatives from the business and IT divisions. There are tailored guidelines for establishing standards and management objectives, and there are processes in place to ensure that these objectives are met. Expectations based on defined data quality dimensions can be expressed, documented, and integrated within a (conceptual) service model. The use of technical components is standardized at both service and implementation layers.

3.3.4 Managed

At the managed level, the data quality program fully incorporates business impact analysis with the ability to express data quality expectations and measure conformance to those expectations. These measurements form the basis of clearly defined criteria for performance in relation to meeting business objectives. Metrics composed of these weighted measurements are used in evaluating statistical process control at different service levels. Measured performance characteristics can be used to assess overall system performance against success criteria. Data quality is proactive, with data flaws identified early in the information workflow. Remediation is governed by well-documented procedures, information is shared, and overall performance against quality expectations is predictable.

3.3.5 Optimized

At the optimized level, the data quality maturity governance framework is in place such that enterprise-wide performance measurements can be used for identifying opportunities for improved systemic data quality. The ability to assess success and identify causes for process variation may suggest actions to adapt standards, policies, and processes for incremental or fundamental quality improvements. Strategic improvements and continuous process monitoring of the data life cycle using dashboards are applied throughout the organization.

3.4 Mapping Framework Components to the Maturity Model

3.4.1 Data Quality Expectations

The challenge of defining data quality expectations often is tied to the convergence of understanding between the information technologists and their business clients. Although the

Table 3.1 Component Maturity Description for Data Quality Expectations

Level	Characterization
Initial	• Data quality activity is reactive • No capability for identifying data quality expectations • No data quality expectations have been documented
Repeatable	• Limited anticipation of certain data issues • Expectations associated with intrinsic dimensions of data quality (see chapter 8) associated with data values can be articulated • Simple errors are identified and reported
Defined	• Dimensions of data quality are identified and documented • Expectations associated with dimensions of data quality associated with data values, formats, and semantics can be articulated using data quality rules • Capability for validation of data using defined data quality rules • Methods for assessing business impact explored
Managed	• Data validity is inspected and monitored in process • Business impact analysis of data flaws is common • Results of impact analysis factored into prioritization of managing expectation conformance • Data quality assessments of data sets performed on cyclic schedule
Optimized	• Data quality benchmarks defined • Observance of data quality expectations tied to individual performance targets • Industry proficiency levels are used for anticipating and setting improvement goals • Controls for data validation integrated into business processes

responsibility for addressing data quality issues lies solely with IT, it is difficult to establish protocols for long-term improvement; but as the partnership between IT and the business side grows stronger, the ability to effectively define and measure against data quality expectations grows as well. The mapping of the maturity model to data quality expectations is shown in Table 3.1.

3.4.2 Dimensions of Data Quality

The ability to predict where data quality becomes critical to achieving business objectives enables data quality management to become systemic. This depends on translating the occurrence of specific business impacts into a taxonomy that systematically allows the practitioner to measure, assess, and

Table 3.2 Component Maturity Description for Defining and Using Data Quality Dimensions

Level	Characterization
Initial	• No recognition of ability to measure data quality • Data quality issues not connected in any way • Data quality issues are not characterized within any kind of management taxonomy
Repeatable	• Recognition of common dimensions for measuring quality of data values • Capability to measure conformance with data quality rules associated with data values
Defined	• Expectations associated with dimensions of data quality associated with data values, formats, and semantics can be articulated • Capability for validation of data values, models, and exchanges using defined data quality rules • Basic reporting for simple data quality measurements
Managed	• Dimensions of data quality mapped to a business impact taxonomy • Composite metric scores reported • Data stewards notified of emerging data flaws
Optimized	• Data quality service level agreements defined • Data quality service level agreements observed • Newly researched dimensions enable the integration of proactive methods for ensuring the quality of data as part of the system development life cycle

improve information value. Table 3.2 describes the mapping of the maturity model for defining and using data quality dimensions.

3.4.3 Policies

As the organization matures, the approach to managing conformance to information policies will transition from an informal approach that has limited documentation to one that completely integrates business activities, information policies, and auditable conformance, as is shown in Table 3.3.

3.4.4 Procedures

A measure of a high-performance organization lies in its well-defined processes and protocols for ensuring information quality, and this is described in Table 3.4.

Table 3.3 Component Maturity Description for Information Policies

Level	Characterization
Initial	• Policies are informal • Policies are undocumented • Repetitive actions taken by many staff members with no coordination
Repeatable	• Organization attempts to consolidate "single source of truth" data sets • Privacy and limitations of use policies are hard-coded • Initial policies defined for reacting to data issues
Defined	• Tailored guidelines for establishing management objectives are established at line of business • Certification process for qualifying data sources is in place • Best practices captured by data quality practitioners • Data quality service level agreements defined for managing observance of policies
Managed	• Policies established and coordinated across the enterprise • Provenance management details the history of data exchanges • Policy-based data quality management • Performance management driven by data quality policies • Data quality service level agreements used for managing observance of policies
Optimized	• Automated notification of noncompliance to data quality policies • Self-governing system in place

3.4.5 Governance

Table 3.5 shows how to map a data governance program to the different levels of the maturity model. The emergence of organizational data governance evolves both from the bottom up, as opportunities for information sharing are provided, and from the top down as the responsibilities are formalized.

3.4.6 Standards

Interoperability is a key to coordinated information activities, and the maturity of the organization is reflected in the way it defines and implements data standards, as is described in Table 3.6.

Table 3.4 Component Maturity Description for Data Quality Protocols

Level	Characterization
Initial	• Discovered failures are reacted to in an acute manner • Data values are corrected with no coordination with business processes • Root causes are not identified • Same errors corrected multiple times
Repeatable	• Ability to track down errors due to incompleteness • Ability to track down error due to invalid syntax/structure • Root cause analysis enabled using simple data quality rules and data validation
Defined	• Procedures defined and documented for data inspection for determination of accuracy and validity • Data quality management is deployed at line-of-business level as well as at enterprise level • Data validation is performed automatically and only flaws are manually inspected • Data contingency procedures in place
Managed	• Data quality rules are proactively monitored • Data controls are designed for incorporation into distinct business applications • Data flaws are recognized early in information flow • Remediation is governed by well-defined processes • Validation of exchanged data in place • Validity of data is auditable
Optimized	• Data controls deployed across the enterprise • Participants publish data quality measurements • Data quality management practices are transparent

3.4.7 Technology

As the maturity of the organization grows, the focus on data quality improvement transitions from acquiring tools to assembling a service-oriented approach for the entire enterprise, as is described in Table 3.7.

3.4.8 Performance Management

Creating a performance-based organization requires a focus on defining performance objectives and using the tools, methods, and protocols to measure conformance to those objectives

Table 3.5 Component Maturity Description for Data Governance

Level	Characterization
Initial	• Little or no communication regarding data quality management • Information technology is default for all enterprise data quality issues • No data stewardship • Responsibility for data corrections assigned in an ad hoc manner
Repeatable	• Best practices are collected and shared among participants. • Key individuals from community form workgroup to devise and recommend data governance program and policies • Guiding principles and data quality charter are in development
Defined	• Organizational structure for data governance oversight defined • Guiding principles, charter, and data governance management policies are documented • Standardized view of data stewardship across the enterprise and stewardship program is in place • Operational data governance procedures defined
Managed	• Data governance board consisting of representatives from across the enterprise is in place • Collaborative data quality governance board meets regularly • Operational data governance driven by data quality service level agreements • Teams within each division or group employ similar governance framework internally • Reporting and remediation frameworks collaborate in applying statistical process control to maintain control within defined bounds
Optimized	• Data quality performance metrics for processes are reviewed for opportunities for improvement • Staff members rewarded for meeting data governance performance goals

and ultimately meet those performance goals. The mapping of the maturity model to performance management is shown in Table 3.8.

3.5 Summary

One of the more important objectives of the process of defining a data quality strategy and framework is to better understand how to integrate performance-based data quality activities into the entire system. Measurements and metrics are designed

Table 3.6 Component Maturity Description for Data Standards

Level	Characterization
Initial	• No data standards defined • Similar data values represented in variant structures • No data definitions
Repeatable	• Data element definitions for commonly used business terms • Reference data sets identified • Data elements used as identifying information specified • Certification process for trusted data sources being defined • Data standards metadata managed within participant enterprises • Definition of guidelines for standardized exchange formats (e.g., XML)
Defined	• Enterprise data standards and metadata management • Structure and format standards defined for all data elements • Exchange schemas are defined
Managed	• Certification of trusted data sources in place • Master reference data sets identified • Exchange standards managed through data standards oversight process • Data standards oversight board oversees ongoing maintenance of internal standards and conformance to externally defined standards
Optimized	• Master data concepts managed within a master data environment • Taxonomies for data standards are defined and endorsed • Conformance with defined standards is integrated via a policy-oriented technical structure • Straight-through processing is enabled for standard data

around the understanding of how poor data quality impacts the business. An organization's level of maturity of data quality management can be assessed, and performance objectives can be defined. Architecting a framework that is essentially driven by governance and performance, intended to achieve a targeted level of maturity, will enable the description of a program with well-defined milestones and deliverables.

Table 3.7 Component Maturity Description for Data Quality Technology

Level	Characterization
Initial	• Internally developed ad hoc routines employed • "Not invented here" mentality
Repeatable	• Tools for assessing objective data quality are available • Data parsing, standardization, and cleansing are available • Data quality technology used for locate, match, and linkage
Defined	• Standardized procedures for using data quality tools for data quality assessment and improvement in place • Business rule–based techniques are employed for validation • Technology components for implementing data validation, certification, assurance, and reporting are in place • Technology components are standardized across the federated community at the service and at the implementation layers
Managed	• Automatic data correction guided by governance policies and defined business rules • Impact analysis and what-if scenarios supported by dashboard and reporting tools
Optimized	• Nontechnical users can define and modify data quality rules and dimensions dynamically

Table 3.8 Component Maturity Description for Performance Management

Level	Characterization
Initial	• Impacts are manifested and recognized long after failure events take place
Repeatable	• Characterization of areas of impact of poor data quality • Data profiling used to identify data failures in process
Defined	• Impact analysis framework in place • Data quality service components identify flaws early in process • Data quality service components defined • Issues tracking system in place to capture issues and their resolutions
Managed	• Data quality metrics fed into performance management reporting • Auditing based on conformance to rules associated with data quality dimensions • Consistent reporting of data quality management for necessary participants • Performance dashboards are in place • Role-based access to performance information • Well-defined visualization of data quality component contribution to business impacts
Optimized	• Enterprise-wide performance can be improved through policy modification via rules environment

ENTERPRISE INITIATIVE INTEGRATION

Approaching data quality management from an enterprise perspective means that the data quality program cannot operate in a vacuum, especially as other organizational initiatives are under way. The context and landscape in which data quality management will be deployed are important considerations when designing an effective data quality program. The impact that the data quality initiative will have on these initiatives must be considered, along with the impacts of those initiatives on the data quality program.

As organizations are gradually recognizing that the interconnectivity between the operational and analytic aspects of the business is driven by high quality data, there will be a recurring need to ensure that any major initiative is aligned with the data governance and data quality management processes described in this book. This chapter looks at a number of types of enterprise initiatives and their relationship with data quality management. In addition, the chapter looks at scoping the integration of data quality management along a variety of dimensions.

4.1 Planning Initiatives

Although maintaining a competitive edge requires forethought by senior management, many organizations are plagued by the absence of strategic objectives that should be intended to drive innovation and excellence in the marketplace. Organizations that engage in defining a vision and planning a strategy are more likely to be focused on achieving well-defined objectives. This section looks at examples of planning initiatives and the interdependency with data quality management.

4.1.1 Performance Management and Key Performance Indicators

From a strategic perspective, organizational performance must be defined in the context of identified business objectives. Structured methods for defining performance objectives, such as Norton and Kaplan's Balanced Scorecard [1], direct the senior managers to define business goals aligned along different perspectives relating to financial management, relationships with customers, internal processes, and internal learning and growth. From the strategic point of view, organizational goals should be defined realistically – they should be specific, measurable, and achievable, with numeric targets assigned for each objective. Some examples are:

- Set a target number of new customers to be acquired by the end of a 12-month period.
- Achieve a 90% collection rate for outstanding balances within agreed-to terms of payment.
- Improve utilization rate of existing hardware to 85%.
- Reduce corporate spend by 10% over a two-year period.

Key performance indicators (KPIs) are intended to measure how well the organization is performing against the defined performance goal. To continue our examples, corresponding key performance indicators might measure:

- New customers acquired by time period,
- Total dollars in "past due" receivables organized by time period,
- Existing hardware under repair, and
- Total dollars of corporate spend by time period.

In turn, each of these example key performance indicators captures rolled-up statistics associated with reported measures that rely on high quality information. In other words, even from the reporting aspects of performance management and KPIs, the quality of the underlying data is critical to a successful performance improvement activity. However, from the operational perspective, the quality of the data is even more important,

[1] See The Balanced Scorecard – Measures that Drive Performance, Harvard Business Review (Feb. 1992).

because KPIs indicative of failures to achieve performance goals will be the focus of drill-down, and the underlying measures that compose a key performance metric will need to accurately reflect the reported business activities so that actions can be taken to properly address any process gaps.

4.1.2 Process Improvement

A holistic approach to managing improvements across an organization involves understanding the interactivity of different business processes and implementing continuous improvements through modifications to both automated processes and their interactions with staff members using those automated processes. Some examples of process improvement programs, such as BPM (business process management), lean production, and six sigma, essentially look at the interactions of processes from across the organization, their interdependencies, and where inefficiencies or ineffectiveness can be identified and eliminated.

Aspects of business process improvement programs involve:

- Aligning the identified business objectives with existing business processes;
- Mapping and documenting those end-to-end business processes, especially ones that involve interaction with external entities (customers, suppliers, vendors, etc.);
- Collecting data from critical junctures within those end-to-end processes that reflect productivity or other operational performance measures in order to gain increased visibility into the mechanics of those processes;
- Adjusting the functional infrastructure (and the corresponding data management infrastructures) to identify overlaps, dependencies, and replication of data and functionality and define common services that can simplify maintenance of existing systems as well as define and implement new systems; and
- Optimizing the organization to reduce or eliminate bottlenecks, leading to improvements in efficiency and effectiveness.

Of course, these activities are intended to provide a framework for adjusting or even overhauling the methods by which those end-to-end business processes are designed and deployed in order to implement optimizations. Any attempts at exploiting enterprise business process improvements are by necessity inextricably linked to the use of information; alternatively, an enterprise data quality improvement program must be aligned with any adjustments or overhauls of business processes.

4.1.3 Organizational Change

Organizations, like people, do not remain static. Rather, they change, sometimes slowly and other times rapidly. So if the intention of instituting data quality is to establish an ongoing program, the policies, processes, and procedures must be able to persist even in the face of change. Here are some examples of organizational change that have ramifications in association with the data quality program:

- Reorganization and downsizing: As part of our approach to data quality management, we suggest the introduction of clearly defined roles mapped to specific individuals within an organization. Those individuals are trained in performing the tasks associated with those roles and are expected to fulfill a set of responsibilities to continually and proactively manage the assurance of high quality data. However, reorganizations and organizational downsizing can have radical impacts on the stability of a data quality initiative, especially as key senior sponsors are moved to new and different roles, or when data quality staff members are reassigned or downsized. For a data quality program to survive reorganizations, the roles, responsibilities, policies, and processes must be properly documented in a way that is dissociated from the individuals implementing the program, and the resulting "run-books" for data quality management can be used to bridge any staffing gaps or changes.

- Outsourcing: Outsourcing is intended to reduce total costs of operations through the ability to modulate staff hiring, reduce labor costs by paying for temporary or short-term development, control capital acquisition costs, and generally reduce some of the risks related to starting up new development. However, any time that one introduces additional layers of control within a system development process or assignation of an operational process (such as managing a call center), the challenges of miscommunication are amplified, especially in translation of what are expected to be commonly used business terms, reference data domains, and exchanged data elements. When considering outsourcing, one must integrate the data quality team to ensure that data exchanges are controlled within the expectations of the consuming business processes.

- Offshoring: If outsourcing poses challenges associated with communication between the organization and external parties, then offshoring, which is basically having outsourced business activities or processes performed in another country, can be even more problematic. Regulations, privacy rules, and most importantly the cultural and language barriers that exist in other countries will detract from using common business terms and definitions, leading to confusion and potential inconsistencies.

- IT management changes: Whether the changes are taking place at the senior level, or incremental replacements at other places along the organizational spectrum, there will always be some degree of instability when there are staff changes in the IT department. Because the IT staff embodies the technical aspects of the best practices for data management, IT management changes will, by necessity, impact the continuity of the data quality program.

In each of these instances, the challenges associated with changes to organizational staff, either through reorganization, downsizing, or allocation of responsibilities to external staff, will impact the continuity of the data quality program. Therefore, when implementing the program, make sure that you accommodate for the possibilities of how staff turnover and organizational changes will affect the program.

How is this done? Some ideas include:

- Making sure there is a clear distinction between the *roles* and the individuals who are assigned those roles,
- Developing a concrete program plan with discrete tasks,
- Defining processes and procedures and carefully documenting those procedures so that the knowledge can be easily transferred,
- Developing training material aimed at different levels so that new team members can come up to speed rapidly, and
- Identifying more than one key senior sponsor who will remain as stakeholders after reorganizations.

4.1.4 Strategic Planning

Organizations that have embarked on developing a strategic plan need to align their planned initiatives with their data management practices. For example, consider these strategic directions and their relationship on quality data:

- New products and services: The circumstances in which new products and services are developed, priced, manufactured, marketed, sold, and delivered rely on accurate information relating to the prospective market, the ability to build and/ or deliver those products and services, and performance according to expectations. In turn, the quality of the new products and services may depend on the right information. This suggests that strategic initiatives relating to new products must be assessed to determine the dependence on information and clearly defined performance metrics whose measures are accessible and computable within the right time to decide future investments in marketing, advertising, product development, or even product termination.

- Cost control and spend management: Corporate sourcing and procurement organizations should always look for opportunities to introduce efficiencies, reduce costs, and negotiate desirable terms with vendors and suppliers. These opportunities are revealed in a number of ways, such as demand aggregation, improved supplier performance assessment, assurance of regulatory compliance, determination of rebates and refunds, and identification of noncompliant spend. All of these business benefits can accrue as a result of a process for reviewing and analyzing spend data. However, few companies have the ability to gain a comprehensive perspective of the products and services purchased and their associated providers. Even when improvements such as negotiated product prices have been identified, ensuring that the negotiated savings can be achieved in practice requires additional visibility into purchasing, supplier fulfillment, and delivery data. Yet the top challenges for spend analysis include "poor data quality," "too many data sources," and "lack of standardized processes" [2]. In essence, the biggest challenges to procurement improvements have to do with information, and the benefits of spend analysis can only be achieved when the spend analysis tools have access to the right data.

- Revenue improvement: There are a number of methods for improving revenue, ranging from concentration on new customer acquisition, reducing attrition, identifying high net worth customers, reducing cost of goods sold, identifying underserved regional markets – and this is just the top of the list. Implementing any of these methods relies on accurate querying and reporting of current states of the different revenue channels and associated processes. For example, identifying high net worth individuals requires accurate views into individual net worth and standardized calculations for assessing value, often using data pulled from multiple sources with inconsistent semantics. Therefore, increasing revenue is tightly coupled with information availability and utility.

- Mergers and acquisitions: As companies are acquired or when two companies agree to merge, there are significant challenges in merging their information technology infrastructures. The

[2] Spend Analysis: Working Too Hard for the Money, Aberdeen Group, August 2007.

challenge of coalescing two client data sets into a single customer database is relatively straightforward. However, there are even more complex challenges one will face, such as integrating underlying core data management frameworks, assessing the enterprise scope of information requirements, integration of system functionality, determination of new data requirements, and alignment of reference data and hierarchies. This range of tasks can only add to a growing list of data expectations that need to be aligned with the organization's data quality activities.

- Environmental considerations: Initiatives associated with environmental issues are directly related to information. Whether the organization is intending to comply with environmental material handling and its associated reporting regulations, intending to drive new marketing campaigns in relation to "green" behavior, or identifying cost savings based on analyzing energy spend (among other strategies), the benefits are going to depend on accurate information.

- Competitive environment: Assessing the size of a market and identifying an approach for capturing, maintaining, and potentially growing a percentage of that market are tasks involving data collection, organization, and reporting. For example, construction and plant management services are directly linked to the manufacturing, sales, and delivery of the machinery supporting those activities, and collecting that information and managing it as a corporate asset provides a strategic advantage. That knowledge, when coupled with results of competitive actions (such as responding to requests for proposals and bids for contract work) provide insight into market share (along a number of dimensions) based on which proposals were accepted, which were not accepted, and which of your competitors won the ones your company lost. In this case, the accuracy of those competitive and market share estimates drive projections for bidding for and acquiring business moving forward, and even small miscalculations or missing data can skew earnings projections, which can have significant impact internally, and for public companies, externally as well.

In any of these strategic initiatives, the data quality practitioners should be incorporated into the planning and implementation to integrate quality data directly into the program.

4.1.5 Centralized versus Decentralized Control

In a centralized information technology environment, all IT resources are provided by a single IT business unit. In a decentralized environment, individual lines of business maintain control over the information technology resources necessary to run the applications supporting that line of business. Although there are benefits and disadvantages of either approach, the decision for one over the other does impact the approach to enterprise data quality management.

Because a centralized environment supports centralized control over the IT infrastructure as well as vendor relationships, this approach is better suited for a data quality approach that emphasizes data standards, common metadata management and data quality control, and reduction in replicated (and inconsistent) functionality supporting data quality. However, because all activity is managed by the centralized environment, there may be a risk that alternate demands for support of application functionality or other system requirements may be assigned a higher priority than that given to addressing data quality issues.

Decentralized systems may benefit a data quality program because the IT group for each line of business will tend to be more responsive to data issues that impact successful operations for the line of business. However, because of the decentralized control, the organization may replicate functionality supporting data quality, and reduced collaboration will lead to inconsistency in metadata, data element definitions, and ultimately in application of data controls, standardization, and enhancements to similar or even the same data sets.

4.2 Framework Initiatives

Typically, the organically grown application environment is a collection of business applications developed to support specific vertical line-of-business needs. However, the perception that the organization should operate holistically in a way that optimizes for general corporate benefit suggests that there should be an alignment of business processes and associated applications along horizontal lines and not just along the vertical lines of business.

4.2.1 Enterprise Architecture

Informally, enterprise architecture is a framework for describing all aspects of the structure of how an enterprise works, broken down into systems, then into associated subsystems, while exposing the relationship among the systems/subsystems, as well as internal and external interfaces. Enterprise architecture frameworks typically focus on the business activities and business architecture, then look at the systems that support the business architecture, then delve down into the information and technology architectures showing how information and control flow across the organization.

The objective of enterprise architecture is to provide a high-level view of the interactions, dependencies, and bottlenecks that can be reviewed, improved, and optimized. The challenge for data quality in how it fits with enterprise architecture is that the impacts of poor data quality are reflected at the business level but are manifested as technical issues. In other words, the challenge of data quality is pervasive along both the description of the business and the descriptions of the technologies supporting the business. Therefore, the data quality practitioners must work with the enterprise architects to understand and document where data quality must be incorporated as an inherent component of the enterprise architecture.

4.2.2 Enterprise Resource Planning

Enterprise resource planning (or ERP) systems integrate system functionality along common business activities in one monolithic system intended to facilitate business operations. ERP systems integrate financial management, the sales cycle, human resources, product design and development, supply chain management, inventory and warehouse management, and so on.

Because of their monolithic characteristics, there are many data-oriented activities associated with implementing an ERP system, such as identifying overlaps between existing business services and the ERP system, selecting applications for replacement, data migration, data integration, as well as implementing interfacing between other legacy or proprietary applications and the ERP system. Alternatively, the ERP system may be the proprietary system, requiring interfaces to the other existing applications. To some extent, ERP systems are somewhat rigid and immune to customization, and this makes instituting embedded data quality controls difficult. In addition, there are issues when attempting to integrate large-scale ERP systems with other enterprise data initiatives, such as metadata management or master data management, since the ERP systems may be closed systems, leading to conflicts in aligning those programs.

4.2.3 Build versus Buy

A fundamental question often asked by IT professionals is whether new applications should be designed and developed internally or purchased from product vendors. While in many situations vendor applications fit the organization's business application needs, from a data quality perspective one might question how well data quality controls have been engineered into the vendor's software package. Since these products often incorporate internal, proprietary data sets, there is little visibility into the ways the product guards against data errors, and it may be difficult, if not impossible, to gain native access to the product's data. Special hooks, queries, or "pipes" may be necessary to extract the data to subject it to data validation.

Alternatively, deciding to build new applications means that the data quality validation and control need to be designed and engineered directly into the software. In this case, there will need to be expectations that data requirements are analyzed along with the functional and technical requirements, and that the system designers will incorporate data validation, inspection, and monitoring into the system design.

4.2.4 Retirement of Legacy Systems

Applications that have been in production for a long time may be robust and dependable, but as the staff members involved in the development and maintenance of those systems leave the organization, the ability to capture and manage the undocumented lore that surrounds the system eventually dissipates. At the same time, older systems may not have been designed in a way that can be extended or adjusted to meet changing business needs or environments. Decisions are made to incorporate ERP systems whose functionality overlaps with those of the existing legacy applications.

At some point there will be a decision to retire older systems, and there are impacts on the data quality program, including issues associated with assessing the quality of the legacy data sets, data migration, and integration with the replacement system. At the same time, ensuring the quality of the replacement system and verifying that it does not operate in a way that is inconsistent with user expectations become important drivers for the data quality practitioner.

4.3 Operational and Application Initiatives

Aside from organizational and framework initiatives, there are operational and application initiatives that impact the entire organization, especially in relation to data quality management, In this section we consider a few examples: compliance, business intelligence, and the purchase and deployment of proprietary systems.

4.3.1 Compliance

Regulatory compliance is one of those necessary activities that, to some extent, are not perceived to add significant value to the bottom line. However, complying with regulations is generally mandatory, and that means that there will be staff dedicated to ensuring compliance. Compliance basically means demonstrating that the organization is in accordance with defined guidelines. That being said, from the information technology perspective, much of compliance centers on two tasks: reporting and auditability.

To accurately address reporting guidelines, the organization may have to accumulate data extracted from multiple data sets across different lines of business, transform and aggregate that data, and reorganize it into a format that meets the regulatory requirements. As with any data integration task, compliance reporting is going to be plagued by inconsistencies in structure and semantics, not to mention the host of other potential data errors such as incompleteness, inaccuracy, and currency. Depending on the seriousness of the organization in accurate and auditable compliance reporting, the data quality team must work closely with the compliance team to define data quality expectations and incorporate data validation, inspection, and notifications when the data does not live up to defined reporting standards.

Auditability suggests not only that the reports are accurate, but that the processes used to materialize the reports can be reviewed and shown to be sound. However, by virtue of the application of best practices in instituting data quality control and data governance across the compliance process, the organization can demonstrate that not only are there quality metrics for the reported data, but that the processes for inspection and monitoring are defined, documented, and rigorously followed, and can be independently validated as proper.

4.3.2 Business Intelligence and Data Warehousing

The major objectives of business intelligence systems and their underlying data warehouse infrastructure are querying and reporting for decision support, compliance, operational reporting, performance management, and integration of the results of analyses and predictive modeling to enhance existing operational activities. The challenge from the data quality perspective is that selection of data to be migrated into a data warehouse is typically done so as an afterthought. Little planning of data is done for quality assurance for the data within the source system other than what is expected by the source application.

As a result, when the data sets are used for purposes other than those originally intended, the results coming out of the data warehouse will be inconsistent with the original systems, leading to confusion and an almost continuous need for revisions, reconciliations, and rework. Embarking on an enterprise data warehouse initiative will depend on an enterprise data requirements analysis process (see chapter 9) in which the performance objectives desired from a decision support system or a business intelligence program will be turned into specific data requirements imposed on the data at the point of creation or integration.

4.3.3 Proprietary Systems

As suggested in section 4.2.3, there are significant challenges associated with assuring the quality of data managed within proprietary systems, for a number of reasons, such as:

- Inability to access the data in a native manner,
- Subtleties in the internal system design masked by hard-coding in software (such as mappings and transformations),
- Deficiencies in the models hidden behind the proprietary interface,
- Embedded data dependencies that are hidden behind the proprietary interface,
- Inability to integrate data validation or inspection of data quality rules,
- Need for "connector" tools to access the data,
- Undocumented data structures,
- Structure of data elements not aligned with organizational standards,
- Semantics of commonly used data concepts that differ from the rest of the organization, and
- Inconsistency between proprietary data and that stored in other data sets.

There are some industries that are largely run on applications suites purchased from external vendors, whereas enterprise systems (such as ERP, as described in section 4.2.2) may be "closed" as well. When purchasing proprietary systems, be aware that additional integration of data quality processes will be necessary.

4.4 Scoping Issues

The assigned area in which data quality management is deployed can be influenced based on a number of factors. In this section we look at scoping issues and their impact on data quality management.

4.4.1 Global versus Local

Global organizations may have different subsidiaries aligned along different dimensions – by line of business, large geographic regions, country, and so on. However, crossing borders introduces scoping issues regarding the reach of governance and oversight for information, and different countries establish different regulatory criteria associated with data management. Some examples are:

- Privacy: Some countries impose restrictions on management and use of personal identifying data; they also prevent its being stored or viewed from other countries.
- Language: Differences in language will complicate the management of consistent semantics, which is already difficult enough in a single language.
- Culture: Even when the languages used are the same, cultural differences introduce variance in the ways that data sets are used and managed.

This raises the question as to whether data governance, data quality, and other data management initiatives such as master data management are deployed across a global scope, or within a region or country. The data quality team must also consider the methods for deploying data quality and data governance consistently, whether the scope is local or global, as well as methods for oversight and collaboration.

4.4.2 Vertical versus Horizontal

Almost as a companion issue to considerations of enterprise architecture and centralized versus decentralized control, is data quality managed more effectively vertically within line-of-business silos or imposed horizontally across the collection of organizational business processes? There are benefits to the siloed approach, especially because the scope is limited to defining and managing data validity and accuracy associated with discrete operational expectations. Line-of-business data quality activities can have success in improving the efficiency and trustworthiness of a select set of related processes. A vertical scope is best suited to organizations that are largely operational and do not share data for reporting or analytic purposes.

However, there are likely to be common data definitions, business terms, and data elements used across the organization, and scoping the data quality management program horizontally will allow the different lines of business to maintain consistency. In turn, a horizontal scope will address the needs of organizations with expectations for enterprise reporting and for exploiting analytics across multiple business applications.

4.4.3 Internal versus External

It would be unusual for any organization to not have to consider the management of data within its own administrative boundaries. Yet in some cases one must consider the management of the quality of data outside of the organization. For example, intermediaries that coordinate the activities of multiple organizations (such as third-party administrators, oversight boards, consortia overseeing industry data sharing) must consider data controls that are for the benefit of its constituent community.

This scoping issue looks at the roles and responsibilities for data governance and data quality once the data is no longer under your discrete control. An externally scoped data quality management scheme will look at what happens to data in transit, defining data sharing standards, exercising controls within the boundaries of other organizations' applications, creating "data quality firewalls" within a data sharing network, and overseeing participant compliance with defined data quality rules.

4.5 Summary

Data quality management has a finite scope as a collection of best practices, and the next chapters will look at those practices in greater detail. However, the maturity of the program is not just defined in terms of functional capability; it must also be reviewed in the context of how the data quality practitioners can integrate a continuous program that supports organizational change and upheaval, new initiatives, or other broad-based activities within (and sometimes external to) the organization. Scoping out the data quality mission and planning a road map and a program plan that can accommodate adjustments to the enterprise will help improve the chances of data quality success.

DEVELOPING A BUSINESS CASE AND A DATA QUALITY ROAD MAP

One of the most frequently asked questions about developing a data quality program is "how do we develop a convincing business case for investing in information quality improvement?" In this chapter we look at how our characterization of risks associated with ignoring data quality problems can be presented to senior management as an opportunity for developing competitive advantage, and what considerations for staffing and planning can be compiled into a tactical road map for deploying a data quality strategy.

One of the major issues is that the senior managers who already recognize the value of improved data quality don't need justification to initiate a data quality program. However, organizational best practices require that some form of business case be assembled and presented to a governing body to justify the investment in any kind of activity. A data quality improvement program is a serious commitment on behalf of an organization, and its importance deserves to be effectively communicated to the all of the business managers who may participate, either as sponsors or as beneficiaries.

In chapter 1, we identified key impact dimensions and corresponding impact categories associated with poor data quality. The process of building a business case to justify both the technology and the organizational infrastructure necessary to ensure a successful program requires additional research and documentation, namely:

- Quantification of identified financial impacts,
- Assessment of the actual financial impacts,
- Determination of the source of the actual root causes in the information processing that are correlated to those impacts,
- Diagnosis of the root cause of the process failure,
- Determination of potential remediation approaches,
- The costs to remediate those process failures, and
- A way to prioritize and plan the solutions of those problems.

All of this information can be accumulated into a pair of templates: one for impact analysis and the other for estimating the opportunity for value improvement or creation. In particular, the impact template is used to document the problems, issues, business impacts, and quantifiers. Together all this information enables the practitioner to estimate a quantified yearly incurred impact attributable to poor data quality.

5.1 Return on the Data Quality Investment

What is the purpose for developing a return on investment (ROI) model? In many situations, the ROI formulation is used before starting a project purely for the purpose of project approval and initiation and is then forgotten. In other environments, the ROI calculation is made after the fact as a way of demonstrating that some activity had some kind of positive business impact. In either situation, the ROI model is a marketing device. But while one might consider this approach as appropriate for projecting a return on investment, it is also reasonable to consider whether the expected "returns" are directly (and predictably) attributable to operations that are within the organization's control.

As an example, let's say the national tax collection agency (in the United States that is the Internal Revenue Service) has built a business case for the investment of a large amount of money to reengineer its software systems, using an expected increase in tax collections as the business justification. The ROI model suggests that building a more modern application system will result in greater collections. The improved system may account for more precision in calculating and collecting taxes, but in reality the amount of taxes collected depends on more than just the computer application. A downturn in the economy might result in more people out of work, legislation may mandate a freeze on the minimum wage or lower the tax rates, or natural disasters may result in migratory populations that are difficult to track down and contact. In essence, justifying the creation of a new application system based on increased collections ignores the fact that the expected performance results depend on a number of other variables beyond the organization's control.

5.2 Developing the Business Case

Therefore, the intention is not just to provide information that can be used to justify a data quality program, it is to provide a foundation for continuing to use the knowledge acquired during this phase to manage performance improvement over the data quality life cycle. If the impacts are truly related to poor data quality, then improving data quality will alleviate the pain in a measurably correlated manner.

In turn, then, the ROI model becomes a management tool to gauge the effectiveness of the program. If improving data quality really will lead to improvements in achieving the business objectives (as is to be claimed by the business case), then the same measures used to determine the "value gap" can be used to monitor performance improvement!

The process for developing a business case is basically a quest to identify a "value gap" associated with data quality – the area of greatest opportunity for creating new value with the optimal investment. Following the process summarized in Figure 5.1 will help the analyst team identify the opportunities with the highest value and, therefore, the highest priority.

5.3 Finding the Business Impacts

It is highly probable that not only will there be an awareness of existing data quality issues, there will also be some awareness of the magnitude of the impacts these issues incur. The value of

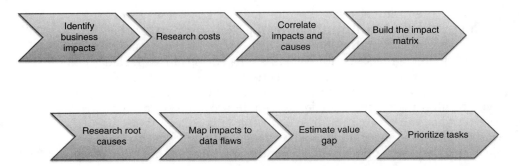

Figure 5.1 Developing a business case for data quality management.

the impact taxonomy developed based on the material in chapter 1 is twofold. First, by clearly specifying the many different impacts, it is possible to trace some of the issues back through the processing stages and determine whether some number can be attributed to a single process failure. Second, it shows how the results of different data quality events can be grouped together, which simplifies the research necessary to determine financial impact.

5.3.1 Roles and Responsibilities

Although there may be some awareness of existing issues, as a practical matter, the process of identifying and categorizing impacts is best performed as a collaborative effort among the line-of-business managers and their supporting information technology staff. The early process of identification, by necessity, relates poor data quality to business issues, which require knowledge of both business processes and how applications support those processes. Therefore, a small team consisting of one business representative and one IT representative from each line of business should assemble to expose those issues that will drive the business case.

This meeting should be scheduled for an extended block of time (half a day) and convene at a location that is away from distractions such as telephone and email. One attendee should be included as a scribe to document the discussion.

5.3.2 Clarification of Business Objectives

Because data quality management is often triggered by acute events, the sentiment may be reactive ("what do we do *right now* to improve the quality?"), perhaps with some level of anxiety.

To alleviate this, it is necessary to level-set the meeting and ensure that every participant is aware that the goal is to come up with clearly quantifiable issues attributable to unexpected data.

To achieve this, it is useful for each group's business partici-pant to prepare a short (10 minutes) overview of that group's business objectives – what services the group provides, what investment is made (staffing and otherwise) in providing those services, and how success is quantified. Next, each group's IT participant should provide a short overview of how information is used to support the group's services and achieve the business objectives.

5.3.3 Identification and Classification

The next step, then, in developing the business case is to clearly identify the issues attributable to poor data quality and to determine if they indeed are pain points for the organization. Again, we can employ the impact categories described in chapter 1 in this process, mostly from the top down by asking these questions:

- Where are the organization's costs higher than they should be?
- Are there any situations in which the organization's revenues are below expectations? (Note: for nonprofit or govern-mental organizations, you may substitute your quantifiable objectives for the word *revenues*.)
- Are there areas where confidence is lowered?
- What are the greatest areas of risk?

The answers to these questions introduce areas for further concentration, in which the questions can be refined to focus on our specific topic by appending the phrase "because of poor data quality" at the end (e.g., "Where are the organization's costs higher than they should be because of poor data quality?"). The analyst can again employ the taxonomy at a lower level, asking questions specifically about the lower levels of the hierarchy. For example, if the organization's costs are higher, is it due to error detection, correction, scrap, rework, or any other area of increased overhead costs?

5.3.4 Identifying Data Flaws

At the same time, it will be necessary to understand how the impact is related to poor data quality. Most often a direct relation can be assessed – each issue has some underlying cause that can be identified at the point of manifestation. For example, extra costs associated with shipping ordered items occur when the original shipping address is incorrect and the item is returned and needs to be shipped a second time.

Data flaws are the result of failed processes, so understanding the kinds of data flaws that are causing the impacts will facilitate root cause analysis. At the end of this stage, there should be a list of data flaws and business impacts that require further investigation for determination of financial impact, assessment of measurement criteria, and setting performance improvement goals.

5.4 Researching Costs

The next step in the process is to get a high-level view of the actual financial impacts associated with each issue. This step combines subject matter expertise with some old-fashioned detective work. Because the intention of developing a business case is to understand gross-level impacts, it is reasonable to attempt to get a high-level impact assessment that does not require significant depth of analysis. To this end, there is some flexibility in exactness of detail. In fact, much of the information that is relevant can be collected in a relatively short time.

In this situation, anecdotes are good starting places, since they are indicative of high-impact, acute issues with high management visibility. Since the current issues probably have been festering for some time, there will be evidence of individuals addressing the manifestation of the problem in the past. Historical data associated with work/process flows during critical data events are a good source of cost/impact data.

To research additional impact, it is necessary to delve deeper into the core of the story. To understand the scope, it is valuable to ask these kinds of questions:

- What is it about the data that caused the problem?
- How big is the problem?
- Has this happened before?
- How many times?
- When this happened in the past, what was the remediation process?
- What was done to prevent it from happening again?

Environments with event and issue tracking systems have a head start, as the details will have been captured as part of the resolution workflow. Alternatively, organizations with formal change control management frameworks can review recommended and implemented changes triggered as a result of issue remediation.

An initial survey of impact can be derived from this source – detection, correction, scrap and rework, and system development risks are examples of impact categories that can be researched through this resource.

At the same time, consult issues tracking system event logs and management reports on staff allocation for problem resolution and review external impacts (e.g., stock price, customer satisfaction, management spin) to identify key quantifiers for business impact.

5.5 Correlating Impacts and Causes

The next step in developing the business case involves tracking the data flaws backward through the information processing flow to determine at which point in the process the data flaw was introduced. Since many data quality issues are very likely to be process failure, eliminating the source of the introduction of bad data upstream will provide much greater value than just correcting bad data downstream.

Consider the example in Figure 5.2. At the data input processing stage, a customer name and contact information are

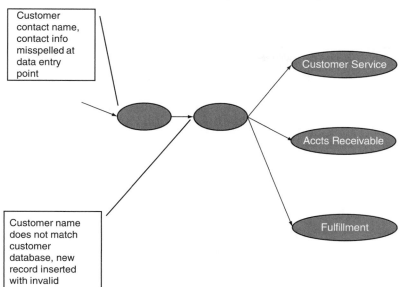

Data Flaws Incur Business Impacts – An Example

Customer contact name, contact info misspelled at data entry point

Customer name does not match customer database, new record inserted with invalid information

Customer Service

Accts Receivable

Fulfillment

Figure 5.2 An example of how one data flaw causes multiple impacts.

incorrectly entered. The next stage, in which an existing customer record is located, the misspelling prevents the location of the record, and a new record is inadvertently created. Impacts are manifested at Customer Service, Accounts Receivable, and Fulfillment.

In this supply chain example, it is interesting to note that each of the client application users would assume that their issues were separate ones, yet they all stem from the same root cause. The value in assessing the location of the introduction of the flaw into the process is that when we can show that one core problem has multiple impacts, the value of remediating the source of the problem will be much greater.

5.6 The Impact Matrix

The answers to the questions combined with the research will provide insight into quantifiable costs, which will populate an impact matrix template. A simple example, shown in Figure 5.3, is intended to capture information about the different kinds of impacts and how they relate to specific problems. In this example, there are five columns in the impact matrix:

Figure 5.3 An example of an impact template.

Problem	Issue	Business Impact	Quantifier	Yearly Incurred Impact

1. **Problem** – this is the description of the original source problem.
2. **Issue** – this is a list of issues that are attributable to the problem. There may be multiple issues associated with a specific problem.
3. **Business Impact** – this describes the different business impacts that are associated with a specific issue.
4. **Quantifier** – this describes a measurement of the severity of the business impact.
5. **Periodic Accumulated Impact** – this provides a scaled representation of the actual costs that are related to the business impact over a specified time frame, such as the "yearly impact" shown in Figure 5.3.

We will walk through an example of how the template in Figure 5.3 can be populated to reflect an example of how invalid data entry at one point in the supply chain management process results in impacts incurred at each of three different client application areas. For each business area, the corresponding impact quantifiers are identified, and then their associated costs are projected and expressed as yearly incurred impacts.

In our impact matrix, the intention is to document the critical data quality problems, so that an analyst can review the specific issues that occur within the enterprise and then enumerate all the business impacts incurred by each of those issues. Once the impacts are specified, we simplify the process of assessing the actual costs, which we also incorporate in the matrix. The resulting matrix reveals the summed costs that can be attributed to poor data quality.

5.7 Problems, Issues, Causes

The first column of the impact matrix to be filled describes the problems and the associated data quality issues. Figuring out the presumptive error that leads to business impacts grounds the later steps of determining alternatives for remediation.

In our example, shown in Figure 5.4, it had already been determined that the source problem is the incorrect introduction of customer identifying information at the data entry point. The issue, though, describes *why* it is a problem. Note that there may be multiple data issues associated with each business problem.

5.8 Mapping Impacts to Data Flaws

The next step is to evaluate the business impacts that occur at all of the line-of-business applications. These effectively describe the actual pain experienced as a result of the data flaw and provide

Problem	Issue	Business Impact	Quantifier	Yearly Incurred Impact
Customer contact name, contact info misspelled at data entry point	*Inability to clearly identify known customers leads to duplication*			

Figure 5.4 Identifying problems and their issues.

greater detail as to why the source problem causes organizational pain. In our example, as seen in Figure 5.5, there are specific business impacts within each vertical line of business. These business impacts are added to the impact matrix, as shown in Figure 5.6.

These business impacts are the same ones identified using the process in section 5.3. Although these are categorized in the impact matrix in relation to the source problem, it is valuable to maintain other classifications. For example, the different areas of shading reflect the application or line of business. We could also track how each impact falls into the business impact categories of chapter 1.

5.9 Estimating the Value Gap

The next step is to enumerate the quantifiers associated with the business impact and calculate a cost impact that can be projected over a year's time. Realize that not all business impacts are

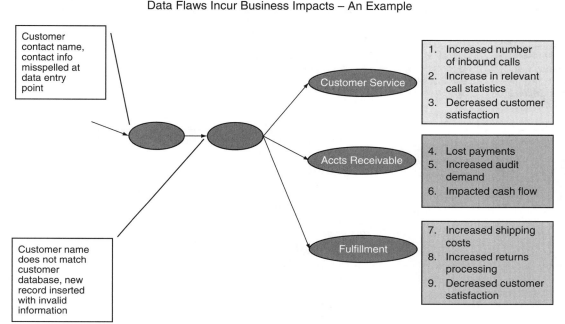

Figure 5.5 Determining the actual business impacts and how they relate to the source problem.

necessarily quantified in terms of money. In our example, shown in Figure 5.7, some of the quantifiers are associated with monetary amounts (e.g., staff time, overdue receivables, increased shipping costs), whereas others are quantified with other organizational objectives (e.g., customer satisfaction, call center productivity). If the quantifier does not specifically relate to a monetary value, we will document it as long as the impact is measurable.

In the version of the impact matrix in Figure 5.7 we have identified hard quantifiers and, based on those quantifiers, some sample incurred impacts rolled up over a year's time. For example, the increase in inbound calls resulted in the need for additional staff time allocated to fielding those calls, and that additional time was summed up to $30,000 for the year. Auditing the accounts receivables might show that $250,000 worth of products have been ordered and shipped, but not paid for, an impact on revenues. Products shipped to the wrong location, returned, and reshipped had an average cost of $30, and took place 50 times per week, which equals $78,000.

Problem	Issue	Business Impact	Quantifier	Yearly Incurred Impact
Customer contact name, contact info misspelled at data entry point	*Inability to clearly identify known customers leads to duplication*	Increased number of inbound call center calls		
		Increase in relevant call statistics		
		Decreased customer satisfaction		
		Lost payments		
		Increased audit demand		
		Impacted cash flow		
		Increased shipping costs		
		Increased returns processing		
		Decreased customer satisfaction		

Figure 5.6 Adding business impacts for each of the issues.

One of the big challenges is determining the quantifiers and the actual costs, because often those costs are buried within ongoing operations or are not differentiable from the operational budget. One rule of thumb to keep in mind is to *be conservative*. Documenting hard quantifiers is necessary since they will be used for current state assessment and identification of long-term target improvement goals. The objective is to come up with estimates that are both believable and supportable, but most of all, can be used for establishing *achievable* performance improvement goals. If the numbers are conservatively developed, the chances that changes to the environment will result in measurable improvement are greater.

We are not done yet; realize that a business case doesn't just account for the benefits of an improvement program – it also must factor in the costs associated with the improvements. Therefore, we need to look at the specific problems that are the root causes and what it would cost to fix those problems. In this

Problem	Issue	Business Impact	Quantifier	Yearly Incurred Impact
Customer contact name, contact info misspelled at data entry point	*Inability to clearly identify known customers leads to duplication*	Increased number of inbound call center calls	Staff time	$30,000.00
		Increase in relevant call statistics	Average call duration, throughput, hold time	
		Decreased customer satisfaction	Call drop rate, re-calls	
		Lost payments	Overdue receivables	$250,000.00
		Increased audit demand	Staff time	$20,000.00
		Impacted cash flow	Cash flow volatility	
		Increased shipping costs	Increased shipping costs	$78,000.00
		Increased returns processing	Staff time	$23,000.00
		Decreased customer satisfaction	Attrition, order reduction (time or size)	

Figure 5.7 Quantifiers and estimated costs.

step, we evaluate the specific issues and develop a set of high-level improvement plans, including analyst and developer staff time along with the costs of acquiring data quality tools. We can use a separate template, the remediation matrix (shown in Figure 5.8), that illustrates how potential solutions solve the core problem(s), and what the costs are for each proposed solution.

Figure 5.8 shows an example remediation matrix, documenting the cost of each solution, which also allows us to allocate the improvement to the documented problem (and its associated impacts). Again, at this stage in the process it may not be necessary to identify the exact costs, but rather to get a ballpark estimate.

5.10 Prioritizing Actions

Because multiple problems across the enterprise may require the same solution, this opens up the possibility for economies of scale. It also allows us to amortize both the staff and technology

Problem	Issue	Solution	Implementation Costs	Staffing
Customer contact name, contact info misspelled at data entry point	*Inability to clearly identify known customers leads to duplication*	Parsing and Standardization, record linkage tools for cleansing	$150,000.00 for license 15% annual maintenance	.75 FTE for 1 year .15 FTE for annual maintenance

Figure 5.8 Quantifiers and estimated costs.

investment across multiple problem areas, thereby further diluting the actual investment attributable to each area of business impact.

Essentially, we can boil the prioritization process down to simple arithmetic:

- Each data issue accounts for some conservatively quantifiable gap in value over a specified time period.
- The root cause of each data issue can be remediated with a particular initial investment plus a continuous investment over the same specified time period.
- For each data issue calculate the opportunity value as the value gap minus the remediation cost.

One can then sort the issues by the opportunity value, which will highlight those issues whose remediation will provide the greatest value to the organization. Of course, this simplistic model is a starting point, and other aspects can be integrated into the calculations, such as:

- Time to value,
- Initial investment in tools and technology,
- Available skills, and
- Learning curve.

Any organization must cast the value within its own competencies and feasibility of execution and value. Although these templates provide a starting point, there is value in refining the business case development process to ensure that a valid return on investment can be achieved while delivering value within a reasonable time frame.

5.11 The Data Quality Road Map

We now have two inputs for mapping out a plan for implementing data quality management program. Pragmatically, they are the value gap analysis described in this chapter and the data quality maturity model described in chapter 3. The road map combines the two by considering the level of maturity that is necessary to address the prioritized issues in the appropriate order of execution.

Though one may aspire to achieve the highest level of maturity across all of the data quality framework components, the complexity introduced by the different kinds of challenges, combined with the oftentimes advisory role played by the data quality manager limits the mandate that can be imposed on the enterprise. Instead, it is desirable to propose a data quality vision that both supports the business objectives of the organization yet remains pragmatically achievable within the collaborative environment of the enterprise community. A practical approach is to target a level of maturity at which the necessary benefits of data quality management are achieved for the enterprise while streamlining the acceptance path for the individuals who will ultimately be contributing to the data quality effort.

Given that targeted level of maturity, the next step is to lay out a road map for attaining that objective, broken out by phases that have achievable milestones and deliverables. These milestones and deliverables can be defined based on the descriptions of the component maturity in chapter 4. A typical implementation road map will contain five phases:
1. Establishing fundamentals
2. Formalize data quality activities
3. Deploy operational aspects
4. Establish level of maturity
5. Assess and fine-tune

At the end of the final phase, there is an opportunity to review whether the stated objectives are met and whether it is reasonable to target a higher level of maturity.

For example, consider this road map for attaining level 3 in the maturity model, which requires establishing the components detailed within levels 2 and 3 in chapter 3. The data quality strategy is deployed in five phases, with the objective of each phase of implementing the best practices that are specified in the detailed data quality maturity model.

5.11.1 Establish Fundamentals

Phase 1 establishes the fundamental organizational concepts necessary for framing the transition towards a high quality environment, with the following milestones:

- A framework for collaboration and sharing of knowledge between application manager, business client, and IT practitioners is put in place.
- Technology and operational best practices are identified, collected, and distributed via the collaboration framework.
- The relevant dimensions of data quality associated with data values are identified and are recognized as relevant by the business sponsors.
- Privacy, security, authorization, and limitation of use policies are articulated in ways that can be implemented.
- Tools for assessing objective data quality are available.
- Data standards are adopted.
- There is a process for characterizing areas of impact of poor data quality.
- Data quality rules are defined to identify data failures in process.

5.11.2 Formalize the Data Quality Activities

During phase 2, steps are taken to more formally define data quality activities and to take the initial steps in collaborative data quality management:

- Key individuals from enterprise form a data quality team to devise and recommend data governance program and policies.
- Expectations associated with dimensions of data quality associated with data values can be articulated.
- Simple errors are identified and reported.
- Root cause analysis is enabled using data quality rules and data validation.
- Data parsing, standardization, and cleansing tools are available.
- Data quality technology is used for entity location, record matching, and record linkage.
- Data quality impact analysis framework is in place.

5.11.3 Operationalizing Data Quality Management

Many of the ongoing operational aspects of a data quality program are put into place during phase 3:

- Data governance board consisting of business and IT representatives from across the enterprise is in place.

- Expectations associated with dimensions of data quality related to data values, formats, and semantics can be articulated.
- Standards defined for data inspection for determination of accuracy.
- Standardized procedures for using data quality tools for data quality assessment and improvement in place.
- Data standards metadata managed within participant enterprises.
- Data quality service components identify flaws early in process.
- Data quality service components feed into performance management reporting.

5.11.4 Incremental Maturation

Phase 4 establishes most of the characteristics of the level 3 maturity:
- Guiding principles, charter, and data governance are in place.
- Standardized view of data stewardship across different applications and divisions, and stewardship program is in place.
- Capability for validation of data is established using defined data quality rules.
- Performance management is activated.
- Data quality management is deployed at both participant and enterprise levels.
- Data validation is performed automatically and only flaws are manually inspected.
- Business rule–based techniques are employed for validation.
- Guidelines for standardized exchange formats (e.g., XML) are defined.
- Structure and format standards are adhered to in all data exchanges.
- Auditing is established based on conformance to rules associated with data quality dimensions.
- Consistent reporting of data quality management is set up for necessary participants.
- Issues tracking system is in place to capture issues and their resolutions.

5.11.5 Assess, Tune, Optimize

The activities at phase 5 complete the transition to maturity level 3:
- Data contingency procedures are in place.
- Technology components for implementing data validation, certification, assurance, and reporting are in place.

- Technology components are standardized across the enterprise at the service and at the implementation layers.
- Enterprise-wide data standards metadata management is in place.
- Exchange schemas are endorsed through data standards oversight process.

5.12 Practical Steps for Developing the Road Map

As a practical matter, these steps can be taken to lay out a road map for building a data quality program:

- Assess the current level of data quality maturity within the organization in comparison with the maturity model described in chapter 3.
- Determine those data quality issues with material impact.
- Articulate alternatives for remediation and elimination of root causes.
- Prioritize the opportunities for improvement.
- Assess business needs for processes.
- Assess business needs for skills.
- Assess business needs for technology.
- Map the needs to the associated level of data quality maturity.
- Develop a plan for acquisition of skills and tools to reach that targeted level of maturity.
- Plan the milestones and deliverables that address the needs for data quality improvement.

5.13 Accountability, Responsibility, and Management

Another important aspect of the data quality road map involves resource management, and addressing the challenge of coordinating the participants and stakeholders in a data quality management program is knowing where to begin. Often, it is assumed that starting an initiative by assembling a collection of stakeholders and participants in a room is the best way to begin. Before sending out invitations, however, consider this: *without well-defined ground rules, these meetings run the risk of turning into turf battles over whose data, definitions, business rules, or information services are the "correct" ones.*

Given the diversity of stakeholders and participants (and their differing requirements and expectations), how can we balance each individual's needs with the organization's drivers for data quality? There are a number of techniques that can help in organizing the business needs in a way that can in turn manage the initial and ongoing coordination of the participants. These include establishing processes and procedures for collaboration before kickoff, developing ground rules for participation, and clarifying who is responsible, accountable, consulted, and informed regarding the completion of tasks.

5.13.1 Processes and Procedures for Collaboration

Assembling individuals from different business areas and applications will expose a variety of opinions about the names, structures, definitions, sources, and reasonable uses for data concepts used across the organization. In fact, it is likely that there is already a lengthy corporate experience regarding the definition of common terms (e.g., "what is a customer?"), and to reduce replication of effort, take the time to establish rules for interaction in the context of a collaborative engagement where the participants methodically articulate their needs and expectations of their representative constituencies. The process should detail the approach for documenting expectations and provide resolution strategies whenever there are overlaps or conflicts with respect to defining organizational business needs.

5.13.2 Articulating Accountability: The RACI Matrix

In chapter 2 we discussed characteristics of the participants and stakeholders associated with a data quality management program. To ensure that each participant's needs are addressed and that their associated tasks are performed appropriately, there must be some delineation of specific roles, responsibilities, and accountabilities assigned to each person. One useful model is the RACI (Responsible, Accountable, Consulted, and Informed) model. A RACI model is a two-dimensional matrix listing tasks along the rows and the roles listed along the columns. Each cell in the matrix is populated according to these participation types:

- R if the listed role is *responsible* for deliverables related to completing the task;
- A if the listed role is *accountable* for delivering the task's deliverables or achieving the milestones;

- C if the listed role is *consulted* for opinions on completing the task; or
- I if the listed role is *informed* and kept up to date on the progress of the task.

Figures 5.9 and 5.10 provide a sample RACI matrix associated with some of the data quality processes described in chapter 2. Again, this template and assigned responsibilities is a starting point and is meant to be reviewed and refined in relation to the roles and relationships within your own organization.

5.14 The Life Cycle of the Data Quality Program

At the beginning of a data quality initiative, there may seem to be a never-ending list of issues that need to be addressed, and as a team works its way through this list, you will find that two interesting counterintuitive phenomena will become clear. The first is that tracking down and fixing one reported issue often results in the correction of some other problems reported to the list. The other is that even though you eliminate some problems, as these issues are resolved, new issues will emerge from the existing test suites.

Sitting back and thinking about this provide some insight into the process, and ultimately suggests an interesting idea about planning for any quality management program. There are good explanations for both of these results, and examining the life cycle of the quality management process should help in developing a winning argument for the support of these programs.

Consider the first by-product, in which fixing one problem results in other problems mysteriously disappearing. Apparently, even though more than one issue is reported, they all share the same root cause. Because the people reporting the issue only understood the application's functionality (but did not have a deep knowledge of how the underlying application was designed or how it worked), each issue was perceived to be separate whenever the results or side effects differed. Yet when issues share the same root cause, the process of analyzing, isolating, and eliminating the root cause of the failure also eliminates the root cause of the other failures. The next time you evaluate the errors, the other issues sharing the same root cause will no longer fail.

The second by-product is a little less intuitive, because one would think that by finding and fixing problems, the result should be fewer issues, when in fact it is likely to result in more

	Senior Manager	Business Client	Application Owner	Data governance manager	Data quality manager	Data steward	Data quality analyst	Metadata analyst	System developer	Operations staff
Business impact analysis	A	CI			C		R			CI
Data quality requirements analysis		A	CI	R	C		C		CI	
Data quality assessment – Bottom-up		I	CI	I	A	I	R	I	CI	C
Data quality assessment –Top-down		A	CI	I	I	I	R	I	I	CI
Engage business data consumers		CI	CI	A	R	C	C	C	CI	
Define, review, prioritize DQ measures		A	CI	R	C	C	C	C	CI	CI
Define data quality metrics	A	CI	CI		R	C	C	C		
Set acceptability thresholds	A	CI	CI		R	C	C	C		
Data standards management			CI	A	C	C	C	R	C	
Active metadata management			CI	A	C	C	C	R	CI	
Define data validity rules		A	CI	I	R	C	C	C		
Data quality inspection and monitoring		I	I	A	I	R				
DQ SLA	A	CI	CI	R	C	C	C		CI	CI

Figure 5.9 Sample data quality RACI matrix – part 1

	Senior Manager	Business Client	Application Owner	Data governance manager	Data quality manager	Data steward	Data quality analyst	Metadata analyst	System developer	Operations staff
Enhanced SDLC for DQ	A	I	CI	R	C	C	C	C	CI	
Data quality issue reporting		CI	CI	A	CI	R				I
Data quality issue tracking				A	I	R	C		I	I
Root cause analysis			CI		A	R	R		CI	
Data correction		CI	CI	I	A	R	CI		CI	
Process remediation		I	A	I	I	C	C		CI	CI
Data standardization and cleansing		I	C	I	A			C	C	
Identity resolution		A	CI	CI	R	C	C		CI	I
Data enhancement		A	R	I	C	C	C	C	CI	

Figure 5.10 Sample data quality RACI matrix – part 2

issues. What actually happens is that fixing one reported problem enables a test to run past the point of its original failure, allowing it to fail at some other point in the process. Of course, this (and every other newly uncovered) failure will need to be reported to the issue list, which will initially lead to an even longer list of issues.

Rest assured, though, that eventually the rate of the discovery of new issues will stabilize and then decrease, while at the same time the elimination of root causes will continue to shorten the list of issues. If you prioritize the issues based on their relative impact, as more problems are eliminated, the severity of the remaining issues will be significantly lower as well. At some point, the effort needed to be expended on researching the remaining issues will exceed the value achieved in fixing them, and at that time you can effectively transition into proactive mode, decreasing your staffing needs as the accountability and responsibility is handed off to the application owners. In other words, this practical application of the Pareto principle demonstrates how reaching the point of diminishing returns allows for better resource planning while reaping the most effective benefits.

There are some lessons to be learned with respect to data quality issue analysis:

1. Subjecting a process to increased scrutiny is bound to reveal significantly more flaws than originally expected.
2. Initial resource requirements will be necessary to address most critical issues.
3. Eliminating the root causes of one problem will probably fix more than one problem, improving quality overall.
4. There is a point at which the resource requirement diminishes because the majority of the critical issues have been resolved.

These points suggest a valuable insight that there is a life cycle for a data quality management program. Initially there will be a need for more individuals focusing a large part of their time in researching and reacting to problems, but over time there will be a greater need to have fewer people concentrate some of their time on proactively preventing issues from appearing in the first place. In addition, as new data quality governance practices are pushed out to others across the organization, the time investment is diffused across the organization as well, further reducing the need for long-term dedicated resources. Knowing that the resource requirements are likely to be reduced over time may provide additional business justification to convince senior managers to support establishing a data quality program.

5.15 Summary

The life cycle of the data quality management program dovetails well with the maturity model described in chapter 3. The lower levels of the maturity model reflect the need for reacting to data quality issues, while as the organization gains more expertise, the higher levels of maturity reflect more insight into preventing process failures leading to data issues.

As a practical matter, exploring areas of value for developing a successful business case will help in mapping out a reasonable and achievable road map. Consider an initial exercise that involves working with some senior managers to seek out those "house on fire issues," namely by following these steps as reviewed in this chapter:

1. Identify five business objectives impacted by the quality of data
2. For each of those business objectives:
   a. Determine cost/impacts areas for each flaw
   b. Identify key quantifiers for those impacts
   c. At a high level, assess the actual costs associated with that problem
3. For each data quality problem:
   a. Review solution options for that problem
   b. Determine costs to implement
4. Seek economies of scale to exploit the same solution multiple times

At the conclusion of this exercise, you should have a solid basis of information to begin to assemble a business case that not only justifies the investment in the staff and data quality technology used in developing an information quality program, but also provides baseline measurements and business-directed metrics that can be used to plan and measure ongoing program performance.

METRICS AND PERFORMANCE IMPROVEMENT

How does ongoing data quality correspond to business performance? There is a challenge in presenting the results of ongoing measurement in a way that effectively articulates the relationship between the measurement and the business value implied by rule compliance. Our goals are to provide a means to communicate our confidence that business is not being impacted by violation of our data quality rules and to explore how a trending improvement or regression in data quality compliance relates to operational efficiency or competitive advantage. The ability to support these goals relies on defining key data quality performance metrics and associating a set of rules that roll up into those metrics. This also requires the means to capture measurements of those metrics, a system to maintain a history of those measurements over long periods, and a front-end presentation of each performance metric and its associated longitudinal view.

6.1 Performance-Oriented Data Quality

As has been alluded to in other chapters, there is a significant difference between the reactive adoption of technical tools to correct or cleanse data and the proactive approach of preventing the introduction of defective or erred data by way of process improvement and proactive validation, inspection, and monitoring. And while we can attest to the kinds of business impacts caused by poor data quality and use them as drivers for a business case, the conceptual return on investment to be achieved (even as we described in chapter 5) is secondary to the value improvement overall by eliminating the introduction of data flaws in the first place.

This suggests a different approach that can be used to establish improvement goals – one that is driven by performance objectives instead of remediation. If we have done our homework by identifying the critical dimensions of data quality, providing quantifiable metrics to measure conformance to expectations, and determining achievable objectives for improvement, then the organization will be better able to reach the desired maturity level. The impact analysis exercise is valuable in this process:

- It identifies business issues that can be related to data failures.
- It helps prioritize the issues that need to be addressed.
- It documents those problems impacted by causes or variables beyond our control.

Better yet, it distinguishes between the problems that are relevant and the ones that are irrelevant, and this provides a basis for determining business needs for technology and prioritizing tool procurement. Contributing to the business needs assessment prevents acquiring unneeded products and services and allows management to more effectively plan for improvement.

Performance-oriented data quality specifies the improvement objectives and drives a business case with a positive message: we have identified opportunities for improvement and are driving our data governance strategy based on reaching stated goals. Even aside from alleviating the specific business impacts discussed in chapter 1, the rewards of performance improvement are fundamental – reduced organizational complexity, increased speed of development, improved communications, harmonized semantics – all benefits that increase competitive advantage.

Basically, performance-oriented data quality management supports the way that data governance contributes to the organization's vision. The tools required for performance-based data quality management include mechanisms for validating data, tracking performance, reviewing longitudinal activity, and providing drillable dashboards or scorecards that reflect key data quality indicators.

6.2 Developing Data Quality Metrics

Program and product managers often desire the ability to summarize an organization's "business productivity" for senior managers using pithy representations that are expected to carry deep meaning and, at the same time, reduce the attention required to absorb that meaning. Business productivity management systems engage key performance indicators whose values are posted to executive dashboards for the CEO's periodic (be it daily or hourly) review. The intention of these applications is to provide a presentation of the current state of the environment in the context of reasonable expectations. In other words, a business manager wants to have an overview of the "value creation" of the entire system, much the same way a nuclear engineer gauges different metrics associated with the safety status of the nuclear reactors.

In most areas of a business, the metrics that back up the key performance indicators may be relatively straightforward. For example, in a shoe factory, one might gauge the number of shoes coming off the production line, the rate at which shoes are being produced, the number of flawed shoes coming off the line, or the number of accidents that occur each day. Each of these metrics may be represented using various visual cues, each of which provides a warning when the performance indicator reaches some critical level.

When it comes to the world of data quality, though, the analogy seems to break down, mostly because there is a difference between what can be measured and what the value of that measurement means. For example, one may count the number of times a value is missing from a specific column in a specific table, but in the absence of any business context, it is not clear how those missing values affect the business, or even if it affects the business at all.

Yet we all know that poor data quality does affect the business, and if so, then there should be some kind of performance indicator that can capture and summarize the relationship between data that does not meet one's expectations and the organizational bottom line. The challenge, then, is to devise a strategy for identifying and managing "business-relevant" information quality metrics.

6.2.1 What Makes a Good Metric?

More challenging, though, is that the individuals typically tasked with devising good information quality metrics are better trained at data analysis than business performance monitoring. So part of this strategy is to understand the characteristics of a reasonable business performance metric, and then explore how to map those characteristics to the measurable aspects of data quality. The following list of characteristics, which is by no means complete, should give us some guidance as to how to jump-start our strategy:

- Clarity of definition
- Measurability
- Business relevance
- Controllability
- Representation
- Reportability
- Trackability
- Drill-down capability

6.2.2 Clarity of Definition

Because the metric is intended to summarize a particular piece of information about an aspect of business performance, it is critical that its underlying definition clearly explains what is being measured. In fact, each metric should be subject to a rigorous "standardization" process in which the key stakeholders participate in its definition and agree to the definition's final wording. In addition, it is advisable to provide the metric's value range, as well as a qualitative segmentation of the value range that relates the metric's score to its performance assessment.

6.2.3 Measurability

Any metric must be measurable and should be quantifiable within a discrete range. Note, however, that there are many things that can be measured that may not translate into useful metrics, and that implies the need for business relevance.

6.2.4 Business Relevance

The metric is of no value if it cannot be related to some aspect of business operations or performance. Therefore, every desirable metric must be defined within a business context with an explanation of how the metric score correlates with a measurement of performance. More desirable is if that performance measurement can be directly associated with a critical business impact; this is probably the most important characteristic of a data quality metric.

6.2.5 Controllability

Any measurable characteristic of information that is suitable as a metric should reflect some controllable aspect of the business. In other words, the assessment of an information quality metric's value within an undesirable range should trigger some action to improve the data being measured.

6.2.6 Representation

Without digressing into a discussion on the plethora of visual "widgets" that can be used to represent a metric's value, it is reasonable to note that one should associate a visual representation that logically presents the metric's value in a concise and meaningful way.

6.2.7 Reportability

From a different point of view, each metric's definition should provide enough information that can be summarized as a line item in a comprehensive report. The difference between representation and reportability is that the representation will focus on the specific metric in isolation, whereas the reporting should show each metric's contribution to an aggregate assessment. In turn this allows the manager to evaluate the priority of any issues needing resolution.

6.2.8 Trackability

A major benefit of metrics is the ability to measure performance improvement over time. Tracking performance over time not just validates any improvement efforts, but once an information process is presumed to be stable, tracking provides insight into maintaining statistical control. In turn, these kinds of metrics can evolve from performance indicators into standard monitors, placed in the background to notify the right individuals when the data quality measurements suddenly indicate a deviation from expected control bounds.

6.2.9 Drill-Down Capability

In recognition of the summarization aspect of a representation of a data quality metric, the flip side is the ability to expose the underlying data that contributed to a particular metric score.

The natural instinct, when reviewing data quality measurements, is to review the data instances that contributed to any low scores. The ability to drill down through the performance metric allows an analyst to better understand any patterns (if any exist) that may have contributed to a low score, and consequently use that understanding for a more comprehensive root cause analysis. This kind of insight allows your organization to isolate the processing stage at which any flaws are introduced and in turn enables eliminating the source of the introduction of data problems (instead of the typical, counterproductive reaction of correcting the data values themselves).

6.3 Measurement and Key Data Quality Performance Indicators

Given those guidelines for developing metrics, we can assemble a hierarchy of metrics that rolls into three levels of data quality measurement. At the lowest level, we use the data quality dimensions to gauge validity of the data models and the data values consumed and produced by each participant across the enterprise. At the middle level, we assess the quality of the conformance and participation of each group within the organization, as described by the protocols. At the highest level, the data quality performance management is used to assess enterprise-wide performance in meeting data quality expectations.

We use key performance indicators (KPIs) to monitor the data quality performance for the enterprise. KPIs characterize organizational data quality and are derived from the dimensions, processes, protocols, and data quality maturity model.

Dimensions frame the primary data quality metrics for data. The data quality and governance protocols specify the data quality management practices of the participants within the enterprise. Measuring participant conformance to data quality best practices provides an operational assessment of data quality. Finally, data quality maturity levels frame a vision for improving data quality through the adoption of specific best practices.

Data quality performance management sets the focus for monitoring data quality performance at the group level. Performance goals may be adjusted over time to synchronize with the dimensions and as protocols within the governance framework are solidified. As this occurs, the operational processes and key performance indicators may need to change to accommodate new performance improvement initiatives and business needs.

6.3.1 Key Data Quality Performance Indicators

Key performance indicators are used to provide a measure of the level of conformance to the data quality results expected by the line-of-business representatives. KPIs, as the name implies, should reflect the key performance areas that are critical to performance management. For data quality, the number of KPIs should not exceed five of the most critical characteristics derived from the dimensions of data quality.

Consider this example set of basic KPIs:

- **Trustworthiness:** Any organization that shares or exchanges information relies on the trustworthiness of the data being shared. Trustworthiness performance is derived from the conformance characteristics and is assessed by determining the degree to which each participant publishes their data quality statistics and the degree to which participants provided transparency into their data quality management practices. This rolls up from periodic reporting of data quality dimension metrics (at all points of data consumption or publication) and reported issues. Missing or incomplete reports from participants indicate potential underlying data quality issues. Mutual reporting of metrics at both consumer and producer sites allows for mutual verification of meeting expectations.

- **Availability:** Access to information is necessary to support the critical nature of the services most organizations provide. Some dimensions that can be used to assess the availability performance measure include periodically examining the comprehensiveness and completeness of line-of-business data and measuring completeness of critical data elements, timeliness, and response times.

- **Consistency:** Ensuring that there is synchronization across the lines of business on data element definitions, structures, meanings, and presentation reflects a well-managed enterprise information architecture. Dimensions that are relevant to consistency include measuring semantic and structural consistency, presentation completeness, and verifying that data entry and exchange edits are defined and that there is compliance with these edits.

- **Policy compliance:** Policies such as those governing privacy, security, or limitations of use are needed. Continually monitoring the different application or line-of-business groups across the enterprise to ensure compliance with these policies is equally critical.

- **Identifiability:** In some instances (e.g., financial application or health care provision), the consequences of misidentifying entities are greater than not identifying the entity. Therefore, identifiability can be a key performance indicator, tracking uniqueness of entity identification, uniqueness of identifier, the percentage of search and match errors, and the promulgation of corrections and updates regarding entity identification.

6.3.2 Hierarchical Drill-Through

Ultimately, it is valuable to define how metrics at the different levels (data, group, enterprise) dovetail with the key performance indicators, especially when the proper organizational structures are in place to take actions based on the measured performance. One approach is to provide a taxonomy or hierarchy of how metrics at each level contribute to the KPI.

For example, if we consider availability, this KPI might be composed of comprehensiveness, metadata completeness, data value completeness, and timeliness. These metrics may be assessed at the application, line-of-business, and enterprise levels. As is shown in Figure 6.1, availability is reported as a score computed as a function of the underlying metrics captured for those four dimensions at the line-of-business level. In turn, each application will be collecting measurements for each of the dimensions, and their combined scores will contribute to the

Figure 6.1 Drilling through key performance indicators.

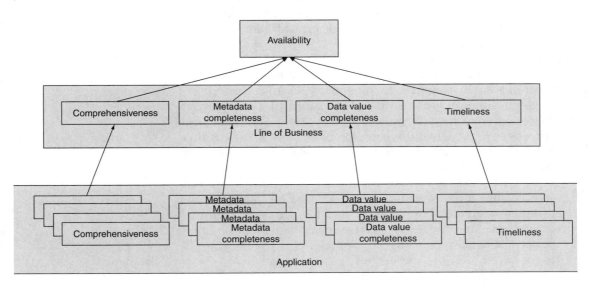

score at the line-of-business level. Consequently, any measured variation at the enterprise level can be drilled through to the lower levels in the hierarchy to determine which line-of-business and specific application is responsible for the variance.

Providing this drill-through capability enables analysts to quickly isolate the sources of monitored data flaws and provide insight as to both where and why the problem occurred. This reporting process will be integrated with the data quality issue tracking and the root cause analysis protocols, described in chapter 17.

6.4 Statistical Process Control

Given a set of data quality dimensions, there are still two necessary components to measure and report on data quality management. The first is the ability to provide quantifiable measures, and we have begun that process through the refinement of the criteria and metrics. The second is a process for initiating the measurement and for determining at a gross level the degree of conformance to data quality standards and a means for evaluating faults and defects.

In the early 1920s, Walter Shewhart, a Bell Laboratories staff member, performed a number of sampling studies that led to the development of a quality management tool known as Statistical Process Control (SPC). By evaluating the occurrence of faults, defects, and errors in the manufacturing process, Shewhart discovered that there are several variations that can occur during a manufacturing process, and that by studying the different kinds of variations (i.e., the ones that generate unusable end products), and by evaluating the root causes behind these variations, the occurrences of poor quality can be identified, which would enable the processes causing those irregularities to be improved.

This can equally apply to data quality; SPC provides a context for a continuous data quality improvement cycle. It is a process of instituting measurements during a manufacturing process to both control quality and to detect variations in quality as items are being produced, instead of finding them during inspection after production.

6.4.1 Variation and Control

Variation occurs in many contexts, but as we explored in chapter 1, we only are concerned with the variations that have an adverse impact in achieving business objectives that can be controlled by improving the process. By reviewing the different kinds of variations within a system, we can narrow the possibility for unexpected and unwanted variation in the information that feeds enterprise processes. In the data quality sense, we can use the notion of quality control as a means for monitoring data quality throughout a system.

Shewhart's studies focused on distinguishing between expected variations that occurred within a manufacturing process, and any significant fluctuations that indicated that there was a problem with the manufacturing process. He narrowed the causes of variation down to these two:

- **Chance**, or **common**, causes, which are minor fluctuations or small variations in the end product and are not necessarily important to correct.
- **Assignable**, or **special**, causes are those for which a source of the variation can be assigned, causing a significant variation in the level of quality.

Although the specific occurrences of variations due to common causes are not predictable in their own right, their occurrences are likely to form a pattern, and Shewhart's observation was that they formed a normal distribution. In other words, we expect that when we measure variation in a process, there will be limits to the number of variations due to chance causes. This implies that when we see fluctuation in the process that exceeds those limits, it is probably due to a special cause, which should then be investigated.

An example might be tracking the on-time performance of an airline. Each day, we can record the times that airplanes pushed back from the gate and the times that the plane reached the gate at its destination. When reviewing the variations from the scheduled times, it can be expected that from day to day, the planes will likely be either a little early, on time, or a little late. The times that the plane is slightly early or late are due to common causes – increased winds, minor congestion while awaiting takeoff, and so on. But one day, a huge snowstorm creates low visibility and dangerous conditions at a major hub airport; planes at the hub are unable to take off, and planes destined for the hub are routed to other locations, causing system-wide delays. That day, the delays in the system are due to an assignable cause.

As another example, let's consider a simple information collection process and look at the different kinds of variations that might occur. Presume we have multiple people transcribing names and addresses from a set of hard copy lists into a sales database. We can expect that overall, most of the transcribers will make some kind of typing mistake, perhaps substituting one letter for another. These errors are all due to common causes. But let's say all of a sudden, the "e" key on one computer keyboard breaks. Now, there are erroneous records being entered from that data entry location, and they all share similar error characteristics; this is an example of an error due to a special cause.

6.4.2 Statistical Control

According to the ANSI/ISO/ASQC standard A3534-1993 (Statistics – Vocabulary and Symbols), the state of statistical control is the state in which the observed sampling results can be attributed to a system of chance causes that does not appear to change with time. This is a characterization of stability – a process is in control (i.e., it is *stable*) if each of its quality measures is in a state of statistical control.

This means that, having selected a set of variables or attributes of a process to measure based on random sampling, we will expect that if the system is in control, there will be a normal distribution of variations and the specific occurrences of variations will be random. If we observe that this is not the case, there must be some special cause to which this pattern or variation can be attributed, which then must be further explored.

6.5 Control Charts

To determine whether an information process is in control, it is reasonable to sample data to see how well they conform to our expectations of data quality. These data samples may be taken at predesignated points or at different points in the information flow. The samples are taken and reviewed over a period of time to see whether there is any significant change with time. These data samples and corresponding data quality measures can be recorded and mapped over a selected time period to highlight the differences between chance causes of variation and assignable causes of variation. This tool is called a *control chart*, which is a graphical representation of the variations produced from a process.

Simply, a control chart has the values of a time series or a sample series plotted along with upper and/or lower **control limits.** A **central line** can be plotted to display the typical (or mean) behavior of the system and can be used to detect trends toward either of the control limits. Control limits are lines plotted above and below the central line to bound the space in which expected variations will occur. Control limits are not

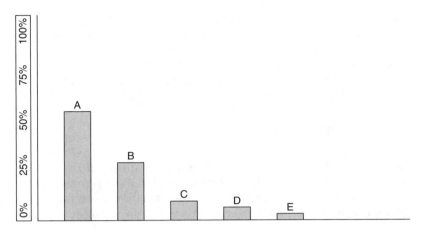

Figure 6.2 Example of a Pareto chart.

defined by the customer, but instead are determined by observing behavior over the series. Because the common causes form a normal distribution, we first need to determine how that distribution is reflected within the normal expectations. A process is said to be **stable** as long as all the points fall between the control limits.

6.5.1 The Pareto Principle

A common observation is that in any system with causes and effects, a significant bulk of the effects is caused by a small percentage of the causes. This notion, called the Pareto principle, has been integrated into common parlance as the "80-20 rule," in which the claim is made that 80% of the effects result from 20% of the causes. This rule is often used to establish the degree of effort to be expended on a particular project; if the rule of thumb is that 80% of the benefit can be achieved with 20% of the work necessary for completion, then the project will go forward, at least until the 80% benefit has been achieved.

In fact, the Pareto principle has a more interesting application in that we use Pareto analysis to determine what aspects of a system (or in our case, data quality) are to be incorporated into the SPC process. A Pareto chart (see the example in Figure 6.2) is a bar chart representing the measurement of different aspects of a system. The presentation of the chart is based on cumulative frequency measurements of particular metrics, ordered from the greatest to the least frequency. The chart highlights those areas that are responsible for the greatest percentage of a problem, and which variables are involved in those areas.

Another interesting corollary to the Pareto principle is that as the larger problems are solved, there is a diminished opportunity for subsequent improvements. In other words, once we have attacked and conquered the first three or four problems, it is not likely that we will achieve significantly more improvements from attacking any additional problems. This is actually quite reassuring, since it means that we can limit the amount of effort to be expended on improving a particular area!

An example of the use of Pareto analysis is in performance improvement. A computer program that is not running up to speed is subjected to a series of profiling processes that gauge the time spent in each individual functional component. The professional performance technician then looks at the function in which the most time was spent, with an eye towards improving the performance of that function. Let's say we had the following data points:

Function	Total Seconds
Foo	56
Bar	26
Baz	8
Boz	6
Raz	4
Faz	2

Together, these six functions account for 100% of the run time of the program, totaling 102 seconds. If we can speed up function Foo by a factor of two, we will have reduced the run time of the entire application by 28% (half of the time of function Foo), making the total time now 74 seconds. A subsequent improvement in the next function down the list, Bar, by a factor of two will result in only an additional 13% improvement over the original run time (actually, the effect is 18% of the current run time, due to the previous reduction in run time from improving Foo).

If we then focus on improving the run time of function Baz by a factor of two, the best speedup we can achieve is now a mere 4 seconds, which will only slightly improve our performance from 61 seconds to 57 seconds. The same improvement in function Boz only reduces the speed by another 3 seconds. As you can see, the same amount of effort expended on making improvements results in diminishing returns.

By performing a Pareto analysis, we can use the results to focus attention on the areas that are contributing the most to the problem. The variables that contribute to these areas become the variables or attributes that are to be incorporated into the control chart.

6.5.2 Building a Control Chart

Our next step is building a control chart. The control chart is made up of data points consisting of individual or aggregated measures associated with a periodic sample, enhanced with the center line and the upper and lower control limits.

These are the steps for building a control chart for measuring data quality:

1. Select one or more data quality dimensions that will be charted. Make use of the Pareto analysis to help determine the variables or attributes that most closely represent the measured problem, since trying to track down the most grievous offenders is a good place to start.

2. If the goal is to find the source of particular problems, make sure to determine what the right variables are for charting. For example, if the dimension that is being charted is timeliness, consider making the charted variable the "number of minutes late," instead of "time arrived." Keep in mind while choosing variables that the result of charting should help in determining the source and diagnosis of any problems.

3. Determine the proper location within the information chain to attach the measurement probe. This choice should reflect the following characteristics:
   a. It should be early enough in the information processing chain that detection and correction of a problem at that point can prevent incorrectness further along the data flow.
   b. It should be in a location in the information chain that is easily accessed and retooled, so as not to cause too much chaos in implementing the charting process.
   c. It should not be in a place such that observation of the sample can modify the data being observed.

4. Decide which kind of control chart is to be used. The choices are:
   a. **Variables chart,** which measures individual measurable characteristics; a variables chart will provide a lot of information about each item being produced.
   b. **Attributes chart,** which measures the percentage or number of items that vary from the expected; an attributes chart summarizes information about the entire process, focusing on cumulative effects rather than individual effects.

5. Choose a center line and control limits for the chart. The center line can either be the average of past measurements, the average of data that has not yet been measured or collected, or a predefined expected standard. The upper control limit (UCL) is set at three standard deviations ($+3\sigma$) above the center line, and the lower control limit (LCL) is set at three standard deviations (-3σ) below the center line.
6. Choose the sample. The sample may consist of measuring individual data values, or measuring a collection of data values for the purpose of summarization. The sampler should be careful not to take a sample at a point in the process or a point in time when there is only a small possibility that the taking of the sample can have any changing affects.
7. Choose a method for collecting and logging the sample data. This can range from asking people to read gauges and write down the answers in a notebook to having an integrated mechanism for measuring and logging sample results.
8. Plot the chart and calculate the center line and control limits based on history.

6.6 Kinds of Control Charts

There are many different varieties of control charts, and for a detailed description of various control charts, see *Juran's Quality Handbook*, 5th edition (McGraw-Hill), chapter 45. The author presents a summary of variables and attributes of control charts.

Since our goal is to measure nonconformance with data quality expectation, we will concentrate on certain attributes of control charts associated with measuring nonconformity. Our statement of the data quality requirements will be using the rules and assertions associated with the dimensions of data quality described in chapter 8. Sample measurements will be based on defining the granularity of the data item being observed (e.g., record versus data attribute), defining a set of data quality rules, and then testing the data items against those rules. Each sample will consist of a number of measured items.

6.6.1 Percentage Nonconforming

The first chart we look at is called a *control chart for percentage nonconforming* and is also known as a *p* chart. A *p* chart is an attributes chart whose data points represent a percentage of the data items that do not conform to our requirements.

The distribution of this data set is a binomial distribution, if we assume that the process is constant, and most data points should fall within 3 standard deviations of the mean. For binomial variables, the standard deviation is computed as:

$$\sigma_p = \sqrt{\frac{p(1-p)}{n}}$$

where p is the probability of occurrence and n is the sample size.

To set up a p chart, we first collect a small sample size over a small amount of time (in most cases, 25 to 30 time points will be enough), and compute the average P by counting the number of nonconforming items in each sample, totaling the number of items in each sample group, and then dividing the total number of nonconforming items by the total number of sampled items. For p charts, the control limits are calculated using the binomial variable standard deviation; the UCL is computed as $P + 3\sigma_p$, and the LCL is computed as $P - 3\sigma_p$. If the LCL is computed to be a negative number, we just use 0 as the LCL.

6.6.2 Number Nonconforming

In this chart, instead of plotting the percentage of nonconforming data objects, we will be plotting the number of nonconforming items. In the p chart, the percentage p is equal to the number of nonconforming items divided by the number of observed items, n. Clearly, the number of nonconforming items is equal to np, and therefore this chart is called an np chart.

For an np chart, the UCL is computed as $nP + 3\sqrt{nP(1-P)}$, and the LCL is computed as $nP - 3\sqrt{nP(1-P)}$, where P is the average of the number of nonconforming items and n is the size of the sample.

6.6.3 Number of Nonconformities

It is not out of the realm of possibility that each data item being observed may have more than one error! In this case, we may not want to just chart the number of nonconforming data items, but instead also include the total of all nonconformities. This kind of attributes chart is called a c chart, and the UCL is calculated as $C + 3\sqrt{C}$, the LCL is calculated as $C - 3\sqrt{C}$, where C is the average number of nonconformities over all the samples.

6.6.4 Number of Nonconformities per Item

If our samples consist of multiple observed data errors, then we might want to look at more than just the number of nonconformities, but rather the number of nonconformities per item. This chart is called a u chart, and the UCL is computed as $U + 3\sqrt{\dfrac{U}{n}}$, the LCL as $U - 3\sqrt{\dfrac{U}{n}}$, where U is the average number of nonconformities, and n is the number of items.

6.6.5 Defining the Control Limits

In the previous subsections, we have discussed the calculations of the upper and lower control limits as a function of the statistical distribution of points in the data set. This is not to say that we can only define these limits statistically.

In reality, as quality overseers, it is our duty to specify the acceptable limits for data quality. For example, when it comes to the acceptable level of incorrect values in certain kinds of databases, we can specify that there is no tolerance for error; in this case, the UCL for errors would be 0. In many cases of examining data quality, there is no need for a lower control limit either. Ultimately, it is up to the users to determine their tolerance for expected variations and errors, and use that as a guideline for setting the control limits.

6.6.6 Example: Invalid Records

In this example, each day a number of records are passed through an automated data validation system, where each record is compared against a number of data validation rules. If the record fails any of the rules, it is tagged as an invalid record and a count of invalid records is incremented. This process was repeated for 24 days, yielding the following table:

Day	Number of Records Processed	Number of Bad Records	Percent Bad
1	10,000	300	0.03
2	10,000	600	0.06
3	10,000	532	0.0532
4	10,000	476	0.0476
5	10,000	620	0.062
6	10,000	546	0.0546
7	10,000	665	0.0665
8	10,000	331	0.0331
9	10,000	337	0.0337
10	10,000	328	0.0328
11	10,000	345	0.0345
12	10,000	358	0.0358

(Continued)

Day	Number of Records Processed	Number of Bad Records	Percent Bad
13	10,000	403	0.0403
14	10,000	341	0.0341
15	10,000	347	0.0347
16	10,000	395	0.0395
17	10,000	342	0.0342
18	10,000	334	0.0334
19	10,000	346	0.0346
20	10,000	347	0.0347
21	10,000	378	0.0378
22	10,000	365	0.0365
23	10,000	351	0.0351
24	10,000	432	0.0432

Over this time, the overall average percentage of bad records was computed to be 0.0409, which we use as the center line; the UCL and LCL were computed in accordance with the computation for the p chart to be 0.0469 and 0.0349, respectively. The corresponding control chart is shown in Figure 6.3.

In this example, since we are trying to limit the error percentage to below a certain point, we can essentially ignore the lower control limit, since the fewer errors, the better. As we can see, early on in the history, the process was not in control, because

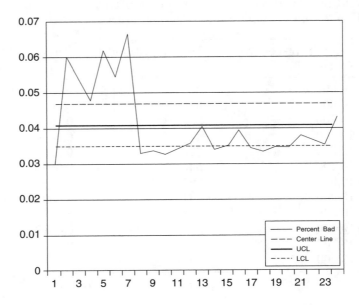

Figure 6.3 Example control chart.

there were a number of days (days 2 through 8) in which the upper control limit for errors was exceeded. At that point, the number of errors each day begins to move into a more predictable pattern, even sometimes moving below the lower control limit. Near the end of the measurement period, the process displays errors well within the acceptable limits.

6.7 Interpreting Control Charts

6.7.1 The Goal of Statistical Process Control

Statistical process control is a tool that makes use of measurements of certain aspects of quality of a process or a product over time to gain insight into the differences between expected, common variations, and the unexpected special variations. The use of the control chart to represent the behavior of a process over time is not just used as a means for locating anomalous events; the ultimate goals of SPC are **stability** and **predictability.**

When there are a large number of data points in the control chart outside of the control limits, it means that the process is very unstable. This instability is more than just points plotted against a handful of parallel lines on a graph – it reflects different causes working at cross-purposes to affect the way that the system acts. It is the role of the data quality analyst to review the results of the SPC process to determine whether the instability is due to common or special causes.

As we identify the special causes associated with each set of out-of-control data points, we gradually improve the process, making it more stable. This will be reflected in the control graph moving forward, because as the data points move closer to the mean, they will also begin to fall within the control limits. This exhibits the stabilizing effect that SPC can have on a process.

Another effect is that as the points fall closer together, the standard deviation becomes smaller as well, and since the control limits are defined as a function of the standard deviation, they will also begin to move closer to the center line. This is a different kind of stability, one that focuses on a tightening band within which we expect to see defective information – the narrower the band between the UCL and the LCL, the fewer expected errors! This kind of stability of a system also implies **predictability** – if for the last 30 days, there were fewer than 10 errors every day, we can expect that tomorrow, there will also be fewer than 10 errors.

This notion of predictability is a significant benefit of SPC. By gradually using the SPC tools to understand the nature of problems within a system, using the selected variables measured to help locate the source of the problem, and eliminating the problems, we also gradually bring a system into a state where we can safely predict the behavior from day to day, and know that anomalous activity is due to special causes.

6.7.2 Reviewing the Control Chart

The next step in the SPC process is interpreting a control chart. When a process is stable, the points in the control chart will reflect a natural pattern of occurrences. The data points on the chart should be randomly distributed above and below the center line, and the chart should have these characteristics:

- Most of the points should be close to the center line.
- Some of the points are near the UCL and LCL.
- Rarely, there will be points above the UCL or below the LCL.
- The distribution of points on the chart should not have any nonrandom clustering or trending.

In the interpretation of control charts, our goal is to determine whether a process is stable, and if it is not stable, find and eliminate special causes. So what do we look for in a control chart?

6.7.3 Unnatural Patterns

The first thing to look for is any departure from what is expected to be seen. Any apparent patterns that belie the expected randomness in the chart should be a sign for further investigation. Here are some examples:

- The existence of many points that lie outside of control limits: This clearly indicates that the system is out of control. Note that when the control limits are user-defined, there is a much greater possibility of this happening than if we rely on the equations prescribed for calculating the control limits.
- The appearance of unnatural clusters of points: Clusters most likely represent patterns in which special causes lurk.
- The appearance of shifts in levels seen in the control chart: In other words, is there a sequence of points within one standard deviation, followed by a sequence of points between one and two standard deviations?
- Any trends up or down probably indicate some deterioration in quality.

6.7.4 Zone Tests

Another aspect of unnaturalness in the distribution of data points can be uncovered using what is called a zone test. A zone is an area of the chart, where there are unlikely distributions of data points on the chart, such as two or three successive points outside two standard deviations, four or five successive points outside one standard deviations, or eight successive points on the same side of the center line. All of these occurrences are equally likely to occur when the process is stable, and so if any appear in a way that is not consistent with our expectations, this is likely to be an indicator of a special cause.

6.7.5 Rebalancing

After the root cause of a problem has been identified and corrected, we can claim that at least one aspect of an out-of-control situation has been resolved. In this case, it may be interesting to recalculate the points and control limits on the control chart, ignoring the data points associated with the identified cause. This is likely to help strengthen the control limit calculations as well as point out other locations to explore for special causes.

6.7.6 Refactoring Data

Let's say that we collected many days' worth of data concerning the number of errors that occurred in the data each day, as a function of the total number of records with errors in them. It is possible that by aggregating the recording of errors by record instead of by error, we may have masked out the fact that many records may have failed more than one data validation test. The overall effect of this is that the appearance of a special cause may have been overlooked.

Instead, the data points can be charted again by collecting the data as number of records that failed because of a specific validation test not passing. Doing this may expose that a large number of records are erroneous because of more than one test failing, or that a large number of the erroneous records have failed one test during the first half of the measurement period, but failed a different test during the second half of the measurement period. By separating data points by attribute, or measuring using a finer granularity, we may be able to identify occurrences of variations due to special causes that the standard charting method fails to highlight.

6.8 Finding Special Causes

The last step in the SPC process is to identify the special causes that are echoed in the control chart. Hopefully, the areas of measurement will have been selected in a way that will provide specific insight into the special causes. Data quality expectations can be specified with a set of data quality rules that can be used for validating data records. A log of the number of times a record is erroneous because it failed a particular test can be used to plot the daily conformance for each specific rule.

At the end of the measurement period, a control chart can be built that consolidates data from each of the data quality rules. Because each rule describes a specific aspect of the users' data quality requirements, the problem of identifying a special cause reduces to determining which of the data quality rules accounted for the anomalous behavior.

6.9 Maintaining Control

The goals of statistical process control are stability and predictability. Once a process has been brought under control, it is beneficial to continue using the SPC process to make sure that the process remains under control. As long as the data points continue to fall between the control limits, the process is stable. Attempts may be made at improving the process on a continuous process, either by making the control limits closer or by introducing new variables or attributes to be measured.

This can be facilitated by integrating control charting as a reporting scheme for a data quality scorecard. The hierarchical roll-up of dimensions metrics described in section 6.3 provides the logical structure, and the characteristics of the metrics are as described in section 6.2. The statistical process control techniques can be used to accumulate a view of the metrics, and we can feed all of this information into a data mart to drive a web-based visualization/scorecard/dashboard of the metrics as well as provide for "clickable" drill-through.

6.10 Summary

In this chapter we looked at providing a frame of reference for defining metrics associated with data quality. In turn, we will see how the dimensions that will be described in chapter 8 will encompass the intrinsic aspects of data quality and the ways that metrics can be generally applied to data quality monitoring within an enterprise. By defining data quality rules whose observance can be measured at various levels across the enterprise information architecture, the data quality practitioner can assemble scorecards for evaluating stability and predictability associated with data quality measurements, and can differentiate common causes from special causes of data failures.

Statistical process control is an analysis tool used for measuring and charting the conformance of information to a set of data quality rules. This is useful in resolving data quality issues based on an objective assessment of an organization's level of data quality maturity with respect to those dimensions of data quality.

DATA GOVERNANCE

Managing the organizational framework for defining, agreeing to, and instituting best practices associated with improvements in data quality requires a governance framework that empowers the proper staff members to ensure the most effective use of the enterprise information assets. Conversely, the management of data quality must incorporate the participation, collaboration, and oversight from all the participants. Ultimately, processes must be in place to establish data quality goals in relation to both business objectives and internal and external constraints; integrate methods for measuring, auditing, and reporting data quality metrics; and develop protocols for responsibility and accountability for issues resolution.

Processes to address these organizational requirements are embodied within a governance framework for data quality management and oversight across the enterprise. Governance is introduced at various data touch points throughout the data life cycle to ensure consistency and conformance to the defined business rules, and to measure the degree to which line-of-business activities comply with the desired level of the data quality maturity model.

An enterprise data governance model must incorporate
- Technical leadership,
- Oversight,
- Steering, and
- Stewardship

to ensure that responsible managers are accountable for high quality data. This chapter introduces governance policies that include a data quality charter, a suggested organizational structure, roles and responsibilities, and workflows for participant activities to provide comprehensive oversight for enterprise information quality.

7.1 The Enterprise Data Quality Forum

We can consolidate the view of the data governance program into an enterprise forum that provides the policies and procedures for oversight of the data quality community. The services provided by the forum include:
- Setting priorities and developing and maintaining standards for data quality,
- Reporting relevant measurements of enterprise-wide data quality,
- Providing guidance that facilitates staff involvement,
- Establishing communications mechanisms for knowledge sharing,
- Developing and applying certifications and compliance policies,
- Monitoring and reporting on performance,
- Identifying opportunities for improvements and building consensus for approval, and
- Resolving variations and conflicts.

The constituent participants work together to define the data quality strategy and framework; develop, formalize, and approve information policies, data quality standards and protocols; and certify line-of-business conformance to the desired level of the data quality maturity model.

7.2 The Data Quality Charter

Although data quality is implemented at the operational level as a result of guidance from the Data Quality Forum, the foundation of the forum and establishment of its authority are strategic initiatives and should be documented and approved through senior-level sponsorship. A data quality charter formalizes the governance framework. Its approval simultaneously describes the relevant roles and responsibilities and empowers the people taking on those roles to get the job done. A data quality charter will include the following sections:

- **Data governance overview,** which will provide a high-level overview of the data governance program and how it relates to corporate and information technology governance
- **Mission and guiding principles,** in which the mission articulates the core objectives of the data governance program, and the guiding principles contain core ideas that apply across the enterprise
- **Governance goals,** which describe the business goals and objectives of the data governance program
- **Work items,** which provide a list of data governance activities
- **Success criteria,** which provide the factors that are critical to the success of the data governance program
- **Roles and responsibilities,** which summarize the roles for the governance program (both participants and stakeholders) and the corresponding sponsor, responsibilities, and approval/authority characteristics
- **Accountability and escalation,** which are probably the most critical components of the charter, because they describe how participants are accountable for their responsibilities and the escalation

7.3 Mission and Guiding Principles

The wording of a mission statement should clearly describe the purposes that the data governance program are intended to serve. For example, consider this:

The mission of the Data Quality Forum is to lead the establishment and adoption of a standardized level of data quality and foster collaboration throughout the enterprise. The Data Quality Forum serves several purposes:

- **Promotion of data quality:** The Data Quality Forum helps promote the adoption of data quality through the publication of data quality guidance documents and brochures, through education sessions and day-to-day activities, and through application of data quality policies and procedures.
- **Development of data quality guidance:** The Data Quality Forum identifies the need for data quality policies and procedures, and charters the development of data quality guidance documents covering topics such as the dimensions of data quality, measurement of data quality, operational functions for data quality management, and stewardship of data.

- **Quality identification:** The Data Quality Forum identifies the necessary relevant touch points within the data life cycle for data quality functions, assisting in the identification of participants with a vested interest in developing and using data quality practices, and with managing a knowledge base that contributes to the effort.
- **Data quality best practices endorsement:** Individual organizations, organizational consortia, or workgroups may develop data quality practices to be considered for adoption by the community. The Data Quality Forum provides a defined process and organization to facilitate the community's endorsement of these data quality practices.
- **Certification:** As a certification and audit body, the data quality forum:
  - Provides a structured and documented process for evaluating certification, and
  - Conducts audits to ensure continuous conformance to the policies and processes adopted by the community.

Guiding principles are the core concepts that are asserted to fundamentally drive the governance framework. Some examples include:

- Information is a corporate asset that will be subject to the appropriate safeguards and oversight.
- Enterprise data definitions and standards will be used when they exist.
- Processes will be in place to ensure data accuracy, completeness, and timeliness.
- Industry standards for data formats and definitions will be used when appropriate.
- Data flaws will be eliminated at the source of their introduction.
- Metadata will be maintained for every data element.
- A master repository will be maintained for all commonly used data sets.
- Data values will be validated against corresponding business rules for the intended target systems.

The mission and principles described in this section can be used as a starting point for refinement within your own organization.

7.4 Roles and Responsibilities

The governance model can be described as a three-tiered management hierarchy whose highest level reports to the organization's executive management, as is shown in Figure 7.1.

The activities of the Data Quality Forum are conducted within several advisory groups and workgroups. The advisory groups make up the core structure for the administration of the forum's activities, whereas the workgroups are responsible for the detailed subject matter activities. Although participation is open to all enterprise participants, the Data

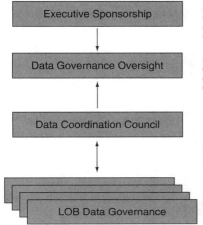

Provide senior management support at the C-level, warrants the enterprise adoption of measurably high quality data, and negotiates quality SLAs with external data suppliers.

Strategic committee composed of business clients to oversee the governance program, ensure that governance priorities are set and abided by, delineates data accountability.

Tactical team tasked with ensuring that data activities have defined metrics and acceptance thresholds for quality meeting business client expectations, manages governance across lines of business, sets priorities for LOBs and communicates opportunities to the Governance Oversight committee.

Data governance structure at the line-of-business level, defines data quality criteria for LOB applications, delineates stewardship roles, reports activities and issues to Data Coordination Council.

Figure 7.1 The data governance hierarchy reports up to executive management.

Quality Forum itself is composed of the following defined functions and roles:
- Data Quality Director,
- Data Quality Oversight Board,
- Data Coordination Council, composed of:
  - Data Quality Steering Committee,
  - Data Standards Advisory Group,
  - Data Quality Technical Advisory Group, and
  - Data Quality Certification and Audit Group.

Within each line of business, Data Stewards are assigned specific tasks that are described in section 7.7. The organization is shown in Figure 7.2.

7.4.1 The Data Quality Director

The Data Quality Director is responsible for the day-to-day management of enterprise data quality. The director provides guidance to all the participants and oversees adherence to the data quality maturity levels and certifications. The Data Quality Director plans and chairs the Data Quality Oversight Board. The director identifies the need for quality improvement initiatives and provides periodic reports on data quality performance.

7.4.2 Data Quality Oversight Board

The Data Quality Oversight Board (DQOB) guides and oversees data quality activities. The DQOB is composed of representatives chosen from across the community. The main responsibilities of the DQOB include:

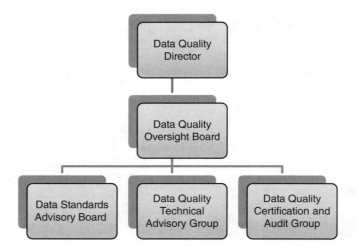

Figure 7.2 The organization of the Data Quality Forum.

- Provide strategic direction for the Data Quality Forum.
- Review corporate information policies and designate work-groups to translate business rules into data rules.
- Approve data quality policies and procedures.
- Identify the necessity for data quality activities.
- Review proposals for data quality practices and processes.
- Endorse data quality certification and audit.

7.4.3 Data Coordination Council

The work within the Data Quality Forum is directed and managed by the Data Coordination Council. The Data Coordination Council operates under the direction of the DQOB. The Data Coordination Council is a group composed of interested individual stakeholders from across the enterprise.

The Data Coordination Council is responsible for adjusting the structure of the Data Quality Forum as appropriate to ensure that the data quality expectations are continually met. As part of this responsibility, the Data Coordination Council recommends the names of appropriate parties whose involvement would add value to committees and advisory groups, and appoints representatives from those constituencies as well as experts to the committees and advisory groups. The Data Coordination Council is responsible for overseeing the work of data stewards. It is also the role of the Data Coordination Council to maximize opportunities to involve the Data Quality Forum in other initiatives as appropriate.

The coordination council will also:
- Provide direction and guidance to all committees and tasked with developing data quality practices;
- Oversee the tasks of the committees advisory groups related to data quality;
- Recommend to the DQOB the endorsement of output of the Data Quality Forum for publication and distribution;
- Recommend data quality standards to the DQOB for final endorsement;
- Recommend to the DQOB the endorsement of certifications and audits;
- Advocate for the Data Quality Forum by leading, promoting, and facilitating the quality practices and processes developed;
- Nominate data stewards;
- Attend periodic meetings to provide progress reports, review statuses, and to discuss and review the general direction of the Data Quality Forum;
- Participate in Data Quality Forum meetings, conference calls, and events; and
- Participate in and liaison with external standards-setting bodies.

7.4.4 Data Standards/Metadata Advisory Group

The Data Standards/Metadata Advisory Group is responsible for overseeing various data standards and metadata activities, and compiling and maintaining metadata and the data standards in progress. The Data Standards/Metadata Advisory Group is tasked with managing and maintaining the status of enterprise data definitions and implementation efforts. The Data Standards/Metadata Advisory Group will guide the Data Coordination Council as to the current data standards activities and their progress, maintain the list of priorities, as well as assist Data Standards workgroups in the process of defining, adopting, and implementing data standards. The Data Standards/ Metadata Advisory Group is responsible for:
- Facilitating data standards activities,
- Providing update reports on data standards activities,
- Managing data standard guidance documentation development,
- Providing training and knowledge transfer,
- Participating in government or industry standards-setting bodies to remain current on all standards activities,
- Providing guidance for the establishment of data standards practices within software and data life cycles, and
- Developing data quality practices to conform to data standards.

7.4.5 Data Quality Technical Advisory Group

The Data Quality Technical Advisory Group consists of participants tasked with the technical aspects of data quality activities. The technical advisory group reports to the Data Coordination Council and is responsible for advising the committee on the technical aspects of data quality, including:

- Updating and maintaining all data quality technical specifications,
- Providing guidance on technical and architectural issues related to data quality, and
- Overseeing the requirements and acquisition process for data quality technology.

7.4.6 Data Quality Certification and Audit Team

The Data Quality Certification and Audit Team is responsible for the certification and audit of participant groups. The team will develop and publish formal certification criteria as well as a process to audit conformance to data quality policies.

7.5 Operational Structure

The governance model is based on facilitating collaboration between groups (at a high level) and individuals (at a low level). Although a framework can describe the expected results of governance activities, it is necessary to specify the details of the processes by which the Data Quality Forum operates. A large part of this focuses on the interaction – when meetings are scheduled, how often the governance bodies meet, what materials need to be prepared ahead of time, what types of feedback are expected from the different roles, and so on. An example is shown in Table 7.1.

7.6 Data Stewardship

The role of the data steward incorporates a number of responsibilities. The data steward's role includes:

- Supporting the user community: The data steward is responsible for collecting, collating, and triaging issues and problems with data. Prioritized issues must be communicated to those individuals who may be impacted. The steward must also communicate issues and other relevant information (e.g., root causes) to those staff members that are in a position to influence remediation.

Table 7.1 Sample Operations Task List

Group	Meeting Frequency	Tasks
Data Quality Oversight Board	Quarterly	• Hear proposals for data quality protocols • Review Data Quality Certification and Audit reports • Review proposed data standards • Set data quality objectives for the 2 upcoming quarters • Review progress of conformance to maturity model
Data Coordination Council	Monthly	• Review organization processes to identify best practices • Select proposals to be presented to DQOB for endorsement • Select certification and audits to be presented to DQOB • Select data standards to be presented to DQOB for endorsement • Nominate and manage data stewards
Data Standards Advisory Group	Monthly	• Review data standards and metadata activities • Review data standards in process • Discuss proposals for new data standards activities • Review external data standards initiatives • Oversee ongoing data standards processes
Data Quality Technology Advisory Group	Monthly	• Review data quality technical specifications • Guide data quality technical issues and architecture • Oversee the requirements and acquisition process for data quality technology
Data Quality Certification and Audit Group	As requested by Data Coordination Council	• Review certification criteria • Develop formal certification auditing processes • Schedule audits • Prepare preaudit questionnaire

- Managing standard business definitions: This includes identifying key business terms for resolution and standardized definition, ensuring compliance with naming conventions and naming standards, facilitating convergence for the correct definitions, associating business term definitions with their authoritative sources.
- Managing metadata: This involves developing and approving business naming standards, data definitions, and aliases, and documenting information about the data domains and mappings, standard entities, attributes, definitions, reference domains, and code mappings.
- Managing data quality standards: The steward must participate in the development of data quality standards that must

be applied to the data sets that are both used and produced within a line of business. These standards are to be communicated to the Data Coordination Council for review.

- Maintaining data: This involves scheduling any periodic updates, making sure that the resources required for data provision are available and working, and acquiring any technology required to maintain the data. Any issues of data aging or retention are handled within the scope of maintenance.
- Overseeing data quality: This includes defining the data quality rules associated with the data sets, and using any technology required to assess and maintain a high level of data quality within each line of business. The steward must oversee the quality, completeness, and consistency of data, communicate changed business requirements, and participate in the enforcement of data quality standards.
- Validating data: This involves validating data as it enters the environment to ensure that the data suppliers are complying with data quality expectations. In addition, this involves applying data validation to data sets that are to be used further downstream by other application groups.
- Distributing information: This involves enabling the capability to disseminate reference data in an efficient manner, which may include replication strategies or data delivery systems using message integration software.
- Managing business rules: This incorporates the documentation of all metadata and associated business rules, and identification and documentation of the way that information is being used and by which users.
- Managing sources: This involves managing the sources of reference information, whether these are internal data providers or external data providers. This integrates with the data quality responsibility listed earlier.
- Authorizing access and validation of security: This involves identifying, authenticating, and authorizing information users; validating security for access to the data; authorizing modifications to reference data; and providing access to the metadata or data standards for the purposes of browsing.
- Managing the data life cycle: There are data quality aspects associated with the creation, modification, sharing, reuse, retention, and back up of data. If any issues regarding the use or availability of data over the data lifetime emerge, it is the responsibility of the steward to resolve them.

Data stewardship is not necessarily an information technology function, nor should it necessarily be considered to be a full-time position. Data stewardship is a role that has a set of responsibilities along with accountability to the line-of-business management. In other words, even though the data steward's activities are overseen within the scope of the Enterprise Data Quality Forum, the steward is accountable to his or her own line management to ensure that the quality of the data meets the needs of both the line of business and of the organization as a whole.

7.7 Data Quality Validation and Certification

All application groups that participate with the Data Quality Forum are expected to achieve a level of data quality proficiency following the maturity model criteria. Conformance will be determined through a certification and validation process. Individual organizations may submit a request for data quality certification.

7.7.1 Requesting Validation/Certification

The initial request must:
1. Be electronic (hard copy submission is acceptable only if accompanied by electronic copies of all items),
2. Include a letter of request (used by the submitter to officially announce to the Data Quality Director its request for certification),
3. Include a narrative that contains:
   a. The role the participant fulfills within the operational community,
   b. The maturity level of certification requested, and
   c. A request for receipt of acknowledgment to the participant.

7.7.2 Data Coordination Council Certification Endorsement

The Data Coordination Council will review the request for certification and task the Data Quality Certification and Audit team to prepare and conduct an audit to verify the participant's compliance with the policies and practices specified in the specific data quality maturity level sought. The Data Quality Certification and Audit team will review the participant's operational, technical, and governance practices and assess the degree to which the participant's practices conform to the best practices specified in the maturity model.

The team will report its findings to the Data Coordination Council, which will publish their assessment to the requesting application group and endorse certification if the participant's practices adequately conform to the maturity practices.

7.7.3 Ongoing Validation

The Data Quality Forum requires periodic formal validation processes to ensure ongoing participant's conformance and consistency to data quality practices within the community. For each participant role, the data quality obligations will be specified, for example, achievement of a data quality maturity level, and conformance to a specified service level agreement (SLA). The validation criteria for each participant obligation determine the degree of conformance. See an example in Table 7.2.

Table 7.2 Ensuring Data Trustworthiness

Participant Role	Description	Obligations	Validation Criteria
Trusted data source	Trusted data sources will be subjected to a certification process; this will include conforming to a threshold level of meeting data quality expectations. To maintain its certified status, the trusted data source will be subjected to data quality audits to ensure a high level of conformance of high quality of data across the defined data quality dimensions.	Maturity level	The participating agency conforms to all of the practices and polices specified in the data quality framework for the specified maturity level.
		Service level agreements	A documented service level agreement for participating in the UHI data exchange is provided.
		Monitoring and reporting	A documented process for monitoring and reporting data quality performance is provided. Periodic reports for internal use and external publication are generated.
		Organization	A data quality organization is defined including roles and responsibilities.
		Problem resolution	Contact information is published to the community and kept current. Data quality issue tracking process is documented and applied.

7.8 Issues and Resolution

All application groups across the enterprise rely on each other to ensure the highest level of quality by conforming to the certification requirements. However, problems may arise and a process is required to ensure problem resolution in a timely and effective way. This section describes a process by which data quality issues are handled and resolved as well as outlining an escalation process. The problem resolution process varies depending on the impact that the issue has on different business initiatives across the organization. For each category of impact, a problem escalation process is defined. An example escalation model is shown in Table 7.3.

7.9 Data Governance and Federated Communities

Collaboration across organizational boundaries introduces its own special requirements when it comes to managing data quality in a federated community. At the simplest level, a federated community is a collection of participants (individuals or organizations), each of which is under its own administrative domain and governance, who agree to collaborate in some way that benefits the participants, both as individuals and as a community. These communities may cross organizational, political, geographic, and jurisdictional boundaries. An easy way to identify the formation of a federation, at least one based on information sharing, is by watching the development of data standards. The need for a standard exists when two parties need to agree on a way to understand each other; an increasing number of parties that join in the activity is evidence that there is general agreement on the benefits of collaboration.

Table 7.3 Sample Escalation Model

Issue Impact	Level 1 Reporting	Level 2 Reporting	Level 3 Reporting
Single participant	Data Quality Director	N/A	N/A
Multiple participants	Data Quality Director	Data Coordination Council	N/A
Entire community	Data Quality Director	Data Coordination Council	Data Quality Oversight Board
Audit failure	Data Quality Director	Data Coordination Council	Data Quality Oversight Board

Assessing the degree to which participants conform to best practices and the various implementations of best practices introduces interesting challenges, especially in the area of data quality management. First of all, within an administered environment, policies regarding the quality of information can be defined and enforced, but as data leave the organization boundary, so too does the ability to control its quality. Second, the quality expectations for data used within a functional or operational activity within one organization may be insufficient for the needs of the "extended enterprise." Third, the existence of data outside the administrative domains suggests the notion of ownerless data, for which no one is necessarily accountable.

Consider this: although data quality cannot necessarily be mandated, the expected benefits of collaborative use of enterprise information can only be achieved when all participants willingly contribute to successful data quality management. Therefore, remember that an important objective of the community is the development of a data quality framework that encourages participants to willingly conform to and broaden the integration of data quality across the entire organization.

7.10 Summary

Applying the concept of governance to data covers both external and internal aspects of oversight. External forces, such as regulations, laws, industry standards, or even generally accepted principles, require that an organization not only abide by the expected behavior, but also be subject to external auditing. Internal oversight is necessary to transition into a more competitive organization, especially as the need for information integration impose rigid data quality standards.

Having protocols and processes in place that can be managed, and for which individuals can be held accountable, enables a streamlined mechanism for enhanced collaboration. The model described in this chapter should be considered to be a template – understand how successful programs are governed within your organization and try to adapt aspects of the model to your own environment.

DIMENSIONS OF DATA QUALITY

According to the famous British mathematical physicist Lord Kelvin, "If you cannot measure it, you cannot improve it." And although the fitness of data for any specific purpose is typically dependent on the characteristics and needs of the business users, the measures of poor data quality are frequently described only using examples and anecdotes. The absence of a rigorous means for measurement limits one's ability to effectively quantify a measure of quality. What is needed is some way to bridge that gap by providing a frame of reference for measurement and quantification in relation to identified business impacts that can lead to those relevant metrics associated with data quality.

Chapter 1 focused on identifying business impacts that could be attributed to poor data quality and the last two chapters looked at developing and employing metrics for performance oversight and data governance. This chapter looks at the practical process of aligning business user data quality expectations that can be measured and then correlated to the identified business impacts. Here we will look at ways to help classify data quality expectations along with ways to measure conformance to these expectations. In turn, these metrics are used to quantify the levels of data quality and will be used to identify the gaps and opportunities for data quality improvement across different applications within the enterprise.

Instead of relating the issue of poor data quality using anecdotes (which limits ones ability to effectively measure true levels of data quality), this chapter arms the practitioner with guidelines for evaluating stability and predictability associated with quality measurements and distinguishing between common causes and special causes of data failures. By measuring fitness of data for any specific purpose based on the characteristics and needs of the business users, this will help in resolving data quality issues based on an objective assessment of an organization's level of data quality maturity with respect to the dimensions of data quality.

8.1 What Are Dimensions of Data Quality?

The concept of a dimension evokes thoughts of measurement, and that is exactly what is meant when the term is used in the context of data quality. A dimension of data quality describes a context and a frame of reference for measurement along with suggested units of measurement.

The dimensions proposed here are based on fundamental data quality principles. Different dimensions are intended to represent different measurable aspects of data quality and are used in characterizing relevance across a set of application domains to monitor against the specified organizational standard of data quality. Once a method for measurement is established for a dimension, the analyst can use the measurements to review data quality performance at different levels of the operational hierarchy.

The collected measurements can populate a dashboard indicating overall line-of-business and then rolled-up enterprise performance with respect to business user expectations. This gives each group within the organization the freedom to introduce its own dimensions with customized characteristics.

Although it is possible to describe a diverse set of measurements, the value of using metrics is being able to weigh the most critical aspects of a process that *need* to be measured against those aspects that are *capable* of being measured. In other words, it is good to define metrics based on quantifiable measurements, but don't let that discourage you from qualitative assessments. But remember that when the measurements are subjective, there is a risk that they can be misinterpreted, so those types of metrics should be used in moderation.

8.2 Categorization of Dimensions

Dimensions of data quality can be logically categorized and ordered in a hierarchy to facilitate governance, technology implementation, the definition of operational processes, compliance, and reporting. Rules associated with different dimensions can be applied to different aspects of organizational data. At the simplest level, there are dimensions that are intrinsic to the values that compose a data set. More complex rules are a result of expected relationships that occur at a record level, then at the data set, followed by the application level. From a different standpoint, there are other types of rules that can be used to govern information compliance with business policy.

The dimensions described in this chapter encompass the intrinsic aspects of data quality that are generally applicable within an enterprise. Figure 8.1 highlights the various levels at which data quality dimensions and data quality rules may be specified. The image shows the levels in a hierarchy to indicate the dependence of each level on the management of quality information associated with the lower levels.

Though the data quality literature proposes many different kinds of dimensions, the practitioner is pragmatically limited to dimensions that are feasibly measured and reasonably socialized across the enterprise. We will only focus on the details of data quality dimensions at the physical and operational levels, and discretely measurable dimensions are presented.

8.2.1 Intrinsic Dimensions

We can consider the measures associated with the data values themselves outside of any association with a data element or a

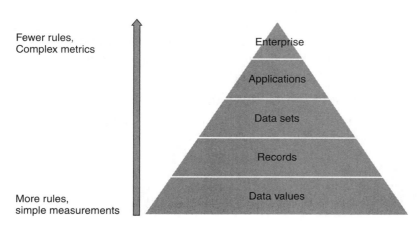

Fewer rules,
Complex metrics

More rules,
simple measurements

Enterprise

Applications

Data sets

Records

Data values

Figure 8.1 Hierarchy of data quality dimension categories.

record as "intrinsic." Intrinsic dimensions relate to the data values themselves out of a specific data or model context. For example, specifying a valid range of temperatures (e.g., −50 to 110 degrees Fahrenheit) is intrinsic to the value, no matter where it is used. As another example, insisting that all data values that represent telephone numbers conform to the standards defined in the North American Numbering Plan format defines a data quality rule associated with the syntax of the value, no matter which table or column that value appears in.

8.2.2 Contextual Dimensions

Measures that look at consistency or validity of a data element in relation to other data elements or from one record to other records can be referred to as "contextual," because they depend on the context. Contextual dimensions depend on various business policies that are implemented as business rules within systems and processes. Yet although information policies (such as those governing security or privacy) are a major source of data quality assertions, because they imply the need for data governance, which is covered in chapter 7. However, some data quality dimensions do have governance implications. As an example, a requirement for assigning identifiers that uniquely reference an individual entity is an information policy; this translates to data quality rules regarding unique identification, identifier anonymity, nonidentifiability, and so on.

8.2.3 Qualitative Dimensions

A third category includes the dimensions that might be deemed "qualitative," and these may reflect the synthesis of the measures associated with the intrinsic and contextual dimensions. Ultimately, this involves combining the measures associated with conformance to the highest level of data quality as intended by the specification of information policies.

8.2.4 Classifying Dimensions

The classifications for the practical data quality dimensions are the following:
1. Accuracy
2. Lineage
3. Structural consistency
4. Semantic consistency

5. Completeness
6. Consistency
7. Currency
8. Timeliness
9. Reasonableness
10. Identifiability

The relationships between the dimensions are shown in Figure 8.2.

The main consideration of isolating critical dimensions of data quality is to provide universal metrics for assessing the level of data quality in different operational or analytic contexts. Using this approach, the data stewards can work with the line-of-business managers to:

- Define data quality rules that represent the validity expectations,
- Determine minimum thresholds for acceptability, and
- Measure against those acceptability thresholds.

In other words, the assertions that correspond to these thresholds can be transformed into rules used for monitoring the degree to which measured levels of quality meet defined and agreed-to business expectations. In turn, metrics that

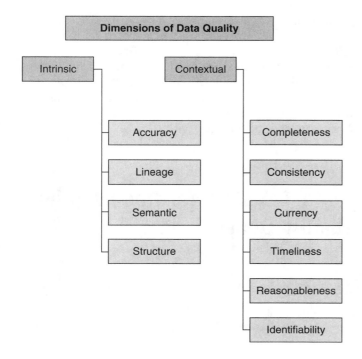

Figure 8.2 Practical dimensions of data quality.

correspond to these conformance measures provide insight into examining the root causes that are preventing the levels of quality from meeting those expectations.

8.3 Describing Data Quality Dimensions

These general areas of concentration frame the discussion for identifying measurable aspects of data quality, but the specifics have to be based on the surveyed business needs. As a way to organize the intended measures, when assembling the list of the relevant data quality dimensions for your organization, it is worth considering:

1. The **characteristic dimension,** which is the aspect of the high level dimension being measured,
2. The **criteria,** which list the specific aspects of the dimension to be measured,
3. The **metric,** which is the quantifiable measure – effectively the way that each criterion is measured, and
4. The **conformance threshold,** which is the level of measurement that indicates conformation.

An example of a table is shown in Table 8.1. Acceptance thresholds can be specified in two ways. Those for which there are truly quantifiable measures will have a quantitative threshold specified as a score or as a percentage of the records that must meet the criteria. Those for which the quantification is less precise can be assessed with general levels that over time can be refined in precision. In this type of situation, for example, the level might indicate a recommended threshold (specified as high, medium, and low) to be adopted in order to provide a benchmark for the level of quality.

Table 8.1 Example of a Template for Documenting Data Quality Dimensions

Characteristic Dimension	Criteria	Metric	Conformance Threshold
Name of the dimension	The relevant aspects of this dimension being measured	Quantifiable measure for the dimension	Acceptable compliance measure

The next set of sections provides some basic characteristic metrics that can be defined as a baseline for your own program. The conformance threshold is deliberately left blank – the threshold should be defined as a function of the needs of your organization! One other note – this list is by no means inclusive, and is expandable to meet the needs of the businesses across the enterprise. The list here is intended to provide guidance for customizing the set for your organization's business needs.

8.4 Intrinsic Dimensions

The intrinsic dimensions focus on the values of data themselves, without necessarily evaluating the context of those values. These dimensions characterize structure, formats, meanings, and enumeration of data domains – essentially the quality of organizational metadata and how it is used.

8.4.1 Accuracy

Accuracy is one of the more challenging dimensions to assess because it refers to the degree to which data values agree with an identified source of correct information. There may be many potential sources of correct information; some examples include a database of record; a similar, corroborative set of data values from another table; dynamically computed values; or perhaps the results of a manual process. In many cases there is no definitive source of correct information.

The characteristics of accuracy include the definition of a system of record or a set of values of record, the precision of data values, value acceptance, and domain definition, as is described in Table 8.2.

8.4.2 Lineage

Trustworthiness of data is of critical importance to all participants across the enterprise. One aspect for the measure of trustworthiness is the ability to identify the source of any new or updated data element. In addition, documenting the flow of information better enables root cause analysis. Therefore, a dimension measuring the historical sources of data, called *lineage*, is valuable in overall assessment.

Table 8.2 Accuracy Dimensions

Characteristic	Criteria	Metric	Conformance Threshold
Systems of record	A registry of data sets that have been identified for accuracy comparison exists.	Policies and protocols for validating and certifying systems of record are followed. In the case where there is no specific system of record for corroborating data accuracy, a manual process should be deployed.	
Precision	Data elements are defined with an amount of precision or detail.	Data value precision conforms to the defined precision or detail.	
Value acceptance	Acceptable values for data are defined.	Each data element supports all the acceptable data values defined for the data element.	
Domain definition	Values for commonly used value domains are defined once.	For every conceptual domain, there is one business definition and enumerations of valid value domains. Value domains are used consistently across the enterprise.	
Value accuracy	Values are accurate.	Each data value is correct when assessed against a system of record.	

Table 8.3 Lineage Dimensions

Characteristic	Criteria	Metric	Conformance Threshold
Originating data source	Record the origins of data	All data elements will include an attribute identifying its original source and date.	
	Record the origins of data	All updated data elements will include an identifier for the source of the update and a date.	
	Record the origins of data	Audit trails of all provenance data will be kept and archived.	

8.4.3 Structural Consistency

Structural consistency refers to the consistency in the representation of similar attribute values, both within the same data set and across the data models associated with related tables. Structural consistency characterizes the care taken by the database modelers, administrators, and stewards in making sure that similar attributes are strongly typed using well-defined representation paradigms.

There are two aspects to measurement. The first examines the percentage of time that commonly used data elements with the same or similar semantics share the same underlying syntactic formats and structures. The second involves ensuring that all used type frameworks are properly documented within the metadata repository. Sample dimensions are provided in Table 8.4.

8.4.4 Semantic Consistency

In general, every enterprise consists of a number of participants, each of which governs its own data environments. This internal governance reflects how information is used within their internal business processes. But in every organization, the

Table 8.4 Structural Consistency Dimensions

Characteristic	Criteria	Metric	Conformance Threshold
Syntactic consistency	Formats of shared data elements that share the same value set have the same size and data type.	Data elements must conform to enterprise length and type standards.	
		Stored representations are consistent with the exchange data size and type (i.e., if a client application stores an exchanged value, the data type of the stored value does not in any way change the representation or meaning, such as shifting from numeric to alphanumeric values).	
Documentation of common types	Data element length and type are specified in the metadata repository.	Percentage of enterprise-wide data types are defined and described within the metadata repository.	

participants often need to exchange or share data, especially as more organizations adopt "single source" master data repositories. Yet as the development of information architectures has largely been driven at the application level, there are bound to be variations in how different individuals (and their managed applications) understand the meanings of commonly used business terms. So for the purposes of information sharing there is a need for agreement on the meanings of the business terms as data moves between applications.

Semantic consistency refers to consistency of definitions among attributes within a data model, as well as similarly named attributes in different enterprise data sets, and it characterizes the degree to which similar data objects share consistent names and meanings. One aspect of semantic consistency involves the meanings of similarly named attributes in different data sets. The meanings of these attribute names should be distinguished, or the attributes should be assigned different names. The conformance to externally defined data standards provides some level of policy for this dimension.

Definition refers to ensuring that all participants understand the names and meanings assigned to the data elements, and that their service and application components employ the data elements in a way that is consistent with the core definition. Table 8.5 provides additional suggestions.

8.5 Contextual

The contextual dimensions provide a way for the analyst to review conformance with data quality expectations associated with how data items are related to each other.

8.5.1 Completeness

A data model should not include extra information, nor should its deployment be missing relevant data values. Unused data, by nature of its being ignored, will tend toward entropy, leading to low data quality levels along with introducing a problem of maintaining data consistency across any copies or replicas. Completeness refers to the expectation that certain attributes are expected to have assigned values in a data set. Completeness rules can be assigned to a data set in three levels of constraints:

1. Mandatory attributes require a value;
2. Optional attributes, which may have a value (potentially under specific circumstances); and

Table 8.5 The Semantic Dimensions of Data Quality

Characteristic	Criteria	Metric	Conformance Threshold
Data definitions	A metadata repository, with all data elements named and defined, is available for all participants.	All data elements are named, and each data element has a definition.	
Data definitions		All participants verify that they can access the names and definitions.	
Data definitions		Definitions conform to enterprise standards.	
Conformance to naming convention	An enterprise naming convention has been documented and all data element names conform to the convention.	Each data element name conforms to the naming convention.	
Name ambiguity	No two elements share the same name.	Participants will obtain all data element names from the metadata repository.	
Semantic consistency	Similarly named data attributes are assured to refer to the same business concept.	Participants will apply data standard terms that are consistent with their related business concept.	

3. Inapplicable attributes (such as maiden name for a single male), which may not have a value.

Completeness can be defined as a directive for a single attribute or can be dependent on the values of other attributes within a record or across records in a data set. Table 8.6 provides some examples of measures associated with the completeness dimension.

8.5.2 Consistency

In any enterprise environment, consistency is relevant to the different levels of the data hierarchy – within tables, databases, across different applications, as well as with externally supplied data. By virtue of the growing trend to consolidate and exchange data across the lines of business, there may be discovered inconsistencies in different data sets that may have eluded scrutiny in the past. Policies and procedures for reporting

Table 8.6 Completeness Dimensions

Characteristic	Criteria	Metric	Conformance Threshold
Population density	Specify the minimum degree of population for each data element.	Measure the frequency of attribute population.	Medium
Optionality	Attributes are expected to have assigned values in a data set. Optionality must be specified for all data elements.	Mandatory attributes require a value. Inapplicable attributes (such as maiden name for a single male), may not have a value.	Medium
Null validation	Null value rules for all data elements are defined. When the null value (or absence of a value) is required for an attribute, there should be a recognizable form for presenting that null value that does not conflict with any valid values. This means that for a numerical field, if the value is missing, it is not an indication that it may be represented to the user as the value 0, because the presence of any number there may have different meaning than the absence of the value.	Null value rules are conformed to.	100%

inconsistencies to the owners of the contributing data sources must be defined to ensure measurable consistency among the participants. Some examples of consistency dimensions are provided in Table 8.7.

8.5.3 Currency

Currency refers to the degree to which information is current with the world that it models. Currency can measure how "up-to-date" information is, and whether it is correct despite the possibility of modifications or changes that impact time and date values. Data currency may be measured as a function of the expected frequency rate at which different data elements are expected to be refreshed, as well as verifying that the data is up-to-date; these may require some automated and manual processes. Currency rules may be defined to assert limits to the

Table 8.7 Consistency Dimensions

Characteristic	Criteria	Metric	Conformance Threshold
Presentation	Common presentation formats for each data element are defined.	Data elements that are presented in a screen or a form will conform to the defined presentation format.	
Presentation completeness	Each data presentation format can convey all information within the attributes.	Every defined presentation format will be verified to ensure that it can present all values the displayed attribute can take.	
Null presentation	Standards for the presentation of missing information for each data type are defined.	Any data element that may be null must have a defined representation for the absent value. If there are multiple reasons for absent values that can be captured in the data (e.g., "unavailable" vs. "not applicable") there will be multiple null representations.	
Capture and collection	Data entry edits and data importation rules should be defined for each data element.	Participants must apply the defined data edit and collection rules.	

lifetime of a data value, indicating that it needs to be checked and possibly refreshed. Examples are shown in Table 8.8.

8.5.4 Timeliness

Timeliness refers to the time expectation for accessibility of information. Timeliness can be measured as the time between when information is expected and when it is readily available for use. Some examples of timeliness measures are provided in Table 8.9.

8.5.5 Reasonableness

General statements associated with expectations of consistency or reasonability of values, either in the context of existing data or over a time series, are included in this dimension. Table 8.10 provides examples.

Table 8.8 Currency Dimensions

Characteristic	Criteria	Metric	Conformance Threshold
Age/freshness	The acceptable time period lifetime between updates for each data element is defined — expiry date.	Data whose lifetime period is expired is considered a data quality issue.	
Time of release	The date/time upon which the data become available is defined. If data is expected to be delivered to specified participants, the release date/time should be specified.	The release of data should be measured against the defined release time.	
Synchronization/ replications	Data synchronizations and replication policies between systems must be specified.	Systems must be updated based on synchronization and replication policies.	
Correction, update promulgation	Polices for promulgation of corrections and updates must be specified.	Corrections and updates must conform to the promulgation policies.	
Temporal	Each data element in a record is temporally related to each other elements. Data elements are relating to or limited by time.	Temporal consistency rules are integrated directly into the validation service and are applied at any time one of the dependent attributes is proposed to be modified. Records whose temporal (e.g., date) attributes are inconsistent are considered data flaws.	

8.5.6 Identifiability

Identifiability refers to the unique naming and representation of core conceptual objects as well as the ability to link data instances containing entity data together based on identifying attribute values. Examples are shown in Table 8.11.

8.6 Qualitative Dimensions

We might characterize additional dimensions for which the ability to get quantitative measurements is less clear. However, providing qualitative dimensions allows you to assess a higher

Table 8.9 Timeliness Dimensions

Characteristic	Criteria	Metric	Conformance Threshold
Accessibility	Newly posted records should be available to enterprise applications within a specified time period. Policies specifying acceptable time delays must be provided.	Time delays must be measured and recorded.	
Response time	Ensure that requested data is provided within the acceptable time period. Expectations for response time must be specified.	Requested data must be received by the requestor within the specified time period.	

Table 8.10 Characteristics of Reasonableness

Characteristic	Criteria	Metric	Conformance Threshold
Multi-value consistency	The value of one set of attributes is consistent with the values of another set of attributes.	Specific rules are defined for measurement.	
Temporal reasonability	New values are consistent with expectations based on previous values.	Comparison of aggregates (sums, totals, averages) is in line with expectations based on history (e.g., the total number of transactions today will not exceed yesterday's total by more than 5%).	
Agreements	Service level agreements (SLA), security agreements, and other authoritative documents governing data provider performance will be defined.	Conformance to agreements will be measured.	
Reasonableness	The data meet rational expectations.	The expectations will be defined.	
Data correction	When possible, poor data quality will be improved by implementing data correction processes.	Measure the percentage of records that can be corrected via automated processes.	

Table 8.11 The Dimension of Identifiability

Characteristic	Criteria	Metric	Conformance Threshold
Entity uniqueness	No entity exists more than once within the system.	Records should not be created if there is an existing record for that entity. Validate that each generated identifier has never been used before.	
Search and match	A probability of a successful or partial match for the identifying information associated with a specific record will be defined.	Performance results for successful and partial matches will be measured.	
Coverage	The central repository is expected to identify the universe of unique entities across the enterprise. The potential total universe of entities by classification must be defined.	The percentage of identified entities measured against the universe of potential entities will be measured.	
Linkage	Links between the central repository and other data records are properly maintained.	Linkages are assessed to measure the number of false negatives and false positives.	

order of oversight – reviewing how well the information meets defined expectations and needs.

One of the more significant challenges in implementing a data quality program is the transition from developing the program at a conceptual level and putting the processes in place that guide conformance to the program. One reason is that transitioning from a reactive organization to a proactive one requires some degree of discipline with respect to identifying performance objectives and ongoing monitoring. Defining and specifying metrics at the outset of a program in a reference document and ignoring them in practice will lead to program failure.

In order to embed data quality in operational environments, ratings can be defined that report on data element quality. These quality ratings can be stored as retrospective attributes of their associated data elements; for example, at the lowest level, a data quality dimension of accuracy can be specified with a "precision" attribute.

Historically the concept of "fitness for use" has reflected the primary data quality measure, although many of the characteristics are subjective and are difficult to be quantitatively measured. However, it is reasonable to incorporate these characteristics and criteria in terms of possible key data quality

Table 8.12 Qualitative Dimensions

Characteristic	Criteria	Metric	Conformance Threshold
Authoritative sources	Trusted data sources are specified. Those data sources charged with providing definitions and other reference related data are identified.	Each definition and reference data attribute contains a reference to an authoritative source.	
Trust	Service level agreements (SLAs) governing enterprise data supplier performance will be defined.	Conformance to service-level agreements will be measured.	
Anonymity/ privacy	Uniquely defined identities that are subject to privacy or security policies have no data or combinations of data by which an individual can be identified.	Decomposition or synthesis of data elements with identifying data elements cannot be used to identify an individual. Identifiers are randomly generated and assigned.	
Quality indicator	Data quality indicators will be specified for all critical data elements. For example, a data element that has been validated by some defined process would be considered higher quality than a data element that has not been validated.	Data quality indicators will be updated based on the associated data quality rules.	
Edit and imputation	Hard edits are used to identify when data is definitely correct. Soft edits are used to identify when data is possibly correct. A rating attribute indicating if hard or soft edits were applied to the data element was applied.	All data elements supplied must specify the edit and imputation rating of hard or soft edits.	
Standards and policies	Enterprise-wide data standards are specified	Conformance to standards and data quality policies will be measured.	

performance indicators, rolled up from some of the other dimension metrics.

8.7 Finding Your Own Dimensions

As was noted earlier in this chapter, the list of dimensions provided here is the starting point for your own organization. Although this enumeration is a basic set of aspects of how data quality can be measured, there are many other aspects that may be specific to an industry (e.g., conformance to industry data standards), a corporation (associated with internal information policies), or even a line-of-business level. Not-for-profit organizations may have different constraints and different productivity measures. Government agencies may have different kinds of collaboration and reporting oversight. No matter what, though, the determination of the critical aspects of data quality should be customized to the organization, since it will feed into the metrics and protocols for assessing and monitoring key data quality performance factors.

8.8 Summary

The basis for assessing the quality of data is to create a framework that can be used for asserting expectations, providing a means for quantification, establishing performance objectives, and applying the oversight process to ensure that the participants conform to the policies. This framework is based on dimensions of data quality – those discussed in this chapter, along with any others that are specifically relevant within your industry, organization, or even just between the IT department and its business clients.

These measures complete the description of the processes that can be used to collect measurements and report them to management (as introduced in chapter 7). Before any significant improvement will be manifested across the enterprise, though, the individuals in the organization must understand the virtues of performance-oriented data quality management and be prepared to make the changes needed for quality management.

DATA REQUIREMENTS ANALYSIS

It would be a disservice to discuss organizational data quality management without considering ways of identifying, clarifying, and documenting the collected data requirements from across the application landscape. This need is compounded as there is increased data centralization (such as master data management, discussed in chapter 19), governance (discussed in chapter 7), and growing organizational data reuse.

The last item may be the most complex nut to crack. Since the mid 1990s, when decision support processing and data warehousing activities began to collect and restructure data for new purposes, there has been a burning question: Who is responsible and accountable for ensuring that the quality characteristics expected by *all* data consumers are met?

One approach is that the requirements, which often are translated into availability, data validation, or data cleansing rules, are to be applied by the data consumer. However, in this case, once the data is "corrected" or "cleansed," it is changed from the original source and is no longer consistent with that original source. This inconsistency has become the plague of business reporting and analytics, requiring numerous hours spent in reconciling reports from various sources. The alternate approach is to suggest that the business process creating the data must apply all the data quality rules. However, this can become a political hot potato, because it implies that additional work is to be performed by one application team even though the results do not benefit that team's direct customers.

That is where data requirements analysis comes into play. Demonstrating that all applications are accountable for making the best effort for ensuring the quality of data for all downstream purposes, and that the organization benefits as a whole when ensuring that those requirements are met, will encourage better adherence to the types of processes described in this chapter.

The chapter first looks at yet another virtuous cycle, in which operational and transactional data is used for business analytics, whose results are streamed back into those same operational systems to improve the business processes. The chapter then provides an introduction to data requirements analysis and follows up by walking through a process that can be used to evaluate how downstream analytics applications use data and how their requirements can be identified and shared with upstream-producing applications. The chapter finishes by reviewing data quality rules defined within the context of the dimensions of data quality described in chapter 8.

9.1 Business Uses of Information and Business Analytics

Business intelligence and downstream reporting and analytics center on the collection of operational and transactional data and its reorganization and aggregation to support reporting and analyses. Examples are operational reporting, planning and forecasting, scorecarding and dashboards presenting KPIs, and exploratory analyses seeking new business opportunities. And if the objective of these analyses is to optimize aspects of the business to meet performance targets, the process will need high-quality data and production-ready information flows that preserve information semantics even as data is profiled, cleansed, transformed, aggregated, reorganized, and so on. To best benefit from a business intelligence and analysis activity, the analysts must be able to answer these types of questions:

- What business process can be improved?
- What is the existing baseline for performance?
- What are the performance targets?
- How must the business process change?
- How do people need to change?
- How will individuals be incentivized to make those changes?
- How will any improvement be measured and reported?

- What resources are necessary to support those changes?
- What information is needed for these analyses?
- Is that information available?
- Is the information of suitable quality?

In turn (see Figure 9.1), the results of the analyses should be fed back into the operational environments to help improve the business processes, while performance metrics are used to continuously monitor improvement and success.

9.1.1 Business Uses of Information

The results of business analyses support various users across the organization. Ultimately, the motivating factors for employing reporting and analytics are to empower users at all levels of decision making across the management hierarchy:

- Strategic use, such as organizational strategic decisions impacting, setting, monitoring, and achieving corporate objectives
- Tactical use, such as decisions impacting operations including supplier management, logistics, inventory, customer service, marketing, and sales
- Team-level use, influencing decisions driving collaboration, efficiency, and optimization across the working environment
- Individual use, including results that feed real-time operational activities such as call center scripts or offer placement

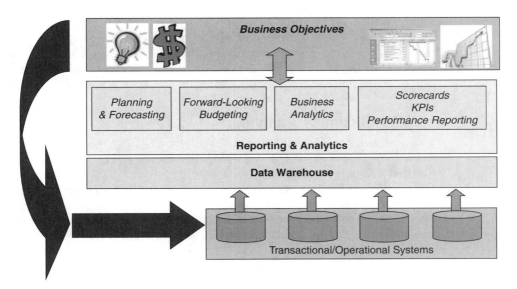

Figure 9.1 The virtuous cycle for reporting and analytics.

Table 9.1 Sample Business Analyses and their Methods of Delivery

Level of Data Aggregation	Users	Delivery
Detailed operational data	Frontline employees	Alerts, KPIs, queries, drill-down (on demand)
Aggregated management data	Midlevel and senior managers	Summary stats, alerts, queries, and scorecards
Summarized internal and external data	Executive staff	Dashboards
Structured analytic data	Special purpose – marketing, business process analysis	Data mining, Online Analytical Processing (OLAP), analytics, etc.
Aggregate values	Individual contributors	Alerts, messaging

The structure, level of aggregation, and delivery of this information are relevant to the needs of the target users, and some examples are provided in Table 9.1. The following are some examples:

- Queries and reports support operational managers and decision requirements.
- Scorecards support management at various levels and usually support measurement and tracking of local objectives.
- Dashboards normally target senior management and provide a mechanism for tracking performance against key indicators.

9.1.2 Business Analytics

The more we think about the realm of "business analytics," we see that is intended to suggest answers to a series of increasingly valuable questions:

- **What?** Predefined reports will provide the answer to the operational managers, detailing what has happened within the organization and various ways of slicing and dicing the results of those queries to understand basic characteristics of business activity (e.g., counts, sums, frequencies, locations). Traditional reporting provides 20/20 hindsight – it tells you what has happened, it may provide aggregate data about what has happened, and it may even direct individuals with specific actions in reaction to what has happened.

- **Why?** More comprehensive ad hoc querying coupled with review of measurements and metrics within a time series enables more focused review. Drilling down through reported dimensions lets the business client get answers to more pointed questions, such as finding the sources of any reported issues, or comparing specific performance across relevant dimensions.
- **What if?** More advanced statistical analysis, data mining models, and forecasting models allow business analysts to consider how different actions and decisions might have impacted the results, enabling new ideas for improving the business.
- **What next?** By evaluating the different options within forecasting, planning, and predictive models, senior strategists can weigh the possibilities and make strategic decisions.
- **How?** By considering approaches to organizational performance optimization, the C-level managers can adapt business strategies that change the way the organization does business.

Answering these questions effectively helps determine if opportunities exist, what information is necessary to exploit those opportunities, if that information is available and suitable, and most importantly, whether the organization can take advantage of those opportunities.

9.2 Business Drivers and Data Dependencies

Any reporting, analysis, or other type of business intelligence activity should be driven from the perspective of adding value to core areas of business success, and it is worthwhile considering a context for defining dimensions of value to ensure that the activity is engineered to properly support the business needs. We can consider these general areas for optimization:

- Revenues: identifying new opportunities for growing revenues, new customer acquisition, increased same-customer sales, and generally increasing profitability
- Cost management: managing expenses and the ways that individuals within the organization acquire and utilize corporate resources and assets
- Productivity: maximizing productivity to best match and meet customer needs and expectations
- Risk and compliance: compliance with governmental, industry, or even self-defined standards in a transparent and auditable manner

Organizations seek improvement across these dimensions as a way to maximize profitability, value, and respect in the market. Although there are specific industry examples for exploiting data, there are a number of areas of focus that are common across many different types of businesses, and these "horizontal" analysis applications suggest opportunities for improvements that can be applied across the board. For example, all businesses must satisfy the needs of a constituent or customer community, as well as support internal activities associated with staff management and productivity, spend analysis, asset management, project management, and so on. The following are some examples used for analytics:

- Business productivity represents a wide array of applications that focus on resource planning, management, and performance.
- Customer analysis applications focus on customer profiling and segmentation to support targeted marketing efforts.
- Vendor analysis applications support supply chain management.
- Staff productivity applications focus on tracking and monitoring operational performance.
- Behavior analysis applications focus on analyzing and modeling customer activity and behavior to support fraud detection, customer requirements, product design and delivery, and so on.

9.3 What Is Data Requirements Analysis?

Though traditional requirements analysis centers on functional needs, data requirements analysis complements the functional requirements process and focuses on the information needs, providing a standard set of procedures for identifying, analyzing, and validating data requirements and quality for data-consuming applications. Data requirements analysis is a significant part of an enterprise data management program that is intended to help in:

- Articulating a clear understanding of data needs of all consuming business processes,
- Identifying relevant data quality dimensions associated with those data needs,
- Assessing the quality and suitability of candidate data sources,
- Aligning and standardizing the exchange of data across systems,
- Implementing production procedures for monitoring the conformance to expectations and correcting data as early as possible in the production flow, and

- Continually reviewing to identify improvement opportunities in relation to downstream data needs.

During this process, the data quality analyst needs to focus on identifying and capturing more than just a list of business questions that need to be answered. Analysis of system goals and objectives, along with the results of stakeholder interviews, should enable the analyst to also capture important business information characteristics that will help drive subsequent analysis and design activities: data and information requirements must be relevant, must add value, and must be subject to availability.

9.3.1 Relevance

Relevance is understood in terms of the degree to which the requirements address one or more business process expectations. For example, data requirements are relevant in support of business processes when they address a need for conducting normal business transactions and also when they refer to reported performance indicators necessary to manage business operations and performance. Alternatively, data requirements are relevant if they answer business questions – data and information that provide managers what they need to make operational, tactical, and strategic decisions. In addition, relevance may be reflected in relation to real-time windows for decision making, leading to real-time requirements for data provisioning.

9.3.2 Added Value

Data requirements reflect added value when they can trace directly to improvements associated with our business drivers. For example, enabling better visibility of transaction processing and workflow processes helps in monitoring performance measures. In turn, ensuring the quality of data that captures transaction volume and duration can be used to evaluate processes and identify opportunities for operational efficiencies, whereas data details that feed analysis and reporting used to identify trends, patterns, and behavior can improve decision making.

9.3.3 Availability

Even with well-defined expectations for data requirements, their utility is limited if the required data is not captured in any available source systems, or if those source systems are not updated and available in time to meet business information and decision-making requirements. Also, in order to meet the availability expectations, one must be assured that the data can be structured to support the business information needs.

9.4 The Data Requirements Analysis Process

The data requirements analysis process employs a top-down approach that emphasizes business-driven needs, so the analysis is conducted to ensure the identified requirements are relevant and feasible. The process incorporates data discovery and assessment in the context of explicitly qualified business data consumer needs. Having identified the data requirements, candidate data sources are determined and their quality is assessed using the data quality assessment process described in chapter 11. Any inherent issues that can be resolved immediately are addressed using the approaches described in chapter 12, and those requirements can be used for instituting data quality control, as described in chapter 13.

The data requirements analysis process consists of these phases:
1. Identifying the business contexts
2. Conducting stakeholder interviews
3. Synthesizing expectations and requirements
4. Developing source-to-target mappings

Once these steps are completed, the resulting artifacts are reviewed to define data quality rules in relation to the dimensions of data quality described in chapter 8.

9.4.1 Identifying the Business Contexts

The business contexts associated with data consumption and reuse provide the scope for the determination of data requirements. Conferring with enterprise architects to understand where system boundaries intersect with lines of business will provide a good starting point for determining how (and under what circumstances) data sets are used.

Figure 9.2 shows the steps in this phase of the process:
1. **Identify relevant stakeholders:** Stakeholders may be identified through a review of existing system documentation or may be identified by the data quality team through discussions with business analysts, enterprise analysts, and enterprise architects. The pool of relevant stakeholders may include business program sponsors, business application

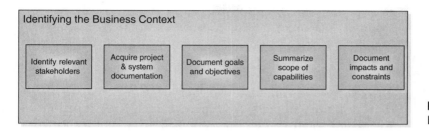

Figure 9.2 Identifying the business contexts.

owners, business process managers, senior management, information consumers, system owners, as well as frontline staff members who are the beneficiaries of shared or reused data.

2. **Acquire documentation:** The data quality analyst must become familiar with overall goals and objectives of the target information platforms to provide context for identifying and assessing specific information and data requirements. To do this, it is necessary to review existing artifacts that provide details about the consuming systems, requiring a review of project charters, project scoping documents, requirements, design, and testing documentation. At this stage, the analysts should accumulate any available documentation artifacts that can help in determining collective data use.

3. **Document goals and objectives:** Determining existing performance measures and success criteria provides a baseline representation of high-level system requirements for summarization and categorization. Conceptual data models may exist that can provide further clarification and guidance regarding the functional and operational expectations of the collection of target systems.

4. **Summarize scope of capabilities:** Create graphic representations that convey the high-level functions and capabilities of the targeted systems, as well as providing detail of functional requirements and target user profiles. When combined with other context knowledge, one may create a business context diagram or document that summarizes and illustrates the key data flows, functions, and capabilities of the downstream information consumers.

5. **Document impacts and constraints:** Constraints are conditions that affect or prevent the implementation of system functionality, whereas impacts are potential changes to characteristics of the environment to accommodate the implementation of system functionality. Identifying and understanding all relevant impacts and constraints to the

target systems are critical, because the impacts and constraints often define, limit, and frame the data controls and rules that will be managed as part of the data quality environment. Not only that, source-to-target mappings may be impacted by constraints or dependencies associated with the selection of candidate data sources.

The resulting artifacts describe the high-level functions of downstream systems, and how organizational data is expected to meet those systems' needs. Any identified impacts or constraints of the targeted systems, such as legacy system dependencies, global reference tables, existing standards and definitions, and data retention policies, will be documented. In addition, this phase will provide a preliminary view of global reference data requirements that may impact source data element selection and transformation rules. Time stamps and organization standards for time, geography, availability and capacity of potential data sources, frequency and approaches for data extractions, and transformations are additional data points for identifying potential impacts and requirements.

9.4.2 Conduct Stakeholder Interviews

Reviewing existing documentation only provides a static snapshot of what may (or may not) be true about the state of the data environment. A more complete picture can be assembled by collecting what might be deemed "hard evidence" from the key individuals associated with the business processes that use data. Therefore, our next phase (shown in Figure 9.3) is to conduct conversations with the previously identified key stakeholders, note their critical areas of concern, and summarize those concerns as a way to identify gaps to be filled in the form of data requirements.

This phase of the process consists of these five steps:

1. **Identify candidates and review roles:** Review the general roles and responsibilities of the interview candidates to guide and focus the interview questions within their specific business process (and associated application) contexts.

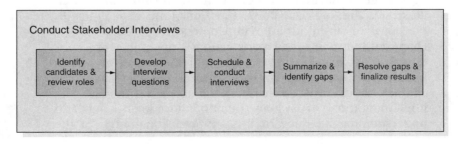

Figure 9.3 Conducting stakeholder interviews.

2. **Develop interview questions:** The next step in interview preparation is to create a set of questions designed to elicit the business information requirements. The formulation of questions can be driven by the context information collected during the initial phase of the process. There are two broad categories of questions – directed questions, which are specific and aimed at gathering details about the functions and processes within a department or area, and open-ended questions, which are less specific and often lead to dialogue and conversation. They are more focused on trying to understand the information requirements for operational management and decision making.

3. **Schedule and conduct interviews:** Interviews with executive stakeholders should be scheduled earlier, because their time is difficult to secure. Information obtained during executive stakeholder interviews provides additional clarity regarding overall goals and objectives and may result in refinement of subsequent interviews. Interviews should be scheduled at a location where the participants will not be interrupted.

4. **Summarize and identify gaps:** Review and organize the notes from the interviews, including the attendees list, general notes, and answers to the specific questions. By considering the business definitions that were clarified related to various aspects of the business (especially in relation to known reference data dimensions, such as time, geography, and regulatory issues), one continues to formulate a fuller determination of system constraints and data dependencies.

5. **Resolve gaps and finalize results:** Completion of the initial interview summaries will identify additional questions or clarifications required from the interview candidates. At that point the data quality practitioner can cycle back with the interviewee to resolve outstanding issues.

Once any outstanding questions have been answered, the interview results can be combined with the business context information (as described in section 9.4.1) to enable the data quality analyst to define specific steps and processes for the request for and documentation of business information requirements.

9.4.3 Synthesize Requirements

This next phase synthesizes the results of the documentation scan and the interviews to collect metadata and data expectations as part of the business process flows. The analysts will review the downstream applications' use of business information (as well as questions to be answered) to identify named data

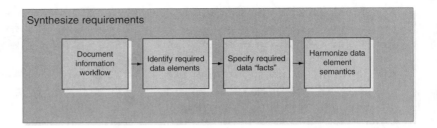

Figure 9.4 Synthesizing the results.

concepts and types of aggregates, and associated data element characteristics.

Figure 9.4 shows the sequence of these steps:

1. **Document information workflow:** Create an information flow model that depicts the sequence, hierarchy, and timing of process activities. The goal is to use this workflow to identify locations within the business processes where data quality controls can be introduced for continuous monitoring and measurement.

2. **Identify required data elements:** Reviewing the business questions will help segregate the required (or commonly used) data concepts (party, product, agreement, etc.) from the characterizations or aggregation categories (e.g., grouped by geographic region). This drives the determination of required reference data and potential master data items.

3. **Specify required facts:** These facts represent specific pieces of business information that are tracked, managed, used, shared, or forwarded to a reporting and analytics facility in which they are counted or measured (such as quantity or volume). In addition, the data quality analyst must document any qualifying characteristics of the data that represent conditions or dimensions that are used to filter or organize your facts (such as time or location). The metadata for these data concepts and facts will be captured within a metadata repository for further analysis and resolution.

4. **Harmonize data element semantics:** A metadata glossary captures all the business terms associated with the business workflows, and classifies the hierarchical composition of any aggregated or analyzed data concepts. Most glossaries may contain a core set of terms across similar projects along with additional project specific terms. When possible, use existing metadata repositories to capture the approved organization definition.

The use of common terms becomes a challenge in data requirements analysis, particularly when common use precludes the existence of agreed-to definitions. These issues become acute when aggregations are applied to counts of objects that may share the same name but don't really share the same meaning. This situation will lead to inconsistencies in reporting, analyses, and operational activities, which in turn will lead to loss of trust in data. Harmonization and metadata resolution are discussed in greater detail in chapter 10.

9.4.4 Source-to-Target Mapping

The goal of source-to-target mapping is to clearly specify the source data elements that are used in downstream applications. In most situations, the consuming applications may use similar data elements from multiple data sources; the data quality analyst must determine if any consolidation and/or aggregation requirements (i.e., transformations) are required, and determine the level of atomic data needed for drill-down, if necessary. Any transformations specify how upstream data elements are modified for downstream consumption and business rules applied as part of the information flow. During this phase, the data analyst may identify the need for reference data sets. As we will see in chapter 10, reference data sets are often used by data elements that have low cardinality and rely on standardized values.

Figure 9.5 shows the sequence of these steps:

1. **Propose target models:** Evaluate the catalog of identified data elements and look for those that are frequently created, referenced, or modified. By considering both the conceptual and the logical structures of these data elements and their enclosing data sets, the analyst can identify potential differences and anomalies inherent in the metadata, and then resolve any critical anomalies across data element sizes, types, or formats. These will form the core of a data sharing model, which represents the data elements to be taken from the sources, potentially transformed, validated, and then provided to the consuming applications.

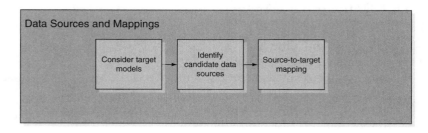

Figure 9.5 Source-to-target mapping.

2. **Identify candidate data sources:** Consult the data management teams to review the candidate data sources containing the identified data elements, and review the collection of data facts needed by the consuming applications. For each fact, determine whether it corresponds to a defined data concept or data element, exists in any data sets in the organization, or is a computed value (and if so, what are the data elements that are used to compute that value), and then document each potential data source.

3. **Develop source-to-target mappings:** Because this analysis should provide enough input to specify which candidate data sources can be extracted, the next step is to consider how that data is to be transformed into a common representation that is then normalized in preparation for consolidation. The consolidation processes collect the sets of objects and prepare them for populating the consuming applications. During this step, the analysts enumerate which source data elements contribute to target data elements, specify the transformations to be applied, and note where it relies on standardizations and normalizations revealed during earlier stages of the process.

9.5 Defining Data Quality Rules

Finally, given these artifacts:
- Candidate source system list, including overview, contact information, and notes;
- Business questions and answers from stakeholder interviews;
- Consolidated list of business facts consumed by downstream applications;
- Metadata and reference data details;
- Source-to-extract mapping with relevant rules; and
- Data quality assessment results,

the data quality analyst is ready to employ the results of this data requirements analysis to define data quality rules.

9.5.1 Data Quality Assessment

As has been presented in a number of ways so far, recall that to effectively and ultimately address data quality, we must be able to manage the following:
- Identify business client data quality expectations
- Define contextual metrics
- Assess levels of data quality
- Track issues for process management

- Determine best opportunities for improvement
- Eliminate the sources of problems
- Continuously measure improvement against baseline

This process is the next step of data requirements analysis, which concentrates on defining rules for validating the quality of the potential source systems and determines their degree of suitability to meet the business needs.

Though Figure 9.6 provides an overview of the data quality assessment process, this is discussed in greater detail in chapter 11. Suffice it to say, though, that one objective is to identify any data quality rules that reflect the ability to measure observance of the collected data quality requirements.

9.5.2 Data Quality Dimensions – Quick Review

This section provides a high-level overview of the different levels of rule granularity, but a much more comprehensive overview is provided in my previous book published by Morgan Kaufmann entitled "Enterprise Knowledge Management – The Data Quality Approach." The rules in this section reflect measures associated with the dimensions of data quality described in chapter 8. However, it is worth reviewing a selection of data quality dimensions as an introduction to methods for defining data quality rules. In this section we will consider data rules reflecting these dimensions:

- **Accuracy,** which refers to the degree with which data values correctly reflect attributes of the real-life entities they are intended to model
- **Completeness,** which indicates that certain attributes should be assigned values in a data set
- **Currency,** which refers to the degree to which information is up-to-date with the corresponding real-world entities

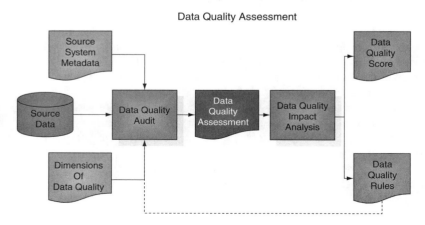

Data Quality Assessment

Figure 9.6 Data quality assessment.

- **Consistency/reasonability,** including assertions associated with expectations of consistency or reasonability of values, either in the context of existing data or over a time series
- **Structural consistency,** which refers to the consistency in the representation of similar attribute values, both within the same data set and across the data models associated with related tables
- **Identifiability,** which refers to the unique naming and representation of core conceptual objects as well as the ability to link data instances containing entity data together based on identifying attribute values

For data requirements purposes, we can add one more category:

- **Transformation,** which describes how data values are modified for downstream use

9.5.3 Data Element Rules

Data element rules are assertions that are applied to validate the value associated with a specific data element. Data element rules are frequently centered on data domain membership, reasonableness, and completeness. Some examples are provided in Table 9.2.

Table 9.2 Examples of Data Quality Rules Applied to Data Elements

Dimension	Description	Example
Accuracy	Domain membership rules specify that an attribute's value must be taken from a defined value domain (or reference table)	A *state* data element must take its value from the list of United States Postal Service (USPS) 2-character state codes
Accuracy	The data attribute's value must be within a defined data range	The *score* must be between 0 and 100
Structural consistency	The data attribute's value must conform to a specific data type, length, and pattern	A *tax_identifier* data element must conform to the pattern 99-9999999
Completeness	Completeness rules specify whether a data field may or may contain null values	The *product_code* field may not be null
Currency	The data element's value has been refreshed within the specified time period	The *product_price* field must be refreshed at least once every 24 hours
Reasonableness	The data element's value must conform to reasonable expectations	The *driver_age* field may not be less than 16
Transformation	The data element's value is modified based on a defined function	The *state* field is mapped from the 2-character state code to the full state name

9.5.4 Cross-Column/Record Dependency Rules

These types of rules assert that the value associated with one data element is consistent conditioned on values of other data elements within the same data instance or record. Some examples are shown in Table 9.3.

9.5.5 Table and Cross-Table Rules

These types of rules assert that the value associated with one data element is consistent conditioned on values of other data elements within the same table or in other tables. Some examples are shown in Table 9.4.

Table 9.3 Cross-Column or Record Rule Examples

Dimension	Description	Example
Accuracy	A data element's value is accurate relative to a system of record when the value is dependent on other data element values for system of record lookup	Verify that the *last_name* field matches the system of record associated with the *customer_identifier* field
Accuracy	A data element's value is taken from a subset of a defined value domain based on other data attributes' values	Validate that the *purchaser_code* is valid for staff members based on *cost_center*
Consistency	One data element's value is consistent with other data elements' values	The *end_date* must be later than the *start_date*
Completeness	When other data element values observe a defined condition, a data element's value is not null	If *security_product_type* is "option" then the *underlier* field must not be null
Reasonableness	When other data element values observe a defined condition, a data element's value must conform to reasonable expectations	*Purchase_total* must be less than *credit_limit*
Currency	When other data element values observe a defined condition, a data element's value has been refreshed within the specified time period	If *last_payment_date* is after the *last_payment_due,* then refresh the *finance_charge*
Transformation	A data element's value is computed as a function of one or more other data attribute values	*Line_item_total* is calculated as *quantity* multiplied by *unit_price*

Table 9.4 Examples of Table or Cross-Table Rules

Dimension	Description	Example
Accuracy	A data element's value is accurate when compared to a system of record when the value is dependent on other data element values for system of record lookup (including other tables)	The *telephone_number* for this office is equal to the *telephone_number* in the directory for this *office_identifier*
Consistency	One data element's value is consistent with other data elements' values (including other tables)	The *household_income* value is within 10% plus or minus the *median_income* value for homes within this *zip_code*
Completeness	When other data element values observe a defined condition, a data element's value is not null (including other tables)	Look up the customer's profile, and if *customer_status* is "preferred" then *discount* may not be null
Reasonableness	When other data element values observe a defined condition, a data element's value must conform to reasonable expectations (including other tables)	Today's *closing_price* should not be 2% more or less than the running average of closing prices for the past 30 days
Reasonableness	The value of a data attribute in one data instance must be reasonable in relation to other data instances in the same set	Flag any values of the *duration* attribute that are more than 2 times the standard deviation of all the *duration attribute values*
Currency	When other data element values observe a defined condition, a data element's value has been refreshed within the specified time period (including other tables)	Look up the product code in the supplier catalog, and if the price has been updated within the past 24 hours then *product_price* must be updated
Identifiability	A set of attribute values can be used to uniquely identify any entity within the data set	*Last_name, first_name, and SSN* can be used to uniquely identify any employee
Transformation	A data element's value is computed as a function of one or more other data attribute values (including other tables)	*Risk_score* can be computed based on values taken from multiple table lookups for a specific client application

9.6 Summary

The types of data quality rules that can be defined as a result of the requirements analysis process can be used for developing a collection of validation rules that are not only usable for proactive monitoring and establishment of a data quality service level agreement (as is discussed in chapter 13), but can also be integrated directly into any newly developed applications when there is an expectation that application will be used downstream. Integrating this data requirements analysis practice into the organization's system development life cycle (SDLC) will lead to improved control over the utility and quality of enterprise data assets.

METADATA AND DATA STANDARDS

People can be very creative in the ways that they opt to represent real-world concepts as information objects. This leads to variation in structure and meaning, resulting in specialized representation of similar ideas across different industries, between companies within the same industry, and even across different divisions and groups within the same company! In some instances, local variations evolve to describe the business objects that are managed and used.

When the pool of participants is small, the impact of this variation is less relevant. For example, when a new person joins a company, he may be handed a glossary of the terms that are used as an aid in coming up to speed. However, as there is a greater demand for information sharing and collaboration (and not just between colleagues or partners, but even with your competitors), slight differentiation between the names, semantics, and formats for shared information objects introduce new hurdles to collaboration.

The absence of a common frame of reference, common business term definitions, and an agreed-to format for exchange makes it difficult for parties to understand each other. Therefore, managing the quality of organizational data is a critical task as information sharing becomes the mantra for the organization. In any enterprise, we'd like to be confident that information exchanges are understood the same way through the definition and use of data standards using common metadata.

In this chapter we look at the use of data standards relying on common metadata definitions as a way to formalize data element metadata, and as a by-product, information structure and meanings. Looking at the relationship between the need for standard data exchange and assessing the various uses of data concepts will help to collate organizational metadata as a way to document data quality assertions in conjunction with data element definitions.

10.1 Challenges

There are some common challenges related to introducing metadata and data standards, usually centered on instituting good practices that are ignored during standard application design and implementation. Some examples include:

- Absence of clarity for object semantics: Relying on the implied meanings associated with business terms may be fine when the system is self-contained, but as soon as there is a need to compare values between two or more environments, subtle differences in meanings become magnified.
- Ambiguity in definition: The ambiguity is typically aligned along application, and subsequently, departmental lines; the exposure of ambiguity will encourage individuals to promote their own semantics to the exclusion of others, and this plants the seeds for organizational conflict.
- Lack of precision: People tend to be less than precise in standard conversations, because humans can derive understanding through context. However, in an imprecise environment, it is difficult to resolve measurements and metrics into a unified view.
- Variance in source systems: Aside from the semantics issues, implementation decisions may create reliance on application frameworks, leading to religious wars (e.g., .NET versus J2EE, XML versus flat data).
- Flexibility of motion mechanisms: The multiple modes by which data is exchanged can expose conflict when trying to create a seamless means for exchange. This may mean creating adapters that can transform data objects between formats, such as between records in flat files and XML documents.

Before embarking on a data standards program, consider the existing factors that may contribute to the overall success of the program:

- Established standards: There are many established standards, issued by government bodies or by recognized standards bodies that may already be in use at your organization. A good example is the use of country codes (US, CA, etc.) that are derived from the International Standards Organization's ISO 3166 standard
- De facto standards: Often there are standards in use that may not have been officially sanctioned, but there is a common understanding that the standard is used. For example, consider the use of U.S. Postal Service (USPS) state codes, which are not a standard sanctioned by an official body, but are well suited for many application purposes and are therefore adopted.
- System design: The way your application is built may exert influence over the way one expects data to be exchanged. Proponents of batch processing on flat files may be more biased toward flat file exchanges and less so toward XML documents.
- Business objectives: A healthy organization drives their development based on their business objectives, and clearly defined objectives will have some influence on the standards process, especially when collaboration is a high-level driver.
- Business rules: Guidance that influences activities within the organization (as well as outside of the organization) is critical to the definition of common business terms. In fact, the sources of those business rules may provide the authoritative definitions that can eliminate ambiguity.

10.2 Data Standards

A data standard is an agreement between parties on the definitions of common business terms and the ways those terms are named and represented in data. A standard incorporates a set of rules that describe how data objects are stored, exchanged, formatted, or presented and encompasses the rules by which information is shared. This includes:

- The identification and definition of common business terms,
- The determination of which data objects will be shared,
- The list of data elements composing those data objects, and
- Data element naming, format/structure, and presentation rules.

10.2.1 Benefits

These rules frame the policies and procedures that align with the data governance framework for ensuring compliance with the standard. Benefits of instituting data standards in alignment with a metadata strategy include:

- Enabling effective communication between multiple parties expressing an interest in sharing data,
- Reducing manual intervention when data is handed off between processes while developing opportunities for increased automation,
- Establishing a shared catalog for enterprise business terms and related exchanged data elements, and
- Supporting ongoing system maintenance and upgrade requirements.

10.2.2 Data Standards Process

A data standards process can be used to synchronize the various metadata aspects of shared or exchanged data objects. By formalizing the process of gaining consensus among the different participants, and enabling their active engagement in both defining and governing the process, we can evolve a collection of well-defined business terms, information object models, and information exchange packages, and a means for mapping these shared object definitions into those models ingrained within our legacy environment. In addition, a data standards process can be used to help harmonize common business language terms and data elements to represent those terms as part of a master data management program.

Why apply a standards process when you are not exchanging information with other organizations? The simple answer is that any time data moves from one system to another, it is considered information exchange. Consequently, an organization may employ a data standard to simplify the construction of data movement procedures even within the company, as in these kinds of projects:

- ETL for data warehousing
- Data aggregation
- EAI
- EII
- Master data management
- Customer data integration
- Consolidated reporting
- Performance metrics

10.3 Metadata Management

Underlying any data standards initiative is metadata, and it is through the metadata that definitions (and by association, data quality rules) are aligned. Managing metadata through a registry, as an information resource, is worthwhile, especially in an environment where emphasis is placed both on information dissemination (i.e., communicating data standards) and on governance (i.e., overseeing the definition an endorsement process). Registries are similar to repositories, capturing metadata at the data element level, except that the registry can capture workflow status. In addition, providing a browsing capability enables a greater potential for reusing business terms and definitions that already have some degree of acceptance. We will briefly explore the ISO standard 11179 on Metadata Registries as the basis for some of the discussion about metadata and data standards.

From both the technical and the process perspectives, data quality management leans heavily on precision and clarity with respect to the specification and definition of data entities and their corresponding attributes. And despite the best intentions of all participants involved in the data management program, there is always some confusion and even contentiousness when it comes to solidifying or standardizing data element specifications. Leveraging the data governance techniques and procedures described in chapter 7 will help address the need for coordination and oversight introduced by the organizational issues that might arise as data definitions are collected and standardized and an enterprise body of *metadata* evolves.

It is easy for us to fall into the trap of referring to metadata by its industry accepted (and benign) definition: "data about the data." Metadata actually proves to be a hard nut to crack for a number of reasons. On the one hand, the quality of data in historically distributed application and data silos is impacted by the variance in meaning and structure that emerges in lockstep with organic application evolution. Providing a model, framework, and architecture that unifies semantics across business applications can enable a control mechanism, or perhaps even a clearinghouse for determining when data elements can be mapped to each other in an appropriate manner, and also importantly, when they cannot.

On the other hand, the metadata associated with an enterprise master data set do more than just describe the size and types of each data element. In fact, the scale of metadata management needed for an enterprise migration differs from the relatively simple data dictionary-style repositories that support individual applications. Sizes and types are just the tip of the iceberg. Integration of records from different data sets can only be done when it is clear that the data elements have the same meaning, that their valid data domains are consistent, that the records represent similar or the same real-world entities. There are more complex dependencies as well: Do the client applications use the same entity types? Do the different applications use different logical names for similar objects? How is access for reading and writing data objects controlled, along with many other important variable aspects? This means that the scope of work for collecting, collating, and assembling a true enterprise metadata repository may exceed the appetite of potential business sponsors.

A conceptual view of metadata starts with basic building blocks and grows to maintain comprehensive views of the information that is used to support the achievement of business objectives. The metadata stack described in this chapter is driven by business objectives from the top down and from the bottom up and is intended to capture as much information as necessary to drive:

- The analysis of enterprise data for the purpose of structural and semantic discovery,
- The correspondence of semantics to data element types,
- The determination of commonly used data element types,
- Mapping data element concepts to business applications,
- Usage and impact scenarios for data element concepts, and
- The data quality directives.

We can look at different types of metadata that are of value to the data quality practitioner, starting from the bottom up:

- Business definitions, which look at the business terms used across the organizations and the associated meanings
- Reference metadata, which details data domains (both conceptual domains and corresponding value domains) as well as reference data and mappings between codes and values
- Data element metadata, focusing on data element definitions, structures, nomenclature, and determination of existence along a critical path of a processing stream
- Information architecture, coagulating the representations of data elements into cohesive entity structures, how those structures reflect real-world objects, and how those objects interact within business processes
- Business metadata, which captures the business policies driving application design and implementation, the corresponding information policies that drive the implementation decisions inherent in the lower levels of the stack, and the management and execution schemes for the business rules that embody both business and information policies

Given this high-level description of a metadata stack, the challenge is to look at how these levels interact as part of an overall metadata management strategy. Much valuable work has been done to standardize concepts for metadata management. Consult the standard for Metadata Registries, ISO/IEC 11179 (http://www.metadata-stds.org), for more detail about metadata management; some of the material in this chapter refers to the 11179 standard.

However, it is still valuable to be vigilant with respect to the scope and potential scale of metadata that can be captured within the metadata model. Limiting the scope to the most critical data elements helps reduce the level of effort. Analysts can iteratively collect enterprise metadata in concert with evaluating information flows and business process models, which can reveal new conceptual data elements. Effective use of metadata relies on its existence as a "living artifact," not just a repository for documentation.

10.4 Business Metadata

We have already considered the fact that variance in data meanings and structures is a significant contributor to data flaws, and this variance evolves from the organic application development and the subsequent divergence of meanings associated with commonly used business terminology. This introduces the opportunity for the data quality practitioner to collect and standardize the definitions for the business terms commonly used across the organization. As concepts are identified, the analysts can engage the subject matter experts to explore differences and commonalities so that the definitions can be standardized when possible, and differentiated when not.

10.4.1 Data Concepts

We'll use the term "data concept" to represent those entities that are both referred to be the business consumers and modeled within the data architecture. Examples include "customer," "product," or "supplier," and each has some core attributes associated with it, such as "birth date" or "product classification." These attributes may refer to data concepts as well. Because similar entities are relevant in different contexts, there will be data concepts relevant to specific business processes and data concepts whose uses transcend specific divisions, organizations, or even industries. A good starting place for identifying key data concepts is a business process model, as are data standards for information exchange among participants within the same industry.

As part of the process of enumerating business concepts, participants may find that there are concepts that are referred to using different words or phrases. At the same time, one may discover that certain words are overloaded and refer to more than a single concept. Collecting the concepts and their names leads to the next concept: business terms.

10.4.2 Business Terms

Many business terms are used so frequently that they eventually lose their precise meaning in deference to a fuzzy understanding of how they relate to data concepts. On the other hand, many organizations have a well-organized set of specialized terms that confuses almost everyone except for the hard-core organizational veterans. These are diametrically opposing aspects of the same problem: organizational knowledge locked inside individual's minds, with no framework for extracting that knowledge and clarifying it in a way that can be transferred to others within the organization. It is this gap that the business terms component is intended to alleviate, and this naturally follows from the identification of the business concepts and the types of words and phrases used to refer to them.

Therefore, the data quality practitioner should endeavor to identify the different terms used to refer to each data concept and document the mappings that can be browsed by the subject matter experts. One approach documents a direct mapping between each data concept and different business terms used to refer to the concept. For example, in a financial services context, for the concept of "customer," the terms *customer* and *account* may both refer to the "customer" entity. The process should not be limited to developing a direct mapping between terms and concepts, but should also include any business terms used in any type of reference. This will include the different terms used for the concept "customer," as well as the terms used for the characteristics of a customer ("customer type," "relationship start date," "contact mechanism," etc.).

10.4.3 Definitions

Metadata management processes are used in determining how each business term is used in different business contexts. A good practice is to evaluate the use of the business term, connect it to a business concept, and seek out a clear definition for each business term in relation to a business concept drawn from an authoritative source. The range of authoritative sources includes both internal documentation and external directives. Again, consider the concept of "customer" – it may be used by the sales staff in relation to definitions and rules from historical emails, internal memos, and corporate dictates. Alternatively, when reporting customer counts for quarterly reports or in regulatory reports to government bodies, the definition of "customer" may be taken from the regulatory guidelines. Both are valid uses of a concept, but it may turn out that the business term "customer" actually is defined in two *different* ways, and that the term is used to refer to two different concepts. These uses must be distinguished, and the variant semantics documented.

These captured definitions drive the harmonization of term usage and enable the distinction of concepts based on classification by authoritative source. Within a metadata repository, for each business term and its definition, the data quality practitioner will provide the listing of authoritative sources and a method of prioritizing those sources so that if there is a conflict between two definitions, the definition that has higher priority is used. Recognize that if one were to assess the different uses of the same business terms and find multiple definitions, it may turn out that despite the use of the same term, we really have multiple concepts that must be distinguished through some type of qualification, indicating a slightly different concept that is being referenced.

10.4.4 Semantics

The aspect of semantics, or the meanings associated with data notions, is intended to capture information about:
- How the identified business terms are mapped to managed information concepts,
- Whether business terms are mapped to multiple concepts,
- Whether concepts are mapped to multiple business terms, and
- How the business concepts are related within the organization.

To some extent, semantics captures the interconnectedness of the business concepts, business terms, and the definitions. Documenting business definitions using prioritized authoritative sources is a relatively formal practice that some people may find constraining, especially when attempting to shoehorn multiple concepts into one specific definition. Allowing for more fluid semantics associated with business terms enables the coexistence of object representations sharing names, as long as their meanings are qualified.

In essence, a separate aspect of semantics allows practitioners to collect similar concepts and terms together, qualify their meanings, and determine if there is any overlap among or between them. If there is, then the relationship is documented; if not, then the specific differences must be clearly specified and a means for distinguishing the meanings in application contexts.

10.5 Reference Metadata

Reference metadata refers to the collections of values that are used to populate the existing application data stores and that are commonly used across the organization. This section will look at two core constructs: data domains and mappings.

10.5.1 Conceptual Domains

An evaluation of the business concepts will reveal relationships and hierarchies associating specific logical notions or objects together. For example, there is a concept of a "US State" that represents a geopolitical subregion of a country (another concept) named "United States of America," which in its own right is a business concept. Though the "US State" conceptual domain is composed of the concepts representing each state of the United States of America – Alabama, Alaska, and so on, through Wyoming, the conceptual domain does not direct the way the concepts are represented; this is done using value domains.

Despite the fact that they are conceptual, there will typically be some basic representation for the objects that compose the domain set. Continuing the "US State" example, there must be some representation of each of the states that conveys the standard agreed-to meaning. Therefore, one of any number of value domains may be selected as that basic representation, as we see in the next section.

10.5.2 Value Domains

A value domain is a collection of representations of the values in a conceptual domain. To continue our example, we can define a collection of character strings that refer to each of the states of the United States of America: "Alabama," "Alaska," and so on.

As is shown in Figure 10.1, there may be different value domains associated with a single conceptual domain. In this

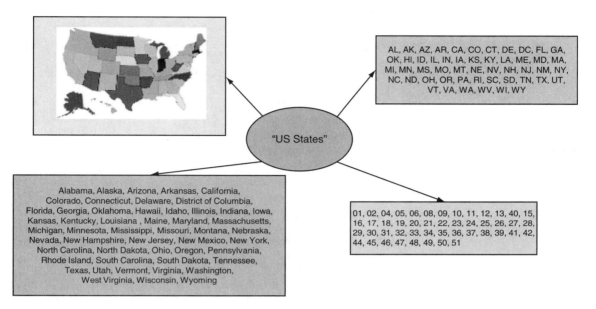

Figure 10.1 Value domains.

case, U.S. states are represented by their full names, by their U.S. Postal Service 2-character codes, by Federal Information Processing System (FIPS) 2-digit codes, or even by graphical images showing each state's boundaries. Each of these data sets is a value domain, each has a unique representation for a concept (each individual state) that is included in the higher-level concept (U.S. States), and in fact, each value in one value domain maps to a corresponding value in the other value domains. This means that we may have data sets intended to represent the same concept yet use different value sets in representation; capturing this information within the metadata repository enables making the necessary links when determining ways to integrate and consolidate data sets.

On the other hand, we may have a value domain that is used to represent different conceptual domains. Figure 10.2 shows a value domain consisting of the numerals 0, 1, 2, 3, 4, 5, and 6 used to represent four different conceptual domains. So even though the same *values* are used, their use across different data does not necessarily imply that the data sets represent the same business concepts. Again, capturing this in a metadata repository is critical in relation to data quality and data standards management.

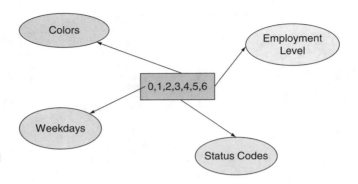

Figure 10.2 One value domain mapped to multiple conceptual domains.

10.5.3 Reference Tables

For any given conceptual domain, there must be a way to document the connection with a specific value domain and how the values within the value domain refer to the objects within the conceptual domain. Reference tables essentially capture this information by providing a direct one-to-one mapping between an enumeration of the basic representation of a value domain representing the conceptual domain and a value domain that is used in an application data context. These are often manifested in the organization as code tables or lookup tables.

For each of the conceptual domains shown in Figure 10.2 that use the same value domain, there is a direct reference table showing the relationship between concept and value; consider one example of "Weekdays."

10.5.4 Mappings

Another artifact of the historical variance of data representations is that different information architects may have selected different value domains to represent the objects within the same conceptual domain. Yet before integrating records drawn from different data sets, one must know when different value domains are used to represent the same conceptual domain. Contrast the reference table in Table 10.2 for weekdays with the one in Table 10.1. The same conceptual domain is associated with two different value domains, and to appropriately establish that two records contain the same weekday value, one must know the mapping demonstrating equivalence between the two value domains.

Data mapping (using data profiling and other analysis tools) can reveal the relationships between value domains within the

Table 10.1 Reference Table for "Weekdays"

Weekday	Value
Sunday	0
Monday	1
Tuesday	2
Wednesday	3
Thursday	4
Friday	5
Saturday	6

Table 10.2 An Alternate Reference Table for "Weekdays"

Weekday	Value
Sunday	SU
Monday	MO
Tuesday	TU
Wednesday	WE
Thursday	TH
Friday	FR
Saturday	SA

context of the conceptual domain. Table 10.3 shows the relationship between the reference data sets for our weekday example.

10.6 Data Elements

The introduction of structured representations of data concepts shows how the definitions and semantics are used to create the information models used in the different application data sets. According to the ISO/IEC 11179 standard, a data element is "a unit of data for which the definition, identification, representation and permissible values are specified by means of a set of attributes." Basically, a data element is the basic building block for data models, and each data element is specified

Table 10.3 Mapping Between "Weekday" Value Domains

Weekday	WD Value 1	WD Value 2
Sunday	0	SU
Monday	1	MO
Tuesday	2	TU
Wednesday	3	WE
Thursday	4	TH
Friday	5	FR
Saturday	6	SA

in terms of a definition, a name, a representation, and a set of valid values.

Data sets designed before the use of structured data modeling tools still conform to the use of data elements, although the associated constraints may not have been formally defined. In these cases, data analytics tools can again be used to evaluate the de facto rules, which can then be reverse-engineered and validated with subject matter experts. Yet realizing the multitude of systems that might already be in production within an organization, one must be careful to consider the scope of analyzing, validating, and formally capturing metadata about every single data element. This may prove to be an overwhelming task, and therefore, it may be worthwhile to initially concentrate on the *critical* data elements.

10.6.1 Critical Data Elements

Critical data elements are those on which the success of business processes and corresponding business applications rely. Yet of the thousands of data elements that could exist within an organization, how would one distinguish critical data elements from your everyday, run-of-the-mill data elements? This suggests a need for a definition of a critical data element within the organization. On the one hand, this definition should frame the specific data elements within the context of the uses of the data element's concept. For example, if it is used within a purely analytic/reporting scenario, the definition might consider the dependent data elements used for quality analytics and reporting (e.g., "A critical data element is one that is used by one or more external reports.")

On the other hand, if the data element is used in one or more operational applications, the definition might contain details regarding specific operational data use (e.g., "A critical data element is one that is used to support part of a published business policy or is used to support regulatory compliance."). Some other examples define critical data elements as:

- "containing personal information protected under a defined privacy or confidentiality policy"
- "containing critical information about an employee"
- "containing critical information about a supplier"
- "containing detailed information about a product"
- "required for operational decision processing"
- "contributing to key performance indicators within an organizational performance scorecard"

Critical data elements are used for establishing information policy, and consequently, business policy compliance, and must be subjected to governance and oversight, as discussed in chapter 7.

10.6.2 Data Element Definitions

Data elements basically instantiate representations of the types of concepts and business terms that are described in this chapter. Therefore, it is important to capture precise definitions of the data elements used in the different contexts, and perhaps one might consider the requirements for precision of definition for data elements to be as great as, if not greater than, that for business terms. Sections 4.1 and 4.2 of Part 4 of the ISO/IEC 11179 standard provide guidance for data definitions, and we can apply these to the definition of a data element.

A definition should state what the data element is (not what it does or what is isn't) using descriptive phrases, not relying on uncommon abbreviations, and be expressed without incorporating definitions of other data concepts or elements. In addition, a definition should state the essential meaning of the data element, be precise and unambiguous, be concise, and avoid circular reasoning. Try to avoid using a data element's functional use as its definition or to include procedural information.

10.6.3 Data Formats

In modern data modeling environments, every data element is attributed by a data type (e.g., integer, varchar, timestamp) and a size or length, but there are still many data environments that are less structured. Older file-based systems were defined with specific data element sizes, but without enforcing any rules regarding data type compliance. As part of the data format component of the metadata repository, each captured data element will also be attributed with the format of the valid value set.

This may be limited to data type, such as CHAR(2) for a "US State" data element that uses a USPS state postal code for its value domain. Alternatively, the format may contain more complex formatting information that reflects a greater degree of constraint, such as limiting North American Numbering Plan telephone numbers to data type of CHAR(12) and a format "999-999-9999," where the 9s represent digits only; any value that does not conform to the format must be invalid. Lastly, specifying an enumerated data value domain to a data element provides a greater degree of format constraint, because the data element's value *must* be selected from that set of values.

10.6.4 Aliases/Synonyms

Recognizing that different data elements ultimately contain data that represent the same underlying business concept allows the metadata analyst to establish a relationship between those data elements in that they are *aliases* or *synonyms*. Synonym data elements may or may not share the same value domains, data element formats, names, and so on, but through their connections within the metadata hierarchy one can determine that they represent the same notions and must be associated.

Note that as one iteratively reviews the use of data element concepts and their representations, one begins to see both relationships and hierarchies inherent in the common use. In turn, the practitioner can determine where two data elements refer to the same concept, even if empirically they look completely different. Let us revisit our example of documenting mappings between value domains associated with the same conceptual domain. In this example, the metadata analyst is presented with two data elements; the first is called "DayOfWeek," with these details:

Data Element Name	Data Element Type	Value Domain
DayOfWeek	Integer(1)	*WD Value 1*

And the other is called "Weekday," with these details:

Data Element Name	Data Element Type	Value Domain
Weekday	CHAR(2)	*WD Value 2*

In isolation, other than slight similarity between the names, empirical analysis of the data elements' values would not suggest that there is any similarity between them, yet the connectivity established in the metadata registry shows that both data elements employ data value domains that are mapped together. Documenting data element synonyms is valuable when determining data extract and transformation rules for master data integration. A more comprehensive process is provided in section 10.8.

10.7 Business Metadata

Metadata management and data standards enable the consolidation of more than just data or even services; doing so will provide expected benefits in terms of data quality improvement and reduction in complexity of developing and maintaining system functionality. It is one thing to consider data integration and another to impose policy constraints, such as those regarding protection of private personal information or segregation of access between different groups. In fact, many policies used to *run* the business correspond to information policies that reflect business rules, and this suggests that another aspect of metadata management involves the documentation of business policies within the metadata environment as well.

Driving policy observance via metadata requires that the business policies themselves be documented, and that their relationship to information policies be made explicit. In turn, the subject matter experts determine how the information policies reflect specific business rules to be applied to the data. The successive refinement of business policies down to information business rules opens opportunities for automating the way that business rule observance is monitored as well as rolling up to gauge business policy compliance.

As an example, consider a business policy that restricts the organization from sharing customer information with trusted partners if the customer is under the age of 13 years, unless the organization has the customer's parental consent. This business policy, expressed in natural language, restricts a business process (information sharing) based on attribution of specific data instances (namely, birth date and parental consent). Therefore, this business policy suggests a number of information policies:

- The organization must capture customer birth date.
- The organization must conditionally capture parental consent.
- Only records for customers over the age of 13 years and those that are under the age of 13 with parental consent may be shared.

Capturing the business rules to be imposed within certain sets of business applications can help with managing data and application transitions and migrations, especially when tools can be used to automate inspection and monitoring observance of those business rules.

10.7.1 Business Policies

At a simplistic level, a business policy is a statement guiding or constraining a business process as a way of controlling the outcome as well as side effects of the business process. Business policies, which may either be documented or undocumented, reflect general practices to be observed by those within an organization along with those that do business with the organization.

Business policies are expressed in natural language, but requiring subject matter experts to capture these policies within the metadata repository is a way to encourage more precision in expressing policies. The objective is to have business policies specified in a way that can be linked to the ways that they are enforced by the applications. Presumably, meeting this objective may be made possible by using information already managed within the metadata repository: concepts, business terms, business definitions, and semantics associated with commonly used business language. Business policies are more likely to be well structured if specified using terms with agreed-to definitions.

10.7.2 Information Policies

The difference between a business policy and an information policy is that a business policy guides the business process, whereas an information policy guides information architecture and application design. An information policy specifies one (of possibly many) information management requirements to support the observance of business policies. In the data sharing example in the previous section, one business policy translated into three information policies. In turn, an information policy may guide the specification of one or more business rules.

10.7.3 Business Rules

A business rule specifies one particular constraint or directive associated with a data element, a collection of data elements, one record, a set of records, and so on. A rule may specify a constraint and be used to filter or distinguish compliant data instances from noncompliant ones and could also trigger one or more actions to be taken should some condition evaluate to true. One or more business rules can be derived from an information policy, and documenting these rules within the metadata repository enables automation of application of the rules via an associated rules engine. The metadata repository provides a centralized location allowing for subject matter expert review before deployment into the rules engine.

10.8 A Process for Data Harmonization

Data harmonization is a process used to standardize the data elements that are used frequently, shared across multiple applications, or are selected for inclusion in a master or reference data model. Harmonizing data elements reduces ambiguity and provides consistency, and essentially begins by taking an inventory of relevant data elements to be administered in a metadata asset and iteratively reviewing the data elements and refining their definitions to accurately capture a consolidated definition (when possible) and distinctions (when necessary).

10.8.1 Data Element Definitions

As described in the ISO/IEC 11179 metadata registry standard, we provide some guidelines for good data definitions. A data definition shall be:

- **Unique:** The data definition should be distinguishable from every other definition within a registry.
- **Singular:** The data definition should always be expressed in the singular.
- **Positive:** A definition must be expressed as a positive, not a negative or what it is not.
- **A statement of concept:** The definition should include the essential characteristics of the concept.
- **Defined with commonly understood abbreviations:** The definition should contain only commonly understood definitions.
- **Without secondary definitions:** A second concept should not appear in the definition, but it could end up being an explanatory comment.

10.8.2 Data Harmonization

A template process is provided in Table 10.4.
The template is shown in Table 10.5.

Table 10.4 Process for Date Element Harmonization

Phase	Tasks
1. Preliminary	1. Perform the initial activities to collect the information needed to perform the harmonization: 1.1. Select the data sets to be harmonized 1.2. Obtain documentations for selected data sets (may include data models, data dictionaries, definitions, forms and related guidance, and any other reference information) 1.3. Analyze reference source documents – review documents, identify critical data elements and important data element metadata 1.4. Enter source data information into data harmonization template
2. Extraction and initial documentation	2. Extract or collect the metadata from the reference sources. Information may be embedded in data dictionaries, text memos, or even in instructions for filling out forms. For each data element, complete the data harmonization template as follows: 2.1. ID – assign a unique identifier to the data element 2.2. Data element name – provide a contextually meaningful unique name for the data element 2.3. Standard name – *not done at this point* (but a name that conforms to a naming standard will be assigned at a later stage) 2.4. Definition – document a definition extracted from an authoritative source document 2.5. Authoritative source – identify reference source for the data element definition; note if there is more than one source, and which source carries the highest priority 2.6. Length – the physical length of the data element 2.7. Type – the data type of the data element 2.8. Business rules – document any constraints on the value set, such as enumerated data domains, format specifications, or value ranges 2.9. Issues/comments – capture observations, assumption, suggestions, questions associated with data element 2.10. Source/application inventory – enumerate the data sets/applications/forms/processes from which the metadata for this data element has been collected; this will be used to assess overlap, similarity, and identical data attributes across multiple data sets 2.11. Validated by – filled by data analyst assigned for validation 2.12. Validation date – filled by data analyst assigned for validation
3. Validate and identify anomalies	3. Verify that data element metadata has been accurately and consistently captured: 3.1. The name must match the original source 3.2. The data element is assigned a unique identifier 3.3. All relevant definitions and business rules appear in the extracted list of data elements

(Continued)

Table 10.4 Process for Date Element Harmonization—*Cont'd*

Phase	Tasks
	3.4. Definitions do not use the data element name as part of definition
	3.5. Definitions are not instructions for providing a value
	3.6. Business rules must be specific to data element
	3.7. Business rules qualify the value set for the data element
	3.8. Note any ambiguous definitions (do not describe the business concept that is stored in the data element, circular definitions, etc.)
	3.9. Inconsistent definitions – definitions from two applications/sources that disagree
	3.10. Business rules as definitions – definitions that are actually rules constraining data value set
	3.11. Inconsistent data types – values are seen in more than one data type (e.g., alphanumeric vs. numeric)
	3.12. Inconsistent formats – data element is seen in conflicting formats
	3.13. Abbreviations – abbreviations used instead of full names
4. Collate and integrate	4. Determine if data elements are similar or identical:
	4.1. Determine identical data elements – data elements that have the same definition, authoritative source, business rules, length, type, and value set can be considered to be identical
	4.2. Provide standardized name – assign each instance of a set of identical data elements with a standard name, and note the relationship between the source data elements; each data element will retain its unique ID
	4.3. Establish data element similarity – data elements are considered similar if the elements share the same definition and authoritative source but disagree about business rules, length, or type
	4.4. Document comments – for each resolved set of data elements, mark the resolution in the issues/comments column
	4.5. Resolve similarity – for data elements marked as similar, research to determine whether the data elements are identical
5. Finalize	5. Finalize the harmonization:
	5.1. Identify final authoritative source – for each resolved data element, choose the authoritative definition source
	5.2. Merge business rules – for each resolved data element, merge the sets of business rules into a single set of business rules
	5.3. Assign a standard name – assign a meaningful standard name to the resolved data element based on a defined naming standard
	5.4. Conform length and type – ensure that the conformed data element has an assigned length and type that supports the merged data elements

Table 10.5 The Data Harmonization Template

Data Element ID	Standard Name	Label	Definition	Authoritative Source	Length	Type	Business Rules	Issues/Comments	Mapping	Validated/Validated By/Validation Date

10.9 Summary

Data standards and metadata management provide a basis for harmonizing business rules, and consequently data quality rules from multiple (and probably variant) sources of data across the organization. Some general processes for data standards and metadata management have been articulated here; evaluating the specific needs within an organization can lead to the definition of concrete information and functional requirements. In turn, the data quality team should use these requirements to identify candidate metadata management tools that support the types of activities described in this chapter.

Lastly, the technology should not drive the process, but the other way around. Solid metadata management supports more than just data quality; a focused effort on standardizing the definitions, semantics, and structure of critical data elements can be leveraged when isolating data quality expectations for downstream information consumers. These processes also highlight the data elements that are likely candidates for continuous inspection and monitoring as described as part of the data quality service level agreement.

DATA QUALITY ASSESSMENT

By now it should be clear that the absence of clearly defined measurements to demonstrate how business impacts are attributable to erred data prevents developing an appropriate business case for introducing data quality management improvement. When resources are allocated to correcting "bad data" without being able to evaluate the root causes, there is no ability to objectively evaluate the relationship between poor data quality and business performance. On the other hand, without being able to identify and prioritize critical issues, it is difficult to access the resources needed to address those problems. This suggests a need for a process to quickly identify high-priority data issues whose remediation can be justified.

In this chapter we look at a combination top-down and bottom-up approach for assessment to quickly generate a report documenting potential data quality issues. This resulting report will describe and prioritize clearly identified data quality issues, recommendations for remediation, and suggestions for instituting data quality inspection and control for data quality monitoring. This review will help identify high visibility data issues as well as characterize the business impacts incurred by those issues. At the same time, opportunities for improvement can be identified, providing an objective assessment of critical data, determine whether the levels of data quality are sufficient to meet business expectations, and, if not, evaluate the value proposition and feasibility of data quality improvement.

This process essentially employs data profiling techniques to review data, identify potential anomalies, contribute to the specification of data quality dimensions and corresponding metrics, and recommend operational processes for data quality inspection. It involves these five steps:

1. Plan for data quality assessment
2. Evaluate business process
3. Prepare for data profiling
4. Profile and analyze
5. Synthesize results

11.1 Planning

Data quality assessment is a challenge because it by necessity combines quantitative analysis of data sets with the qualitative context setting needed to manage the potentially ever-broadening scope of data improvements. But while tools such as data profiling are used for statistical evaluation of data, the analyst's inclination is to continue to drill down through, and across, the data in a continuous search, without a clear understanding of what one is actually searching for. Yet the reason for developing that business case is to improve the ability to address the most critical problems, and that means putting some control in place to limit the breadth of the assessment. That control is achieved through developing and then executing against a well-defined plan that narrows the scope of analysis.

11.1.1 Select a Business Process and Assess Scope

Even before the assessment planning begins, it is necessary to understand what existing activities are in place for data quality assessment and monitoring as potential benchmarks for the review. But because the process is directed at linking data quality issues to business impacts, the starting point is selecting a specific business process that is potentially impacted by poor data quality. Once that business process has been determined, the data quality practitioner must understand the scope in order to assemble a plan for how the assessment will be conducted.

Any selected business process may create, use, or dispose of data, either within the context of persistent storage or as part of a workflow or data flow, so it is necessary to assess the scope of applications that supply data to the business process, either within static data stores or an information flow. This will expose the data sets that need to be analyzed and will help in assessing the scope of the analysis, because one can then note the characteristics of each of the candidate data sets – the number of tables, the number of rows in each table, the number of data elements, as well as the data types, sizes, and so on. In addition, the knowledge workers who are the consumers of the data touched by these applications must be identified, because they will provide the details about business issues related to data and potential data flaws requiring specific investigation.

Given some understanding of the size of the data to be inspected, the business data consumers, as well as the system designers and developers associated with the applications supporting the business process, the practitioners can identify staff resources that must be participating in the data quality analysis process. As the team members are identified, internal preparation tasks can be assigned, with the intention of assembling a plan taking into account staff, resource, and tool/technology availability. The result is an outline plan for meeting with the stakeholders, collecting the source data, profiling that data, documenting the discoveries, synthesizing the results in the context of the interaction with the stakeholders, and prioritizing any critical data errors that have material business impact.

11.1.2 Preliminary Preparation

Because data is potentially created and used throughout the phases of a business process, there are a number of places where an error can be introduced. Not only that, the nature of the data elements, their data types, and their associated value domains may allow a variety of potential errors to be introduced. Therefore, it is valuable to have a clear picture of how those data sets are used within the business process, and that can be facilitated by accumulating any documentation associated with the data to be examined. That request for application and system documentation should include:

- Business process flow diagrams,
- Data models,
- Data dictionaries and any other metadata,
- Existing data edits and data validation rules,
- Previously discovered data issues, and
- Change control log entries documenting application fixes.

A review of the objectives of the business process will provide insight into immediate issues associated with low quality data having potential business impacts. The existing artifacts can be scanned for explicit (or implicit) business or data rules, and along with a review of the data elements, the applications that consume the data, and any noted gaps in the provided documentation. The analyst can then begin to assemble a list of business data quality expectations for discussion with subject matter experts and the business stakeholders.

11.1.3 Prepare and Update Project Plan

At this stage, a data quality assessment plan can be assembled based on the available resources, tools, and staff within the particular environment. Data quality assessment team members are identified, internal preparation tasks are assigned, and the schedule is aligned to best meet the business consumers' needs.

11.2 Business Process Evaluation

This process reviews business processing, systems and data documentation, existing data issues, and business impacts of data quality. The information flow supporting the business process is mapped, identifying the points in the process where data is created, exchanged, or used, and the key locations are identified in the process flow where there are critical dependencies on data that would be appropriate locations to probe the data. While the assessment looks at the data in the context of business processes, the data values are also reviewed intrinsically to identify *any* issues that indicate potential errors that would be considered for remediation or monitoring, regardless of the business context.

11.2.1 Interview Business Data Consumers

Subject matter experts must be interviewed to solicit descriptions of business impacts. The discussion with the subject matter expert is centered on "points of pain" and further drill-down to determine whether noted impacts are related to the use of data. An interview may take this form:

1. Open-ended request to describe most critical business application problems
2. For each problem, ask:
   a. What makes this a critical business problem? (assess level of criticality)
   b. What are the business impacts? (help quantify the issue.)
   c. How is the business problem related to an application data issue? (establish a relationship with data)
   d. How often does the data issue occur? (both time frame and as a percentage of interactions or transactions, to gauge frequency and probability of occurrence)

    e. When the data issue occurs, how is it identified? (determine if there is an inspection process in place)

    f. How often is the data issue identified before the business impact is incurred? (determine if there is an existing data stewardship and data issue remediation process)

    g. What remediation tasks are performed? (note the effort for remediation)

11.2.2 Review Collected Documents and Metadata

If the objective of this phase is to identify the business impacts that are attributable to data quality, one aspect is to look at the existing artifacts for evidence of data problems. One task involves determining if there is a logging and tracking system for data quality issues and, if so, reviewing the logged issues to note:

- The business function/role reporting the issue,
- How and at what point in the business process the issue was discovered,
- Who discovered the issue,
- What business impacts are related to the issue,
- How the issue was remediated, and
- Any business rules or data quality checks recommended.

Next, the data quality analyst reviews existing metadata and/or data dictionaries for the data sets that are used by the business process whose quality is being assessed. For each table, list the data elements and note when:

- The data element's value domain is specified using an internal reference table,
- The data element's value domain is specified using an external or standardized reference table, and
- There are specific data quality assertions or business rules.

Document any reference data sets and code tables used, as well as any questions regarding the use of the data element, validity constraints, or relationship to other data elements within the same table or with data elements in other tables. These include the following:

- Generated keys
- Foreign keys
- Composed keys
- Overloaded attributes (data elements whose values carry more than one meaning)
- Value ranges
- Questionable reference data

11.2.3 Collate Business Impacts

Specific business impacts can be collected and then collated within the categories described in chapter 1, namely financial, satisfaction, productivity, risk, and compliance.

11.2.4 Document Information Production Flow

A documentation review is intended to determine the flow of information across the business process, and map how the data from the raw data sources is transformed into the ultimate information product. Constructing an information production flow diagram is valuable for many reasons:

- It provides an information-centric view of the ways that business processes are executed.
- It focuses on multiple uses of data and information across information system and business process boundaries.
- It reduces the concentration on functional requirements in deference to enterprise data and information requirements across the organizations.
- It documents the way that information flows across business processes and can be used to identify the best locations for inspecting data quality and identifying flaws before any business impacts can occur.

The information production flow notes how information flows through these stages within an application:

1. Data sources that are used by the business process
2. Processing stage, noting any processing performed on the data
3. Storage locations, listing the data elements that are stored and the system where the data is stored
4. Validation points, where there are checks for data quality criteria, and for each location, the list of data quality validations performed at that point
5. Decision points at which the processing stream is directed based on the result of evaluating different conditions

Any data handoffs between processing stages, application boundaries, or system boundaries are also noted.

11.2.5 Identify Dimensions of Data Quality

Having identified the business impacts and considered the data issues associated with those business impacts, the data quality analyst's task is to propose ways to identify when data issues occur and to measure how often the issues occur.

In chapter 8 we discussed how measurements require a dimension and a process for measuring, and suggested that a dimension of data quality is a framework for quantifying observance of a data quality expectation. An example is stating that "the XFER-CD field must be either 'CKA,' 'AKA,' or 'CUST'"; this specifies a value domain and a rule that all values in the XFER-CD field must belong to the value domain.

Commonly used dimensions of data quality focus on accuracy (in comparison to a system of record), timeliness, completeness, and consistency; consult chapter 8 for a more comprehensive baseline list of data quality dimensions. Early identification of dimensions of data quality can guide the data analysis performed using the data profiling tool.

11.3 Preparation and Data Analysis

The typical process of data profiling is undirected, allowing the tool to drive the activity, with the analyst drilling through various measurements with little forethought, seeking any potential anomalies that may indicate a data flaw. But since this process is to assess the quality of the data in the context scoped by the results of the business process evaluation, the focus will be limited to evaluating the quality of the data elements potentially implicated in the identified business impacts based on the expectations of the business users. This incorporates the following activities:

- Isolation of critical data elements: reduce the scope of the data elements to be examined to those that are critical to producing the results that are impacted
- Definition of data quality measurements: review the issues that are reported by the business users to provide specific types of data quality expectations, what is to be measured, and how those measurements reflect the business impacts
- Preparation of data analysis environment: prepare data for analysis, specifically accessing the data and connecting it to some data analysis or profiling tool
- Analysis to capture measurements: analyze the data and then capture analysis statistics and measures

11.3.1 Critical Data Elements

At this point, the analyst should be able to prepare a list of the data sets to be analyzed and limited by the list of the "critical data elements" associated with data quality issues within those data sets. Critical data elements are those that are essential business facts deemed critical to the organization; any organization may define its own criteria for criticality, but some examples include any data element that:

- Is used to support part of a published business policy,
- Is used within a business intelligence application,
- Is used by one or more external reports,
- Is used to support regulatory compliance,
- Is designated as protected personal information (PPI),
- Is designated critical employee information,
- Is recognized as critical supplier information,
- Is designated as critical product information,
- Is designated as critical for operational decision making, and
- Is designated as critical for scorecard performance.

For each table and critical data element, document the description of the data element and any specific metadata defining business rules, data quality checks, or potential data quality issues that have not already been manifested or reported. An example of this is a data element whose values are composed of data values from two different data domains, such as values copied from other systems whose first 4 characters indicate the original source system and the next 10 characters contain the value. Embedding multiple values within one data element is not considered a good data management practice and may lead to complexity and unexpected irregularities in the data.

11.3.2 Data Quality Measurements

Dimensions of data quality characterize measurable aspects of data used to evaluate conformance to thresholds based on user expectations. For each dimension identified for measuring the quality of the data against expectations, the analyst must describe how that measurement will be performed. Many measurement processes are automated using queries or data profiling tools, either through statistical capabilities or through definition of business rules for comparative compliance measurement.

Once an initial set of data quality dimensions has been specified, the analysts can determine a corresponding set of measurements to be performed. Determining suitability requires an understanding of the end users' tolerances for quality, and business users must be solicited to provide acceptability thresholds to be used with the defined measurement processes.

11.3.3 Preparing the Data Analysis Environment

With the preliminary reviews performed, the data quality team members are ready to prepare the data and tools for the analysis.

Verify that the data can be accessed; if there is direct access to the data, determine that the profiling tool and any querying tool can access the data. If not, arrange for the data to be extracted and made available to the profiling tool. It is a good practice to analyze the entire data set, and most profiling tools can accommodate large data sets. However, if extenuating circumstances prevent profiling the entire data set, the best approach is to randomly sample records from the data set. The number of records to be sampled should be the largest that can be accommodated by the environment. Lastly, consider whether there might be a need for any alternate analysis tools that would be used as part of the assessment (examples include parsing and standardization, record linkage, statistical packages, and reporting tools).

11.4 Data Profiling and Analysis

With the data and the environment prepared for analysis, the analysts can profile the data within each column of the selected tables/files for frequency-based statistics for the purpose of anomaly review. In addition, at this point, any knowledge derived from the profiling can be captured: document inferred metadata, compare against estimated levels of acceptability, review statistics of columns of interest, and review with stakeholders. Lastly, determine if it is necessary to identify additional data sets that may be subjected to further analysis.

There are three types of analyses that a data profiler will perform: column analysis, table analysis, and cross-table analysis. Although we will explore the technology behind these techniques in chapter 14, here we look at how those statistics can be used for assessment.

11.4.1 Column Analysis

The profiler will provide frequency-based statistics about the values within each column. Though each situation may differ, there are some common statistics and measures that help highlight potential anomalies, and this list provides a good starting point for noting potential aberrations.

1. Document number of distinct values.
   a. Note any duplicate values when the column should be unique.
   b. Note whether the number of distinct values is consistent with expectations.

2. Evaluate the highest (maximum) values.
   a. Note whether there are values that are greater than expected.
   b. Note comparisons with defined or expected maximum values.
3. Evaluate the lowest (minimum) values.
   a. Note whether there are values that are lower than expected.
   b. Note comparisons with defined or expected minimum values.
4. Document the mean and median value (for numeric data).
5. Document the standard deviation (for numeric data).
   a. If there is a small standard deviation, examine outliers distant from median, and document potential irregularities.
   b. Examine values that are more than three standard deviations from the mean, and document potential irregularities.
6. Note the number of nulls.
   a. Note the existence of nulls if the value should never be null.
   b. Note comparison between null and value population.
7. Discovered patterns, if any.
   a. Document potential irregularities with data values matching infrequent patterns.
8. Evaluate potential overloaded use.
   a. Note when values recognizable as belonging to multiple data domains appear in one column.
9. For each column's set of values:
   a. Verify inferred data type is consistent with document data type.
   b. Verify validity of values.
10. Evaluate the most frequently occurring values.
    a. Note unexpectedly large number of null values.
    b. Note if frequently appearing values represent default values.
    c. Note if frequently appearing values are not valid values.
11. Evaluate the least frequently occurring values.
    a. Note any unexpected or invalid values.
12. Perform a visual inspection.
    a. Sort by value, scan for consecutive values, and document findings.
    b. Sort by value, scan for similar values, and document findings.

11.4.2 Table Analysis

Table analysis focuses on dependencies across the entire table, either between sets of columns or across all records in the data set, such as candidate keys. Particularly interesting are examples of functional dependence between sets of attributes that indicate some general correlations. More detail on this aspect is provided in chapter 14.

11.4.3 Cross-Table Analysis

Cross-table analysis looks at the relational structure inherent in a collection of data tables, such as:
- Assess referential integrity: identify any orphaned records in the related table;
- Validate reference data: confirm that data elements that are expected to draw their values from existing code table comply with the expectations; and
- Seek cross-table (join) duplicates: identify overlapping records across multiple tables where only one record should exist.

11.4.4 Documenting Potential Anomalies

The analysts reviewing the data statistics are on the lookout for situations in which data values could be perceived to miss end user expectations. Observations can be noted in reference to the tables or columns observed, the data quality dimension or inspection measured, such as completeness, consistency, and timeliness, as well as any special processes (other than profiling) used for measurement. The values or results that are of concern or require additional review are noted along with any additional details and suggestions for further investigation. Examples of potential anomalies and observations that are documented include:
- Frequently occurring values (values whose frequencies are greater than expected)
- Infrequently occurring values (values whose frequencies are less than expected)
- Completeness (higher than expected number or percentage of null values)
- Frequently occurring patterns (patterns whose frequencies are greater than expected)
- Infrequently occurring patterns (patterns whose frequencies are less than expected)
- Value cardinality concerns (columns in which the number of distinct values is greater or less than expected)
- Unexpected values (values that do not conform to defined value domain constraints)
- Default values (frequently occurring values or nulls specified as default values)

- Orphans (records with foreign keys that have no matching primary key)
- Mapping concerns (consistency of values between columns in a single table or across tables does not conform to expectations)
- Duplicate records
- Relationship cardinality concerns (relationships that do not observe defined mapping expectations, such as when one primary record maps to more than one foreign record when the relationship is supposed to be one to one)
- Statistical variance (counts, durations, or other computed numeric values that vary from expected statistical norms)

In addition, observation of anything that looks odd or unexpected should be added with a corresponding explanation. Any business rules or validations that showed the absence of anomalies or errors should also be documented (for example, noting that a check for duplicate records showed that there were no duplicates).

11.5 Synthesis of Analysis Results

Even with constraining profiling to those critical data elements, any conclusions regarding the quality of data within the specific business context require review of the analysis results synthesized into a coherent enumeration of potential anomalies, annotated with descriptions indicating their potential relevance. This phase includes these steps:

- List and review: Specifically describe the potential anomalies along with the notes explaining why those anomalies are related to business impacts. Examine the results of the analysis statistics within the context of the business impacts.
- Potential drill-down for additional detail: Some discovered items may require additional drill-down or review, perhaps using other analytic tools.
- Prepare assessment report: This provides a tangible artifact detailing the potential data flaws and also provides a template for iterating the process internally on another data set.

11.5.1 List and Review

During the profiling and analysis phase, the analyst will have identified a number of potential data issues. However, not every apparent issue has an impact to the business, so at this point it is incumbent upon the analysts to review data profiling and analysis results and map those potential issues to any of the business impacts discussed during the business process evaluation. Any observation of a suspected data problem should be annotated with the reasons for suspecting that it has business impact, along with some estimate (if possible) of the scale of the related impact.

The analyst will review the observations with the business data consumers and subject matter experts. During this sequential walk-through, the analyst will describe the observation in the anticipation of soliciting one of these typical types of responses:

- Serious problem: This is an issue with potential business impact requiring immediate action.
- Issue of concern: This is noted as an issue that has potential of business impact, but does not need immediate attention.
- Not a problem: This is not perceived to cause business impact.

Within the set of issues categorized using these response types, each issue is assigned a level of severity and the issues are prioritized. Even though some issues will be classified as not a problem, the analyst will evaluate and propose recommendations for all issues.

11.5.2 Drill-Down

Data profiling provides a relatively basic level of analysis, and there are situations that may require additional drill-down or data preparation to identify potential issues. This task involves determining if any further revision, data segmentation, or inclusion of additional data tables and sets would provide additional insight. Examples include the following:

- Calculation of derived values (derived sums, counts, durations) that are then subjected to profiling
- Regression analysis
- Approximate duplicate analysis using identity resolution tools
- Data segmentation and subsequent profiling (for example, profiling customer records segmented by region instead of the entire customer data set)

11.5.3 Prepare Assessment Report

Connecting potential data issues to business impacts and considering the scope of those relationships allows the team to prioritize discovered issues and document a "fitness score" based on the feedback from the business data consumers. In turn, an additional step is needed to consider the options for addressing the most critical issues and providing recommendations for issue remediation, data quality improvements, and/or ongoing data quality inspection.

The Data Quality Assessment Report is intended to be a stand-alone report documenting the drivers, process, observations, and recommendations from the data profiling process. The report includes recommendations relating to any discovered or verified anomalies that have critical business impact, including tasks for identifying and eliminating the root cause of the anomaly. Some suggestions might include:

- Inspection and monitoring
- Additional (deeper) review of the data
- One-time cleansing
- Review of data model
- Review of application code
- Review of operational process use of technology
- Review of business processes

A rough outline of a Data Quality Assessment Report contains the following sections:

1. Executive summary, providing high-level overview of the task and the results
2. Introduction, describing how data profiling and additional analyses were used to assess the quality of selected data sets
3. Goals, enumerating the specific goals of the analysis, such as "reviewing the quality of data prior to integration in a data warehouse"
4. Scope, detailing the results of the scope assessment and the identified business impacts
5. Approach, describing the details of how the assessment was performed, namely, profiling and other analyses performed, the identified critical data elements, proposed measurements, and the techniques applied
6. Data analysis results, providing the listed observations of potential anomalies and reasons for consideration
7. Recommendations, detailing the suggestions resulting from the synthesis
8. Open issues, listing any unresolved questions
9. Next steps, providing the action items resulting from the recommendations review and any requirements to resolve any of the open issues.
10. Additional supporting material, including such information as raw statistics from the column, table, and cross-table templates and any other (nonprofiling) analyses to support the recommendations

11.6 Review with Business Client

The data quality analysts will meet with the business data consumers to review the discovered anomalies and explore options for remediation. This phase includes:

- Present analysis report and associated measurements: Walk through the anomalies, explain what measurements were performed, and present the scores, including why those scores may be related to identified business impacts.
- Prioritize discovered issues: Based on the business client input, prioritize the issues based on significance, business relevance, and feasibility of remediation.
- Identify remediation tasks: List specific tasks to be performed to correct data, evaluate root causes, and mitigate immediate issues and remediation steps to eliminate the root causes of the introduction of flawed data.

11.6.1 Present Report

Engaging the business data consumers by walking through the observations in the draft report enables a clarification of the assessment process as well as the measures, impacts, expectation, and the actual measured values, all as a way of justifying the observations that were noted. As part of this walk-through, the team can accumulate additional information from business clients and subject matter experts that will lead to a refinement of any proposed data quality metrics (as discussed in chapter 6).

11.6.2 Prioritize Issues

There are a number of factors used to determine priority of the discovered issues. First, focus only on those issues that are relevant to business impact. Those issues can be ordered based on the business value perceived by the business clients from remediation. However, there are two additional factors. The first is whether there are concrete steps that can be taken to eliminate the root causes, and the second is the estimated cost of taking those steps. Even for egregious issues, if the cost to remediate exceeds the negative business impact, it would not make sense to expend resources for a negative return on investment.

11.6.3 Identify Remediation Tasks

As a by-product of the review, specific remediation tasks will have been suggested, such as data cleansing, defining and enforcing data standards, instituting data validity inspection and reporting, application modifications for business processes, applications, or data models. These tasks will be incorporated into the data quality improvement plan.

11.7 Summary Rapid Data Assessment – Tangible Results

The data quality assessment sets the context that is used to establish the business case for investing in data quality improvement. Alternatively, the process can be used to evaluate whether the costs associated with data quality improvement would provide a reasonable return on the investment. Either way, this repeatable assessment process provides tangible results that can either validate or negate the "fuzzy" organizational perception of poor data quality and provides the impetus to make the organizational commitment to measuring, monitoring, and improving data quality.

REMEDIATION AND IMPROVEMENT PLANNING

The data quality assessment process is likely to expose a number of data issues. At the same time, there is typically a growing list of data issues identified and reported by data consumers as the issues manifest themselves during business operations. Often, the data quality team can generate some "quick wins" that address immediate issues having critical business impact. Alternatively, reviewing an issue may suggest a set of data quality assertions that require continuous monitoring and control. But no matter what, when flaws in the data or the processes touching the data are identified, the data quality practitioners must determine the appropriate actions to be taken.

This chapter reviews the approach to developing that action plan, providing guidance for the triage and root cause analysis tasks performed by data quality practitioners when data issues are identified and logged in a data quality incident tracking system. Each identified issue can be prioritized in relation to a number of variables, including severity, impact, and feasibility of resolution. The practitioner can then determine the most appropriate actions to take. The process includes these stages:

- Triage: Evaluate and assess the issue and determine the scope and extent of the problem from both a business impact perspective and from an operational perspective.

- Review the information production flow: Map out how the data from the raw data sources are transformed into the customer information product.
- Root cause analysis: Review the information process map to determine the likely locations for the source of introduction of the problem.
- Corrective measures: Determine strategies for immediately addressing critical problems.
- Preventive measures: Research strategies for eliminating the root causes.
- Execution: Plan and apply operational aspects, including data correction, monitoring, and prevention.

Evaluating criticality, assessing the frequency and severity of discovered issues, and prioritizing tasks for remediation are all part of the data practitioner's role. Formalizing the different tasks to perform when issues of different levels of criticality occur will reduce the effort for remediation while speeding the time to resolution.

12.1 Triage

Limitations to staffing will influence the data quality team to consider the best allocation of resources to address issues. There will always be a backlog of issues for review and consideration, revealed either by direct reports from data consumers or results of data quality assessments. But in order to achieve the "best bang for the buck," and most effectively use the available staff and resources, one can prioritize the issues for review and potential remediation as a by-product of weighing feasibility and cost effectiveness of a solution against the recognized business impact of the issue. In essence, one gets the optimal value when the lowest costs are incurred to resolve the issues with the greatest perceived negative impact.

When a data quality issue has been identified, the triage process will take into account these aspects of the identified issue:

- **Criticality:** the degree to which the business processes are impaired by the existence of the issue
- **Frequency:** how often the issue has appeared
- **Feasibility of correction:** the likelihood of expending the effort to correct the results of the failure
- **Feasibility of prevention:** the likelihood of expending the effort to eliminate the root cause or institute continuous monitoring to detect the issues

The triage process is performed to understand these aspects in terms of the business impact, the size of the problem, as well as the number of individuals or systems affected. Triage enables the data quality practitioner to review the general characteristics of the problem and business impacts in preparation for assigning a level of severity and priority.

12.1.1 The Prioritization Matrix

By its very nature, the triage process must employ some protocols for immediate assessment of any issue that has been identified, as well as prioritize those issues in the context of existing issues. A prioritization matrix is a tool that can help provide clarity for deciding relative importance, getting agreement on priorities, and then determining the actions that are likely to provide best results within appropriate time frames. Collecting data about the issue's criticality, frequency, and the feasibility of the corrective and preventative actions enables a more confident decision-making process for prioritization.

Different approaches can be taken to assemble a prioritization matrix, especially when determining weighting strategies and allocations. In one example, shown in Table 12.1, the columns of the matrix show the evaluation criteria. There is one row for each data quality issue. In this example, weights are assigned to the criteria based on the degree to which the score would contribute to the overall prioritization. In this example, the highest weight is assigned to the criticality. The data quality practitioner will gather information as input to the scoring process, and each of the criteria's weighted scores is calculated, and summed in the total.

Table 12.1 Example Prioritization Matrix

Criteria	Criticality Weight = 4		Frequency Weight = 1		Correction Feasibility Weight = 1		Prevention Feasibility Weight = 2		Total
Issues	Score	Weighted score	Score	Weighted score	Score	Weighted score	Score	Weighted score	

The weights must be determined in relation to the business context and the expectations as directed by the results of the data requirements analysis process (as discussed in chapter 9). As these requirements are integrated into a data quality service level agreement (or DQ SLA, as is covered in chapter 13), the criteria for weighting and evaluation are adjusted accordingly. In addition, the organization's level of maturity in data quality and data governance may also inform the determination of scoring protocols as well as weightings.

12.1.2 Gathering Knowledge

There may be little to no background information associated with any identified or reported data quality issue, so the practitioner will need to gather knowledge to evaluate the prioritization criteria, using guidance based on the data requirements. The assignment of points can be based on the answers to a sequence of questions intended to tease out the details associated with criticality and frequency, such as the following:

- Have any business processes/activities been impacted by the data issue?
- If so, how many business processes/activities are impacted by the data issue?
- What business applications have failed as a result of the data issue?
- If so, how many business processes have failed?
- How many individuals are affected?
- How many systems are affected?
- What types of systems are affected?
- How many records are affected?
- How many times has this issue been reported? Within what time frame?
- How long has this been an issue?

Then, based on the list of individuals and systems affected, the data quality analyst can review business impacts within the context of both known and newly discovered issues, asking questions such as these:

- What are the potential business impacts?
- Is this an issue that has already been anticipated based on the data requirements analysis process?
- Has this issue introduced delays or halts in production information processing that must be performed within existing constraints?
- Has this issue introduced delays in the development or deployment of critical business systems?

The next step is to evaluate what data sets have been affected and what, if any, immediate corrective actions need to be taken, such as whether any data sets need to be recreated, modified, or corrected, or if any business processes need to be rolled back to a previous state. The following types of questions are used in this evaluation:

- Are there short-term corrective measures that can be taken to restart halted processes?
- Are there long-term measures that can be taken to identify when the issue occurs in the future?
- Are there system modifications that can be performed to eliminate the issue's occurrence altogether?

The answers to these questions will present alternatives for correction as well as prevention, which can be assessed in terms of their feasibility.

12.1.3 Assigning Criticality

Having collected knowledge about each issue, the data quality analyst can synthesize the intentions of the data quality requirements with what has been learned during the triage process to determine the level of severity and assign priority for resolution. The collected information can be used to populate the prioritization matrix, assign scores, and apply weights. Issues can be assigned a priority score based on the results of the weightings applied in the prioritization matrix. In turn, each issue can be prioritized, from both a relative standpoint (i.e., which issues take relative precedence compare to others) and an absolute standpoint (i.e., is a specific issue high or low priority). This prioritization can also be assigned in the context of those issues identified during a finite time period ("this past week") or in relation to the full set of open data quality issues.

Data issue priority will be defined by the members of the various data governance groups. As an example, an organization may define four levels of priority, such as those shown in Table 12.2.

Depending on the scoring process, the weighting, and the assessment, any newly reported issue can be evaluated and assigned a priority that should direct the initiation of specific remediation actions. Issues can be recategorized as well. For example, issues categorized as *tolerable* may be downgraded to *acknowledged* once the evaluation determines that the costs for remediation exceed the negative impact. Similarly, once a work-around has been determined for a *business critical* issue, that issue may no longer prevent necessary business activities

Table 12.2 Example Classifications of Severity or Criticality

Classification	Description	Implications
Business critical	The existence of a *business critical* problem prevents necessary business activities from completing, and must be resolved before those activities can continue.	Addressing the issue demands immediate attention and overrules activities associated with issues or a lower priority.
Serious	*Serious* issues pose measurably high impacts to the business, but the issue does not prevent critical business processes from completing.	These issues require evaluation and must be addressed, but are superseded by business critical issues.
Tolerable	With *tolerable* issues, there are identified impacts to the business, but they require additional research to determine whether correction and elimination are economically feasible.	It is not clear if the negative business impacts exceed the total costs of remediation; further investigation is necessary.
Acknowledged	Acknowledged issues are recognized and documented, but the scale of the business impact does not warrant the additional investment in remediation.	It is clear that the negative business impacts do not exceed the total costs of remediation; no further investigation is necessary.

from continuing, in which case it could be reclassified as a *serious* issue.

12.2 The Information Flow Map

Chapter 11 introduced the concept of an information production flow to note how information flows through these types of processing stages within an application. This information production flow map is valuable as part of the remediation process to help with root cause analysis, and more precision in the information production map (or IP-MAP)[1] will supplement root cause analysis and help isolate points in the business process flow where data errors may have been introduced.

In greater detail, then, a more precise information production map documents the flow of information across one or more

[1] See Chapter 7 of R.Y. Wang, E.M. Pierce, S.E. Madnick, C.W. Fisher, Information Quality (Advances in Management Information Systems), M.E. Sharpe, 2005, ISBN 0765611333, which provides much greater details about the creation and use of IP-MAPs.

business processes, and maps how the data from the raw data sources are transformed into one or more customer information products. The information product map provides an information-centric view of the ways that business processes are executed and can be used to show the multiple uses of data and information across information system and business process boundaries.

12.2.1 The IP-MAP Described

The IP-MAP reduces the concentration on functional requirements in deference to enterprise data and information requirements across the organizations. Within each of those information flows across business processes, the analyst can explore the best locations for inserting data inspection "probes" to monitor observance of the defined data requirements. The analyst will review the documentation to identify the components that will be incorporated into the IP-MAP:

1. Raw data sources that are used by the business process. For each raw data source, note the business area and role responsible for the raw data, the system where the data is stored, where the data is created or is brought into the enterprise, and the data elements that compose the raw data source.
2. Processing block, listing any processing performed on the data, which data elements are used, modified, and the business rules and procedures associated with the process.
3. Data stores (temporary and persistent), listing the data elements that are stored and the system where the data is stored.
4. Decision block, points at which the processing stream is directed based on the result of evaluating different conditions.
5. Locations where there are checks for data quality criteria, and for each location, the list of data quality validations performed at that point. There are two potential output streams, one taken when the data is valid and one taken when the data fails a data quality check.
6. Information system boundaries, specifying the information systems that share or exchange data as part of the information production process, and listing the data elements that are shared or exchanged.
7. Business boundaries, where data is handed off from one business area to another, listing the business processes that are exchanging data and the data elements that are exchanged.
8. Customer output product, listing the business area and role that will consume the finished product and the data elements that constitute the final information product.

12.2.2 Constructing an IP-MAP

The eight constructs used in an IP-MAP (shown in Figure 12.1) correspond to the eight items described in section 12.2.1. Once those items have been identified, draft an information flow showing how data enters the environment, which processing stages the data passes through, where quality checks are performed, where decision points are located, where data is accessed from or written to a data store, where data is handed off between information systems, and where data values pass across business area and business process boundaries, until the final customer information product is created.

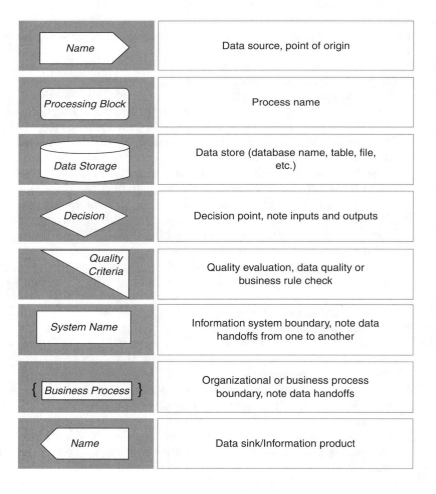

Figure 12.1 IP-MAP constructs and symbols.

12.3 Root Cause Analysis

The point at which the error was identified is not necessarily the point at which the error was introduced, and that means tracking the information flow backward from the point of discover to determine the root cause. Alternatively, once the data quality analysts are aware of a data flaw that has manifested itself along one information flow, it is worthwhile to determine whether any other downstream computations, calculation, business processes, and/or reports are affected by the error.

This task is to assess the landscape (both forward and backward!) and identify the impacted systems and data sets. Given a complete information flow mapping that details data dependency chains, the data quality analysts can review which systems and data sets may have been affected and quickly configure tests or queries to check if there are any changes from expected results. Then, they can document any data sets that may need to be corrected or any business processes that need to be rewound and restarted.

12.3.1 Identifying the Source of Errors

To identify mitigation strategies, it is necessary to understand where the issues originated and where the best places are for fixing and eliminating the root cause. Alternatively, there may be a place in the business process where the introduction of the issue caused system failures. Reviewing the business process model and traversing the processes help determine the root cause and provides input into the determination of recommendations for addressing the issue.

This step involves reviewing the business process models that map the information flow before the point at which the data error was reported. At each boundary where data values are handed off from one processing block to another, data values emerging from the producing block can be reviewed to determine whether they observe the expectations of the consuming block. If the values do not conform to the data quality expectations, the information flow is tracked back to the data handoff point for the current processing block.

This process is repeated until either the data values are found to conform to the data quality expectations or the origination point for the data is found. By identifying the processing stage at which the data is valid before entry and invalid after exit, the data quality analyst is able to narrow down the location within the information flow where the error is introduced.

This isolation process can be repeated on a finer granularity until the data steward, together with the necessary system analysts and programmers, is able to determine exactly where the error is introduced.

12.3.2 Understanding the Introduction of Errors

Once the data quality analyst has isolated the processing stage at which the error is introduced, further analysis must be performed to review any point where the flawed data item is created, imported from an alternate source, or is accessed and modified. Any of those points may be the source of the issue, and each of these situations may have different implications.

If the source of introduction is from an externally imported data set, this suggests that the responsibility for the error lies outside of the administrative domain. If the source is a point of data creation (such as a record newly created via a system interface), this suggests that user data entry errors may be the culprit. When data accesses and updates are implicated, the errors may be introduced through flawed applications or as a result of user error.

Understanding how errors are introduced will inform the analysts as to the alternatives for remediation. Those alternatives are considered in the context of the level of criticality and the most effective ways to prevent negative impacts from being incurred.

12.4 Remediation

There may be different approaches for addressing both the root cause of an issue and the side effects caused by the issue. At this point, the data quality practitioner's job is to determine alternatives for figuring out ways to eliminate the root cause and then assess the feasibility of each of the alternatives. Feasibility is a combined quantitative and qualitative measure that looks at the amount of effort required to eliminate the source of the problem as well as the investment needed to ensure that the error is not introduced again.

If it is not feasible to eliminate the source of the problems, the data quality team members should work with the data consumers to identify sentinel (or leading) measures or assertions for which inspection routines can be used to generate alerts upon nonconformance to expectations. This way, the right operational data governance practices can be put in place using inspection or monitoring routines to flag the issue when it occurs and to enable remedial action to be taken as early as possible in the process.

There are a number of alternatives for remediation, and in this section we look at three:

1. Data correction
2. Root cause elimination
3. Monitoring and prevention

12.4.1 Data Correction and Cleansing

If data errors introduced earlier in the process flow have cascaded through other data sets, it is necessary to review those data sets and assess the damage. Under urgent circumstances, identified data errors can be corrected.

Any modifications that had been made that are based on invalid data will need to be identified and backed out, and when those incorrect modifications cannot be distinguished from correct updates, one must presume that any could be in error. Therefore, any dependent processing stages may need to be rolled back and restarted. The time frame and urgency of data correction will be set according to the criteria set out in the DQ SLA.

Because of the sensitivity of accessing and modifying data directly through "unblessed" channels, both of these tasks must be performed under strict scrutiny and must be documented and reported into the incident reporting workflow. One-off programs intended to perform mass data corrections must be announced to all relevant stakeholders and scheduled to minimize impact on operations.

12.4.2 Root Cause Elimination

If the data quality team and system analysts have determined the specific location and root cause of the introduction of the error, and they have determined that there are flaws in the processes that can be corrected, they can assess the options for correcting the process to eliminate that root cause. At this point, they can:

- Evaluate the level of effort for each alternative;
- Select one of the alternatives as the proposed fix;
- Determine the time frame for the fix;
- Provide a development plan; and
- Provide a test plan.

If the level of effort and the associated costs are reasonable and the resources are available, then it makes sense to execute the plan to eliminate the root cause of the issue.

12.4.3 Monitoring and Prevention

If the level of effort to eliminate the root cause exceeds the organization's capability, resources, or desire, an alternate plan of action is to institute inspections and processes to monitor for known errors. When the inspection routines determine that an error has occurred, the appropriate team members can be notified immediately. Those staff members that are alerted to the issue can then take the appropriate actions to delay or halt the business process until the identified error can be reviewed and for the offending data to be corrected or even removed, if necessary, to allow normal processing to continue.

12.5 Execution

Given the options to eliminate the root cause, institute inspection process, or address the issue in other ways, the next step is to make a decision to move forward. As with all business activities, it is critical to make sure that the steps to be taken are properly planned so that progress and success can be measured in alleviating the pain introduced by the data issue.

12.6 Summary

The objective of remediation and improvement planning is to evaluate the criticality of reported and logged data issues, and prioritize the most effective ways to address those errors. Evaluating criticality helps in determining where to get the best bang for the data quality management buck. At the same time, picking the low-hanging fruit not only helps concentrate efforts for data quality improvement, it establishes credibility across the organization by reducing the time necessary for resolving critical issues.

DATA QUALITY SERVICE LEVEL AGREEMENTS

Data warehouses and data marts are employed for capturing and reporting key success metrics that are used to monitor performance measures of operational activities for the purpose of continuous improvement. The same idea can be applied to data quality management. Establishing expectations for performance is not a new idea. Measuring conformance to defined service levels has long been part of network, server, and desktop management, and therefore it should not be a surprise that these same ideas can be applied to data quality management as well. The difference between hardware service level management and data service level management is in the perceived variability in specifying what is meant by "acceptable levels of service." It is usually clear when the network is too slow or if a server fails, but we have to apply our knowledge of data quality dimensions and measures to set the acceptability thresholds for data quality.

In this chapter we examine how to translate the information needs derived from the business drivers into data quality controls, and how we convert measured observance of those controls into data quality metrics based on the business objectives.

These metrics provide the quantification for reporting a data quality scorecard. This scorecard can be a valuable management tool for observing more than just the quality of the data; we can also determine how well the data stewards are performing in remediation efforts to maintain data quality control.

13.1 Business Drivers and Success Criteria

Data quality expectations are often rooted in actual business rules dictating dependencies on information. As an example, the concept of "compliance" is a strong motivator. Industry organizations dictate expected practices for participation within the community, whereas municipal, state, and federal governments introduce regulations and policies for both data quality processes and data quality itself.

Alternatively, maintaining high transaction processing throughput also inspires the definition of controls; successful implementation of automated business processing streams is related to high quality data, especially if data errors break the processing flow and force that flow to remain halted until there is some manual intervention. The increased use of business intelligence platforms for measuring performance against operational and strategic goals is indicative of a maturing view of what the organization's business drivers are and how performance is supported by all aspects of quality, including data quality.

Establishing the trust of a unified view of business information and decreasing the need for redundant storage and seemingly never-ending stream of reconciliations helps improve operational efficiency. Reviewing the specific ways that information supports the achievement of business objectives helps analysts clarify the business drivers for data governance and data quality, and lays out the parameters of what "acceptable data quality" means within the organization.

For example, business clients making decisions using analytic applications dependent on data in the data warehouse may have to defer making decisions or, even worse, make incorrect decisions when there is no oversight in controlling the quality of the data in the warehouse. The business user would not be able to provide usable insight into which customers to target, which products to promote, or where to concentrate efforts to maximize the supply chain. In this scenario, a business driver is to ensure an acceptable level of confidence in the reporting and analysis that satisfies the business needs driven by the use of enterprise information. Similar drivers can be identified in relation to transaction processing, regulatory compliance, or conformance to industry standards.

In this analytic application example, the success criteria can be noted in relation to the ways that data quality improvement reduces time spent on diagnosis and correction, increases the speed of delivering information, and increases confidence in the decisions. Articulating specific achievements or milestones as success criteria allows managers to gauge and reward individual accountability.

13.1.1 Business Drivers

Identifying the business drivers establishes the operational governance direction by enabling the data governance team to prioritize the information policies in relation to the risk of material impact. Listing the expectations for acceptable data suggests quantifiable measurements, and this allows business analysts or data stewards to specify acceptability thresholds related to the success criteria. By listing the critical expectations, methods for measurement, and specific thresholds, the business clients can associate data governance with levels of success in their business activities.

And this connects two aspects that we have covered: the first is the categorization of business impacts of poor data quality described in chapter 1, and the second is the solicitation of business issues as part of the data quality assessment performed in chapter 11. Instead of just asserting the existence of a business impact, the important questions focus on comparing the costs of ignoring a problem to the costs of addressing it, determining the business risks of ignoring that problem, and determining how the answers to those questions merge to prioritize an action plan for monitoring and remediation.

13.1.2 Business Rules and Data Dependencies

Business processes are constrained by business rules, which are imposed from many different sources. These business rules are derived from regulatory compliance, internal business objectives, and standard operating procedures, among others. In fact, many of these sources are not even intended to imply data quality rules. However, business rules that have explicit or implicit data dependencies will lead to the definition of information rules, which in turn will be composed of data constraints. Usually, some of those constraints will be reflected as assertions whose compliance can be measured.

As one example, anti–money laundering regulations require financial institutions to identify and report suspicious transactions to the financial intelligence offices of the country within which it operates. One aspect of compliance requires ascertaining each customer's identity and monitoring each customer's activity for one or more transactions indicative of suspicious activity. This business rule has information rule implications:

- There is an index of customer identity information available against which each customer can be verified.
- There is a definition of "suspicious activity."
- Each transaction is logged.
- One or more transactions performed by a single customer can be accessed and reviewed against the definition of suspicious activity.
- There is a notification process when suspicious activity has been identified.

Each of these statements can be iteratively refined to identify some dependent data sets and data attributes and their associated valid values, which can be monitored for conformance. In fact, any artifact or document providing business rules is likely to contain some data dependencies. For example:

- A web site's privacy policy may state the circumstances under which the organization will (or will not) share customer data;
- Membership levels in an industry association may be based on organization size by employees, by revenue, or by number of transactions; and
- An airline's customer may be entitled to an automatic upgrade depending on that customer's frequent flyer status.

In each of these business examples, some result is dependent on some data attributes associated with the key data concepts, and there is some expectation of auditable compliance with business rules. If the business rules can be dissected into their corresponding (measurable) data rules, then conformance to the corresponding data rules would demonstrate conformance to the business rules.

13.1.3 Defining Data Quality Acceptability Levels

In turn, each business rule, as it is decomposed into a set of data rules, can be associated with a measure of acceptability. There are basically two approaches to defining these acceptability levels. The first approach is full conformance, in which every critical data element's value (or record) is 100% conformant to the rule(s). Quantifying compliance is simple – each data element's value is either valid or invalid, and any invalid values imply noncompliance with end-user expectations.

The second approach is a relative degree of compliance, measured across a set of data elements or records. In this case, there is some tolerance to noncompliance, and that tolerance is expressed as the acceptability threshold, which may be a percentage of the data attributes (or records) with valid values. That tolerance threshold is directly related to the business impacts of the monitored data issues. For example, the organization may have enough staff available to address five data issues a day, but more than that number would be beyond the organization's ability for remediation. Therefore, the acceptability threshold is five issues per day. The acceptability threshold can depend on other factors, such as the average cost per error, or can be more tolerant of some types of data failures than others. These different tolerance levels can be rolled into a collection of measures that are monitored throughout the day.

Identifying the data quality rules and instituting probes to measure conformance to those rules is the first step in evaluating acceptability levels. Comparing the degree of compliance with the dependent business impacts over a period of time (a few weeks to a month) and gauging when the number of errors becomes intolerable will help define a level of acceptability.

13.2 Identifying Data Quality Rules

The different levels of control granularity suggest a way of refining data consumer expectations into formal rules that can be applied automatically using a rules engine. This approach is a successive refinement of those expectations into more precise (and hopefully, measurable) assertions. The monitoring processes can then use the rules to examine the candidate data at the different levels of granularity. Once the rules are formally defined, the data quality team determines a method for measurement, a unit of measure, and an acceptability threshold, which is the lowest measurement that denotes conformance to business expectations.

For example, consider a consumer expectation for customer address data regarding the existence of a "State" data element value in each record. This expectation is measured using the completeness dimension, and since it involves a specific data element within each record, its granularity is at the data element level. If the number of violating records the consumer is willing to tolerate is as much as 1% of the total number of records, this suggests the unit of measure (percentage of conforming records within the data set) and the acceptability threshold (99%).

13.2.1 Successive Rule Refinement

As a general approach for defining rules, for each specified data quality expectation, the data quality analyst can apply these steps:

1. Determine the dimension of data quality. For starters, focus on a subset of those described in chapter 8, such as accuracy, completeness, currency, reasonability, consistency, and identifiability.
2. Determine the level of granularity (data element, data record, data set).
3. Identify the constraint and dependent data elements to be reviewed. For example, if this is an accuracy rule for product names, then one might select the product identifier, product name, and product description as the dependent variables and provide a system of record against which the product data is to be compared for accuracy.
4. Document the constraint and unit of measure, and select a measurement method.
5. Determine the acceptability threshold.

Despite the potential abstract nature of the dimensions of data quality, rules defined within those categories are eminently transformable into straightforward assertions that can be automated. For example, a data element completeness rule can be stated as an assertion that the data element is never null or missing; a consistency rule might assert that a membership start date is always earlier than a membership end date, and so on.

In fact, many rules can be boiled down to a standard format inspecting specific values. Rules that apply to single data elements, such as structural consistency or domain membership will allow one to inspect the data element's value in comparison to the specified constraint. As an example, specifying that a state code field must belong to the set of United States Postal Service two-character state codes, the assertion may describe the data domain as a reference table and assert that each state code must belong to that table. Syntactic pattern compliance (e.g., telephone numbers) can also be expressed in terms of conformance to a set of formats.

Rules that apply at the record level examine a condition involving more than one data element within the record. For example, ensuring that the start date is earlier than the end date is an assertion relating two data element values within each record. Again, assertion expressions (such as those expressed using SQL) can be used to formalize these data quality rules.

Data set rules compare sets of elements in one data set with sets of elements in another data set, or comparisons against aggregate values derived from more than one record in a data set. For example, key assertions and record uniqueness are rules that are relevant within the data set context. Other examples may involve verifying data element values against averages accumulated over a collection of transactions. Again, expression syntax such as that contained within SQL can be used for these assertions.

13.2.2 The Challenge of Semantics in Free-Form Text

The biggest challenge is the successive refinement of free-formed text to identify the business rules and the corresponding data rules. Any free-formed document may hide data dependencies, yet there may be lots of additional text that help people understand what is being discussed but does not carry any syntactic or semantic information. This means that the analyst must be able to scan the document and highlight those sections that direct (or indirectly imply) data dependencies. Although this is an evolving mix of process and intuition, there are some general guidelines:

1. Identify any reference to any data concept that plays a role in any of the business processes. These are often nouns, and some examples are "customer," "user," "grantor," "payee," "product," "item," "account," and "agreement." For each data concept, verify the existence of a corresponding data object within the business process applications.

2. For each referenced data concept, determine whether it is a core data entity, a characteristic of another data entity, or a description of a relationship between data entities. For example, "term" may be a referenced noun, but it may be a characteristic of an "agreement," which is the key data entity. Another example is that the items noted as characteristics are likely to be attributes of the identified key data concepts.

3. Determine whether the references to both key data entities and characteristics have robust descriptions or definitions. If not, note a requirement for a discussion with subject matter experts to capture additional details.

4. For each referenced attribute, determine if there are any constraints described in the text and document that constraint.

5. If possible, document the constraint using a well-defined expression.

For example consider this sentence taken from a sample privacy policy statement: "We will only share personal information with the user's consent." Here, the data concepts are "we," "personal information," "user," and "consent." "We" obviously refers to the organization publishing the privacy policy. "User" is the party that is the subject of the statement, and we can presume that is a key data concept.

Both "personal information" and "consent" are nouns, but are characteristics of the key data concept of "user." "Personal information" is directly associated with the "user," but this description does not provide enough detail, so there is a need for further investigation to document the details – is "personal information" a data concept with its own model that is related to the "user," or a collection of attributes of the "user"? "Consent" is a little more straightforward, since it represents a value indicating that the "user" is allowing the organization to share personal information. This actually presents the constraint:

"User's personal information may be shared if user's consent is TRUE."

Each time that a constraint can be refined to a point where it can be expressed as a business rule, the associated data rules can be defined as well. In this case we have a dependency between a business action ("sharing personal information") with a specific value of a specific data attribute (that is, a TRUE value for user's consent). In turn, this implies some other data rules (which can follow the guidelines provided in chapter 10 on data standards, metadata, and business rules):

- The user data object must have a data attribute for "consent to share personal information."
- The user's consent to share personal information must have a value (a completeness rule).
- The value of the user's consent attribute must be either TRUE or FALSE (a defined data domain).
- The user's consent data attribute must be reviewed before that user's personal information is shared (an operational data constraint).
- It is a violation of a business policy if a user's personal information is shared if the value of the consent attribute if FALSE.

The last step is assigning the acceptability threshold for these rules. If the business policy does not allow for any violations, then it is never acceptable for any of these rules to be violated. One can institute data quality probes across the business processes that create, update, or read the dependent attributes to ensure compliance with these defined constraints. The collection of these probes helps in establishing data quality control.

13.3 Establishing Data Quality Control

A data quality control framework enables the ability to identify and document emerging data issues, then initiate a workflow to remediate these problems. Operational data quality management leads to an increase in the level of trust in the data, because the ability to catch an issue is pushed further and further upstream until the point of data acquisition or creation. A data quality control process provides a safety net that eliminates the need for downstream users to monitor for poor-quality data. As long as the controls are transparent and auditable, those downstream users can trust the data that feed their applications.

For years, nobody expected that data flaws could directly impact business operations. However, the reality is that errors – especially those that can be described as violations of expectations for completeness, accuracy, timeliness, consistency, and other dimensions of data quality – often impede the successful completion of information processing streams, and consequently, their dependent business processes. However, no matter how much effort is expended on data filters or edits, there are always going to be issues requiring attention and remediation.

Operational data governance combines the ability to identify data errors as early as possible with the process of initiating the activities necessary to address those errors to avoid or minimize any downstream impacts. This essentially includes notifying the right individuals to address the issue and determining if the issue can be resolved appropriately within an agreed-to time frame. Data inspection processes are instituted to measure and monitor compliance with data quality rules, whereas service level agreements (SLAs) specify the reasonable expectations for response and remediation.

Note that data quality inspection differs from data validation. Whereas the data validation process reviews and measures conformance of data with a set of defined business rules, inspection is an ongoing process to:

- Reduce the number of errors to a reasonable and manageable level,
- Enable the identification of data flaws along with a protocol for interactively making adjustments that permit completion of the processing stream, and
- Institute a mitigation or remediation of the root cause within an agreed-to time frame.

The value of data quality inspection as part of operational data governance is in establishing trust on behalf of downstream users that any issue likely to cause a significant business impact is caught early enough to avoid any significant impact on operations. Without this inspection process, poor-quality data pervades every system, complicating practically any operational or analytic process.

13.4 The Data Quality Service Level Agreement

A key component of governing data quality control is an SLA, which will guide the monitoring of data quality levels as data is passed across different stages in the information production flow.

13.4.1 Data Handoffs

A business process enables the communication of the right information to the appropriate targets at the right time, and the process flow consists of an enumeration of the processing stages, their inputs, aspects that control the process, the types of events or triggers that emerge as a result of the processing stage, and the expected output of the processing stage. The basic aspects of each processing stage incorporate descriptive information such as processing stage purpose, timing attributes, triggers, inputs, expected duration, any events to be generated, resources used, and the output(s), and this is reflected in the mapping of the information production flow, as is described in chapter 12.

In addition, individual activities are linked together to show how the outputs of one activity coupled with triggered events from other activities control or influence the behavior of the system. This means that the final production of the process flow is a result of the intermediate sets of data that are handed off between processing stages. And as we know that there are data quality rules that need to be observed across the entire information production flow, we also know that observance of the rules can be monitored at each data handoff point between processing stages. These are the "articulation points" at which data quality rule inspection can take place between the data producer and the data consumer (especially if the data is persisted as part of the hand-off), as is shown in Figure 13.1.

Figure 13.1 A data handoff.

13.4.2 Defining the Data Quality Service Level Agreement

For each of these articulation points within an information processing stream, we can define a data quality service level agreement (DQ SLA) incorporating a number of items:

- The location in the processing stream that is covered by the SLA,
- The data elements covered by the agreement,
- The business impacts associated with data flaws,
- The data quality dimensions associated with each data element,
- The expectations for quality for each data element for each of the identified dimensions,
- The methods for measuring against those expectations,
- The acceptability threshold for each measurement,
- The individual to be notified in case the acceptability threshold is not met,
- The times for expected resolution or remediation of the issue, and
- The escalation strategy when the resolution times are not met.

Figure 13.2 shows how these items are monitored and reported on at an example data hand-off.

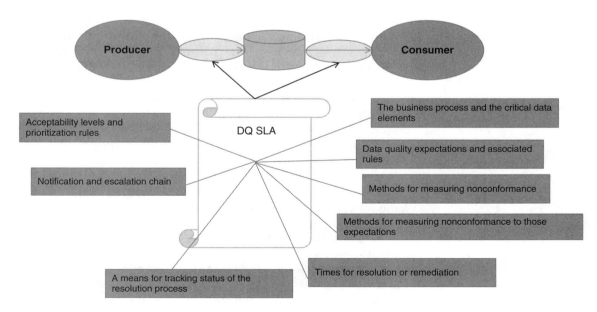

Figure 13.2 Instituting the DQ SLA.

13.5 Inspection and Monitoring

While there are practices in place for measuring and monitoring certain aspects of organizational data quality, there is an opportunity to evaluate the relationship between the business impacts of non compliant data as indicated by the business clients and the defined thresholds for data quality acceptability. The degree of acceptability becomes the standard against which the data is measured, with operational data governance instituted within the context of measuring performance in relation to the data governance procedures. This measurement essentially covers conformance to the defined standards, as well as monitoring staff agility in taking specific actions when the data sets do not conform. Given the set of data quality rules, methods for measuring conformance, the acceptability thresholds defined by the business clients, and the SLAs, we can monitor data governance by observing not only compliance of the data to the business rules, but of the data stewards to observing the processes associated with data risks and failures.

The availability of an assertion for validating data against a defined expectation is the basis for data quality monitoring and tracking. Supporting the terms of the DQ SLA means that when data quality issues are identified, the appropriate people are notified and the agreed-to remediation tasks are initiated. This requires mechanisms for data inspection and monitoring, and process workflows must be defined for the purposes of inspecting data and ensuring that the data elements, records, and data sets meet downstream requirements.

This task involves defining the data quality inspection routines, which may include both automated and manual processes. Automated processes may include the results of edit checks executed during application processing, data profiling or data analysis automation, data integration tools, or customized processing. Manual inspection may require running queries or reports on data sources or even obtaining samples of data which are then examined. Inspection procedures are defined for each relevant data quality dimension. Each system may require different techniques and data quality inspection procedures.

Those procedures support two different approaches to monitoring. Static monitoring can be performed as batch inspections when data sets are handed off from one process activity to another, while inlined monitoring can be integrated directly as part of the end-to-end application workflow. The characteristics of each data quality expectation, its associated acceptability threshold, and the expected level of service will suggest whether it is better suited to static or inlined monitoring.

13.5.1 Static Monitoring

Static monitoring is well suited to environments supported by batch processing, where data sets are "bulk exchanged" from one processing task to another, or where data is extracted and loaded into a target environment in preparation for analysis and reporting (such as data warehouses, data marts, and, to some extent, operational data stores). In these cases, element, record, and data set rules can be applied to a collection of data instances as a whole. Conformance to data quality expectations can be measured in terms of both counts of violation and percentage of non conformant records within the data set. Acceptability thresholds can be set based on either of those units of measure, and therefore data issues that are related to not meeting those thresholds are best suited to static monitoring.

13.5.2 Inlined Monitoring

Inlined monitoring, implemented through the augmentation of applications with verification routines to inspect data elements and records as they are created and/or modified, are best suited to situations in which a single violation requires immediate attention. That suggests that, for the most part, inlined inspection and monitoring works well for data rules to be applied to data element values and to records, but may introduce performance bottlenecks when applied to large data sets.

13.5.3 Measurement Processes

Automated processes can be put into place for both types of monitoring, with the intention of enhancing any existing measurement processes to generate a notification when a violation occurs to the appropriate data steward as specified within a DQ SLA. Data profiling tools and data auditing tools are popular alternatives used for statically assessing conformance to defined rules as well as creating filters that can be embedded within a process flow. Inlined data edits are commonly used for data validation, and these edits can be enhanced to database queries and reports can be configured to measure and present statistics regarding conformance to rules. By embedding queries within polling applications that continually validate data on a periodic basis, any distinct violations requiring attention can be flagged quickly and the proper alerts can be generated.

13.6 Data Quality Metrics and a Data Quality Scorecard

Putting the processes in place for defining a data quality SLA for operational data governance depends on measuring conformance to business expectations and knowing when the appropriate data stewards need to be notified to remediate an issue. This requires two things: a method for quantifying conformance and the threshold for acceptability.

Since business policies drive the way the organization does business, we can say that business policy conformance is related to information policy conformance. Data governance reflects the way that information policies support the business policies and impose data rules that can be monitored throughout the business processing streams. In essence, performance objectives center on maximizing productivity and goodwill while reducing organizational risks and operating costs. In that context, business policies are defined or imposed to constrain or manage the way that business is performed, and each business policy may loosely imply (or even explicitly define) data definitions, information policies, and even data structures and formats.

Therefore, reverse engineering the relationship between business impacts and the associated data rules provides the means for quantifying conformance to expectations. These data quality metrics can then roll up into a data quality scorecard. This suggests that a good way to start establishing relevant data quality metrics is to evaluate how data flaws impact the ability of application clients to efficiently achieve their business goals. In other words, evaluate the business impacts of data flaws and determine the dimensions of data quality that can be used to define data quality metrics. For more information on establishing data quality metrics, consult chapter 6.

13.7 Data Quality Incident Reporting and Tracking

Supporting the enforcement of the DQ SLA requires a set of management processes for the reporting and tracking of data quality issues and corresponding activities. This can be facilitated via a system used to log and track data quality issues. By more formally requiring evaluation and initial diagnosis of emergent data events, encouraging data quality issue tracking helps staff members be more effective at problem identification and, consequently, at problem resolution.

Aside from improving the data quality management process, issue and incident tracking can also provide performance reporting including mean-time-to-resolve issues, frequency of occurrence of issues, types of issues, sources of issues, and common approaches for correcting or eliminating problems. A good issues tracking system will eventually become a reference source of current and historic issues, their statuses, and any factors that may need the actions of others not directly involved in the resolution of the issue.

Conveniently, many organizations already have some framework in place for incident reporting, tracking, and management, so the transition to instituting data quality issues tracking focuses less on tool acquisition, and more on integrating the concepts around the "families" of data issues into the incident hierarchies and training staff to recognize when data issues appear and how they are to be classified, logged, and tracked. The steps in this transition will involve addressing some or all of these directives:

1. Standardize data quality issues and activities: Understanding that there may be many processes, applications, underlying systems, and so on, that "touch" the data, the terms used to describe data issues may vary across lines of business. To gain a consistent and integrated view of organizational data quality, it is valuable to standardize the concepts used. Doing so will simplify reporting, making it easier to measure the volume of issues and activities, identify patterns and interdependencies between systems and participants, and ultimately to report on the overall impact of data quality activities.

2. Provide an assignment process for data issues: Resolving data quality issues requires a well-defined process that ensures that issues are assigned to the individual or group best suited to efficiently diagnosing and resolving the issue, as well as ensure proper knowledge transfer to new or inexperienced staff.

3. Manage issue escalation procedures: Data quality issue handling requires a well-defined system of escalation based on the impact, duration, or urgency of an issue, and this sequence of escalation will be specified within the DQ SLA. Assignment of an issue to a staff member starts the clock ticking, with the expectation that the problem will be resolved as directed by the DQ SLA. The issues tracking system will enforce escalation procedures to ensure that issues are handled efficiently, as well as prevent issues from exceeding response performance measures.

4. Document accountability for data quality issues: Accountability is critical to the governance protocols overseeing data quality control, and as issues are assigned to some number of individuals, groups, departments, or organizations, the

tracking process should specify and document the ultimate issue accountability to prevent issues from dropping through the cracks.

5. Manage data quality resolution workflow: The DQ SLA essentially specifies objectives for oversight, control, and resolution, all of which defines a collection of operational workflows. Many issue tracking systems not only provide persistent logging of incidents and their description, they also support workflow management to track how issues are researched and resolved. Making repeatable and efficient workflow processes part of the issues tracking system helps standardize data quality activities throughout the organization.

6. Capture data quality performance metrics: Because the DQ SLA specifies performance criteria, it is reasonable to expect that the issue tracking system will collect performance data relating to issue resolution, work assignments, volume of issues, frequency of occurrence, as well as the time to respond, diagnose, plan a solution, and resolve issues. These metrics can provide valuable insights into the effectiveness of current workflow and systems and resource utilization, and are important management data points that can drive continuous operational improvement for data quality control.

Implementing a data quality issues tracking system provides a number of benefits. First, information and knowledge sharing can improve performance and reduce duplication of effort. Furthermore, an analysis of all the issues will permit DQ staff to determine if repetitive patterns are occurring, their frequency and impact, and potentially the source of the issue. Tracking issues from data transmission to customer support problem reporting will ensure that a full life cycle view of the data and issues are identified and recorded. And lastly, since we know that issues identified and being resolved upstream of the data life cycle may have critical consequences downstream, employing a tracking system essentially trains people to recognize data issues early in the information flows as a general practice that supports their day-to-day operations.

13.8 Automating the Collection of Metrics

Articulating data quality metrics is valuable, and in fact may supplement metrics or controls that already are in place in some processing streams. However, despite the existence of these controls for measuring and reporting data validity, frequently there is no framework for automatically measuring, logging, collecting, communicating, and presenting the results to those entrusted with data stewardship. Moreover, the objective of data governance is not only to report on the acceptability of data, but also to remediate issues and eliminate their root causes with the reasonable times established within the data quality service level agreement. Identifying the metrics is good; better yet is integrating their measurements and reporting into a process that (at any point where data is shared between activities within a processing stream) automatically inspects conformance to data expectations, compares against the acceptability thresholds, and initiates events to alert data stewards to take specific actions truly makes governance operational and actionable.

13.8.1 Capturing Metrics and Their Measurements

The techniques that exist within the organization for collecting, presenting, and validating metrics must be evaluated in preparation for automating selected repeatable processes. Cataloging existing measurements and qualifying their relevance helps to filter out processes that do not provide business value and helps reduce potential duplication of effort in measuring and monitoring of critical data quality metrics. Surviving measurements of relevant metrics are to be collected and presented hierarchically within a scorecard, reflecting the ways that individual metrics roll up into higher-level characterizations of compliance with expectations while allowing for drill-down to isolate the source of specific issues. As is shown in Figure 13.3, collecting the measurements for a data quality scorecard would incorporate:

1. Standardizing business processes for automatically populating selected metrics into a common repositor,
2. Collecting requirements for an appropriate level of design for a data model for capturing data quality metrics,
3. Standardizing a reporting template for reporting and presenting data quality metrics,
4. Automating the extraction of metric data from the repository, and
5. Automating the population of the reporting and presentation template.

13.9 Reporting the Scorecard

In Figure 13.4 we have an example of a high-level data quality scorecard reflecting three aspects of measurements. The first, **Data Quality Score,** is an accumulated score computed as a function of the underlying data quality metrics. The second, **Data Quality Policy,** refers to the degree to which the data

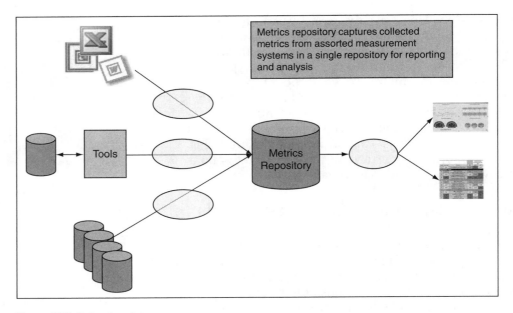

Metrics repository captures collected metrics from assorted measurement systems in a single repository for reporting and analysis

Figure 13.3 Collecting data quality measurements.

	Data Quality Score	Data Quality Policy	Data Governance
Sales			
Marketing			
Human Resources			
Finance			
Fulfillment			
Manufacturing			
Supplier			

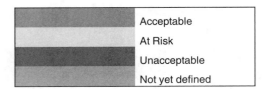

Acceptable

At Risk

Unacceptable

Not yet defined

Figure 13.4 A simple example of a data quality scorecard.

governance team has identified business impacts and defined corresponding metrics, whether those metrics have processes for measurement, and whether acceptability thresholds and DQ SLAs have been agreed to by business clients from the key business areas. The third, **Data Governance,** provides an accumulated score reflecting the observance of the DQ SLAs by the team members and functional area data stewards (such as resolving data quality issues within specified time periods).

In this example, scores are qualified as acceptable (green), at risk (yellow), unacceptable (red), or not yet defined (blue). Sample scores for Data Quality Policy might be to assign green if more than 90% of the metrics have processes and thresholds; yellow if between 50% and 90% do; and red if less than 50% do. If governance processes are not yet in place, we can designate a "not yet assigned" score for Data Governance.

The dimensions of data quality provide a framework for defining metrics that are relevant within the business context while providing a view into controllable aspects of data quality management. The degree of reportability and controllability may differ depending on one's role within the organization, and correspondingly, so will the level of detail reported in a data quality scorecard. Data stewards may focus on continuous monitoring in order to resolve issues according to defined service level agreements, whereas senior managers may be interested in observing the degree to which poor data quality introduces enterprise risk.

Essentially, the need to present higher-level data quality scores introduces a distinction between two types of metrics. The types discussed so far, which can be referred to as "base-level" metrics, quantify specific observance of acceptable levels of defined data quality rules. A higher-level concept would be the "complex" metric representing a rolled-up score computed as a function (such as a sum) of applying specific weights to a collection of existing metrics, both base-level and complex. The rolled-up metric provides a qualitative overview of how data quality impacts the organization in different ways, because the scorecard can be populated with metrics rolled up across different dimensions depending on the audience. Complex data quality metrics can be accumulated for reporting in a scorecard in one of three different views: by **issue,** by **business process,** or by **business impact.**

13.9.1 The Data Quality Issues View

Evaluating the impacts of a specific data quality issue across multiple business processes demonstrates the diffusion of pain across the enterprise caused by specific data flaws. This scorecard scheme, which is suited to data analysts attempting to prioritize tasks for diagnosis and remediation, provides a rolled-up view of the impacts attributed to each data issue. Drilling down through this view sheds light on the root causes of impacts of poor data quality, and it identifies "rogue processes" that require greater focus for instituting monitoring and control processes.

13.9.2 The Business Process View

Operational managers overseeing business processes may be interested in a scorecard view by business process. In this view, the operational manager can examine the risks and failures preventing the business process's achievement of the expected results. For each business process, this scorecard scheme consists of complex metrics representing the impacts associated with each issue. The drill-down in this view can be used for isolating the source of the introduction of data issues at specific stages of the business process as well as informing the data stewards in diagnosis and remediation.

13.9.3 The Business Impact View

Business impacts may have been incurred as a result of a number of different data quality issues originating in a number of different business processes. This reporting scheme displays the aggregation of business impacts rolled up from the different issues across different process flows. For example, one scorecard could report rolled-up metrics documenting the accumulated impacts associated with credit risk, compliance with privacy protection, and decreased sales. Drilling down through the metrics will point to the business processes from which the issues originate; deeper review will point to the specific issues within each of the business processes. This view is suited to a more senior manager seeking a high-level overview of the risks associated with data quality issues, and how those risks are introduced across the enterprise.

13.9.4 Managing Scorecard Views

Essentially, each of these views composing a data quality scorecard requires the construction and management of a hierarchy of metrics related to various levels of accountability for support of the organization's business objectives. But no matter which scheme is employed, each is supported by describing, defining, and managing base-level and complex metrics such that:

- Scorecards reflecting business relevance are driven by a hierarchical roll-up of metrics,
- The definition of metrics is separated from their contextual use, thereby allowing the same measurement to be used in different contexts with different acceptability thresholds and weights, and
- The appropriate level of presentation can be materialized based on the level of detail expected for the data consumer's specific data governance role and accountability.

13.10 Taking Action for Remediation

One of the most important steps in the planning process is developing an action plan for responding to emergent data issues. Depending on the specific measure being observed there may be slightly different processes, but for most issues, certain steps should always be followed:

1. **Confirm** the issue by directly reviewing the data, such as observing specific examples or running queries, profiles, or reports.
2. **Notify** the key stakeholders that a confirmed issue exists and is being researched.
3. **Log** the issue in the data quality issues tracking system.
4. **Diagnose** the issue by researching the source of the issue to determine its root cause.
5. **Evaluate options** for addressing the issue, which may include eliminating the root cause by modifying the processes or introducing new techniques into the information flow, introducing additional monitoring processes, and potentially directly correcting the offending data items.
6. **Correct** offending data; correction may be a temporary mitigation tactic for a data quality issue, and in this case, a more permanent remediation strategy is required to prevent reoccurrence of the problem.
7. **Improve** delinquent processes by identifying the root cause and adjusting the process to eliminate any source of error introduction.

13.11 Summary – Managing Using the Data Quality Scorecard

In this chapter we have described a target state for operational data quality management that is achieved using a data quality scorecard that communicates:

- The qualified oversight of data quality along business lines,
- The degree of levels of trust in the data in use across the application infrastructure, and
- The ability for data stewards to drill down to identify the area of measurement that contributes most to missed expectations.

Processes can be put in place to facilitate the definition of DQ SLAs and the metrics that support those SLAs. The collection of statistics associated with data quality management and data governance and the presentation of the resulting scores to the stakeholders will demonstrate that, with respect to data, the business processes are in control and the data is of a predictable level of acceptable quality. Providing a data quality scorecard provides transparency to the data quality management process by summarizing the usability of the data as defined by the business users. The data quality team will work with the business users to integrate the hierarchies of data quality expectations and rules into the metrics collection and reporting framework and enable drill-through to track down specific issues that impact organizational data. The processes for instituting data quality business rules and data validation can then be used to demonstrate an auditable process for governing the quality of organizational data.

DATA PROFILING

Data profiling has become such a ubiquitous piece of technology that it is often specifically equated with the concept of data quality assurance. And as data profiling has emerged as a critical commodity tool, it should be viewed as a set of technical tools that can be applied in support of numerous information management programs, including data quality assessment, data quality validation, metadata management, data integration and transformation processing, migrations, and modernization projects. The value of data profiling lies in the ability to integrate the capabilities of a technical tool with knowledge of how to apply what can be learned in support of a program's goals.

Data profiling incorporates a collection of analysis and assessment algorithms that, when applied in the proper context, will provide empirical insight into what potential issues exist within a data set. In this chapter we look at some of the analyses and algorithms that are performed and how they are used to provide value in a number of application contexts, including assessment or potential anomalies, business rule discovery, business rule validation, validation of metadata, and data model validation. This chapter will also look at the roles involved, and then provide a guide to the profiling process within each individual context, and show how to operationalize the results.

We have already seen in previous chapters (particularly in chapter 11 on data quality assessment) that profiling is a key

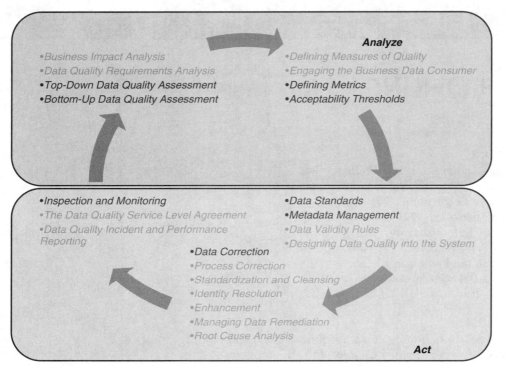

Figure 14.1 Data profiling contributes to key aspects of the virtuous cycle.

technology. Recalling the virtuous cycle described in chapter 2 (see Figure 14.1), this chapter will describe how data profiling contributes to some key aspects of each phase of that cycle. Understanding how these techniques work and how they are used provides additional insight into ways that profiling can be applied.

14.1 Application Contexts for Data Profiling

A retrospective look at the wave of consolidations among vendors in the data quality and data management industry shows one specific similarity across the board – the transition to building an end-to-end data management suite is incomplete without the incorporation of a data profiling product. The reason for this is that many good data management practices are based on a clear understanding of "content," ranging from specific data values, the characteristics of the data elements holding those values, relationships between data elements across records in one table, or associations across multiple tables.

It is worth reviewing some basic application contexts in which profiling plays a part, and that will ultimately help to demonstrate how a collection of relatively straightforward analytic techniques can be combined to shed light on the fundamental perspective of information utility for multiple purposes. We will then provide greater detail in subsequent sections for each of these applications.

14.1.1 Data Reverse Engineering

The absence of documented knowledge about a data set (which drives the need for anomaly analysis) accounts for the need for a higher-level understanding of the definitions, reference data, and structure of the data set – its metadata. Data reverse engineering is used to review the structure of a data set for which there is little or no existing metadata or for which the existing metadata are suspect, for the purpose of discovering and documenting the actual current state of its metadata.

In this situation, data profiling is employed to incrementally build up a knowledge base associated with data element structure and use. Column values are analyzed to determine if there are commonly used value domains, if those domains map to known conceptual value domains, to review the size and types of each data element, to identify any embedded pattern structures associated with any data element, and to identify keys and how those keys are used to refer to other data entities.

The results of this reverse engineering process can be used to populate a metadata repository. The discovered metadata can be used to facilitate dependent development activities, such as business process renovation, enterprise data architecture, or data migrations.

14.1.2 Anomaly Analysis

One might presume that when operating in a well-controlled data management framework, data analysts will have some understanding of what types of issues and errors exist within various data sets. But even in these types of environments there is often little visibility into data peculiarities in relation to existing data dependencies, let alone the situation in which data sets are reused for alternate and new purposes.

So to get a handle on data set usability, there must be a process to establish a baseline measure of the quality of the data set, even distinct from specific downstream application uses. Anomaly analysis is a process for empirically analyzing the values in a data set to look for unexpected behavior to provide that initial baseline review. Essentially, anomaly analysis:

- Executes a statistical review of the data values stored in all the data elements in the data set,
- Examines value frequency distributions,
- Examines the variance of values,
- Logs the percentage of data attributes populated,
- Explores relationships between columns, and
- Explores relationships across data sets

to reveal potentially flawed data values, data elements, or records. Discovered flaws are typically documented and can be brought to the attention of the business clients to determine whether each flaw has any critical business impact.

14.1.3 Data Quality Rule Discovery

The need to observe dependencies within a data set manifests itself through the emergence (either by design or organically through use) of data quality rules. In many situations, though, there is no documentation of the rules for a number of reasons.

As one example, the rules are deeply embedded in application code and have never been explicitly associated with the data. As another example, the system may inadvertently have constrained the user from being able to complete a task, and user behavior has evolved to observe unwritten rules that enable the task to be performed.

Data profiling can be used to examine a data set to identify and extract embedded business rules, whether they are intentional but undocumented, or purely unintentional. These rules can be combined with predefined data quality expectations, as described in chapter 9, and used as the targets for data quality auditing and monitoring.

14.1.4 Metadata Compliance and Data Model Integrity

The results of profiling can also be used as a way of determining the degree to which the data actually observes any already existent metadata, ranging from data element specifications, validity rules associated with table consistency (such as uniqueness of a primary key), as well as demonstrating that referential integrity constraints are enforced properly in the data set.

14.2 Data Profiling: Algorithmic Techniques

14.2.1 Column Analysis

Column profiling provides statistical measurements associated with the frequency distribution of data values (and patterns) within a single column (or data attribute). From a computational perspective, column profiling is relatively simplistic, requiring a scan through the entire table, and a count of the number of occurrences of each value within each column. Technically, this can be implemented using hash tables that map each value that appears in the column to the number of times that value appears.

Despite its simplicity, the frequency distribution of column values exposes some insightful characteristics, and enables a number of interesting analyses, including:

- **Range analysis,** which looks at the values, considers whether they are subject to a total ordering, and determines whether the values are constrained within a well-defined range;
- **Sparseness,** which evaluates the percentage of the elements that are not populated;
- **Cardinality,** which analyzes the number of distinct values that appear within the column;
- **Uniqueness**, which indicates if each of the values assigned to the attribute is unique;
- **Value distribution,** which presents an ordering of the relative frequency (count and percentage) of the assignment of distinct values; and
- **Value absence,** which identifies the appearance and count of occurrences of null values.

The frequency analysis also provides summarization/aggregate values that can be used to characterize the data set, including:

- **Minimum value,** based on the ordering properties of the data set;
- **Maximum value,** also based on the ordering properties of the data set;
- **Mean,** providing the average value (for numeric data);
- **Median,** providing the middle value (if such a thing can be defined); and
- **Standard deviation,** although this is mostly relevant only for numeric values.

Column profiling also looks at descriptive characteristics, feeding these types of analyses:

- **Type determination,** which characterizes data type and size;
- **Abstract type recognition,** which refines the semantic data type association with a specific attribute, often depending on pattern analysis;
- **Overloading,** which attempts to determine if an attribute is being used for multiple purposes; and
- **Format evaluation,** which tries to resolve unrecognized data into defined formats.

Frequency analysis can suggest potential areas for further investigation, as we will see in subsequent sections of this chapter. For example, low frequency values (outliers) are potential data quality violations, and a small number of very high frequency values may indicate a flag or code attribute.

14.2.2 Cross-Column Analysis

There are two main aspects to cross-column analysis:

- **Key analysis:** Especially in older data systems, there are situations in which there is no artificially created primary key, yet there remains a need for unique differentiation between entities stored in a table. Key analysis examines collections of attribute values across each record to determine candidate primary keys.
- **Dependency analysis:** The ability to determine if there are embedded relationships or embedded structures within a data set is enabled through the discovery of functional dependencies. Therefore, it is valuable to review what functional dependencies are and how they can be used as part of the discovery process. A functional dependency between column X and column Y basically says that, given any two records, if the corresponding values of column X are the same, then the corresponding values of column Y will be the same. This implies that the value of column X *determines* the value of column Y, or that column Y is said to be *dependent* on column X. This abstraction can be extended to sets of columns as well. Functional dependency analysis can be used for identification of redundant data as well as determining opportunities for data normalization.

Compared with column analysis, cross-column analysis is much more computationally intensive. The algorithms employed by profiling tools for cross-column analysis require multiple scans through the table, and the results of each iteration of those algorithms must be cached to support each subsequent processing stage.

14.2.3 Cross-Table Analysis

Cross-table analysis examines overlapping value sets across different tables. Some key capabilities include:

- **Foreign key analysis,** which seeks to map key relationships between tables;
- **Identification of orphaned records,** indicative of a foreign key relationship that is violated because a child entry exists where a parent record does not;
- **Determination of semantic and syntactic differences,** such as when differently named columns holding the same values, or same-named columns hold different values.

Redundancy analysis is straightforward, in that the values in each of a pair of columns respectively selected from different tables are evaluated for set intersection. Conclusions drawn from the analyst's review provide the insight: depending on the size of the sets and the degree to which the sets overlap, two columns might be tagged as foreign keys (if the value set is large and mostly disparate) or perhaps as both taking their value from the same reference domain (if the value set is small).

14.2.4 Data Rule Validation

The three types of analyses discussed in this section are used for discovery of anomalies and business rules. A fourth type of analysis uses data profiling in a proactive manner to validate defined assertions. Most data profiling tools allow for the definition of data rules, typically as assertions constructed from expressions. The granularity of these rules may concentrate at the column (attribute) level, at the data instance level, or across multiple data instances. Examples of rules for validation are similar to those described in chapter 9.

Data rule validation can be performed in two ways – as a batch and as a service. In the batch approach, an entire data set can be subjected to validation of a collection of rules at the same time. In the service mode, specific data instances can be submitted for validation. The main difference is in supporting the different levels of granularity. In the batch approach, the entire data set to be evaluated is presented to the profiler, and therefore rules of all levels of granularity can be applied. In the service mode, the types of rules to be validated are limited by the scope of the set of data instances provided. Since the entire data set is usually not provided, the rules are limited to column and data instance rules.

14.3 Data Reverse Engineering

Every structured data collection has an underlying data model, whether it is explicitly defined or not. Many older systems built prior to the use of data modeling tools do have some underlying model, and at some point, either when the data are to be aggregated into a data warehouse or when the application is migrated to an updated architecture, some better understanding of the de facto model is required. The goals of data reverse engineering include identifying the system's information components, reviewing the relationships between those components, and finding any embedded object hierarchies, with the intention of identifying opportunities for model improvement.

14.3.1 Domain Discovery and Analysis

This is the process of identifying sets of values that logically belong together with respect to a well-defined business meaning. Some domain discovery activities include:

- **Identifying enumerated domains and reference data:** This is the process of identifying a set of values that is the source data set for one or more table attributes. Enumerated domains are typically character string value sets with a limited number of entries. Examples of enumerated domains are status codes and department codes.
- **Analyzing range constraints:** This process identifies attributes whose values lie between two well-defined endpoints. Though this often applies to integral values, it can also apply for character string values and dates, as well as other abstract data types.
- **Identifying mapped values associated with conceptual domains:** As a combination of range constraint analysis and enumerated domain analysis, this process evaluates integer domains to determine if the values are mapped to another set of values that can provide some business context. The issue here is that often the same integral value sets may be used for many attributes, even though the numbers relate to different conceptual domains, and therefore the analyst's goal is to identify the mapping between numbers and the values or concepts they actually represent.

- **Abstract data type analysis:** Often there are specific patterns exhibited by value sets that suggest a more complex data type may have some semantic meaning. This process reviews patterns and helps the analyst to suggest potential abstract data type definitions used within the data set.

14.3.2 Embedded Structure Analysis

From the reverse engineering standpoint, understanding the intended structure of a data set will help in clarifying its definition, semantics, and the data quality and data transformations associated with a renovated data architecture or a data migration. The following are some examples:

- **Identifying opportunities for normalization:** Functional dependencies within a single table may be redundant data elements that really represent embedded tables. Identifying these dependencies helps in data migration efforts to identify relational structure in relatively flat data.
- **Identifying opportunities for consolidation:** As an iterative process, identifying common or multiple use of embedded data among multiple data sets allows for consolidating that information as reference data.
- **Understanding relational structure:** This process looks for embedded or exposed foreign key relationships.
- **Data Definition Language (DDL) generation:** As prospective relational and structural suggestions are made, eventually the DDL for a target representation of the data can be generated as part of a migration strategy.
- **Syntactic consistency:** Knowing that two data set attributes (or columns) are intended to represent the same set of values, this is a process to ensure that the value sets share the same format specification (i.e., are syntactically compatible).
- **Semantic consistency:** This is the process of determining that two (or more) columns that share the same value set and are discovered to refer to the same concept have the same name.

14.4 Analyzing Anomalies

The goal of anomaly analysis is to empirically review all the data elements in the data set, examine their frequency distribution, and explore relationships between columns to reveal potential flawed data values. This section looks at some common anomalies that can be identified as a result of data profiling.

14.4.1 Column Anomalies

Common column anomalies include:

- **Sparseness,** which identifies columns that are infrequently populated.
- **Unused columns,** indicated either by being largely unpopulated or populated with the same value in all records.
- **Null analysis,** which is used to determine the percentage of absent values and to identify abstract null representations (e.g., "N/A" or "999-99-9999").
- **Overloaded attributes,** determining when columns are used for storing more than one conceptual data element.
- **Expected frequency analysis,** or reviewing those columns whose values are expected to reflect certain frequency distribution patterns, validate compliance with the expected patterns.
- **Outlier review,** a process for those columns whose values do not reflect the expected frequency distribution; the goal is to identify and explore those values whose frequencies are either much greater than expected or much lower than expected.
- **Range analysis,** used to determine if a column's values fall within one (or more) constrained value ranges. This may involve single range analysis or more complex value clustering.
- **Format and/or pattern analysis,** which involves inspecting representational alphanumeric patterns and formats of values and reviewing the frequency of each to determine if the value patterns are reasonable.
- **Value domain compliance,** in which columns whose values are expected to comply with known data domains are reviewed to identify noncompliant values.
- **Composed value analysis,** which is a process that looks for sets of values that appear to be composed of two or more separable values. As an example, consider a product code that is composed of a unique value appended to a code representing the manufacturing site, such as NY-123, the "NY" representing the manufacturing site.

14.4.2 Cross-Column Anomalies

Types of cross-column anomalies include:

- **Derived value analysis,** which looks for columns whose values are computed as functions of other values within the same record. As an example, a purchase order line total should equal the quantity of items ordered multiplied by the unit cost of that items.

- **Uniqueness analysis,** which reviews all records in the data set (table) to ensure that no exact duplicates exist.
- **Primary key validity,** which, when given a set of attributes expected to form a primary key for the data set, validates that key is unique across each record in the table.
- **Functional dependency validity,** which is intended to discover the existence of functional dependencies across multiple columns, as well as to determine when those functional dependencies are violated.

14.4.3 Cross-Table Anomalies

Examples of cross-table anomalies include:

- **Referential consistency compliance:** Referential integrity asserts that for any foreign key relationship, every foreign key in table B that refers to a primary key in table A must exist in table A. Assuming that we know the existence of a foreign key relationship, this process checks its compliance. This process can check for both orphans (child rows without parents) and childless parents if desired.
- **Syntactic consistency:** This process evaluates columns that are expected to take values from the same data domain and checks consistency with the domain rules. This ensures that there is a common de facto agreement of syntactic form among common attributes.
- **Semantic consistency/synonym analysis:** This is the process of determining that two (or more) columns that share the same value set and are discovered to refer to the same concept have the same name, or mapped to the same conceptual data element. Conversely, this process can explore value sets that are supposed to represent the same concept but have values that occur in one column but not others (nonoverlapping values).

14.5 Data Quality Rule Discovery

Activities that use data profiling are intended to discover rules that correspond to business expectations of the data. Violation of these rules can either prevent a properly automated process from executing properly, result in incorrect implementation of business directives, or skew analytic roll-ups and aggregation and lead to incorrect assumptions and poor decision making.

The goal of these procedures is to collect rules that can be used for ongoing auditing/monitoring of compliance and objective information quality scoring. Profiling may provide some information in determining business rules, but understand that a large part of the process is analyst-oriented.

14.5.1 Column-Oriented Rules

Column analysis will expose such rules as the following:

- **Default values:** There are two kinds of default values: meaningless and meaningful. A meaningless default is equivalent to a true "null" value that represents the absence of a value. A meaningful default value is one used to represent some concept without specifying a value. For example, an all-nine value for a social security number may represent an unavailable value, whereas all zeros may indicate that the individual is a foreigner and does not have a social security number. This process can look for correlations with other fields or high frequency values and explore whether these are defaults in the application, and whether they are reasonable.
- **Missing values:** This is a process to determine if there is are instances where values are missing that should be there. This includes reviewing the use of default values treated as nulls, and also reviews other values which should be interpreted as NULL, such as text values "N/A" or in some instances, zero.
- **Indicator values:** Indicators or flags are fields that have one of two values – some representation of true or false. This procedure evaluates columns to determine if they are indicator fields.
- **Domain definitions:** Discovered domains may have rules governing value membership, either through enumeration, reference (i.e., the values are compiled into another table), or format specification. This procedure is the analysis of domain value sets and the definition of the governing rules for domain value membership. In addition, collecting data domains and providing business names for the value set is part of the metadata management process.
- **Domain membership:** These are rules specifying that certain columns must take their values from specific known domains.
- **Domain nonmembership:** These are rules specifying that certain columns may not take their values from certain known domains. This is particularly relevant when specific default values have been accumulated as a data domain so as to identify those records using defaults for further evaluation.
- **Attribute overloading:** Overloaded attributes are columns that take on more than one virtual attribute. Overloaded

attributes often are used in conjunction with some other attribute that indicates the use. For example, one column may be a SEX indicator for customers, but since this attribute is irrelevant for organizational customers, the column might be used to indicate organization size. A separate column such as the ORG_INDICATOR would toggle the use between SEX and SIZE. Therefore, part of the business rules discovery process is to determine if there are overloaded attributes, and if so, what attributes are used to toggle the different uses. A different type of attribute overloading occurs when one field holds multiple values of the same attribute, sometimes separated by a comma or other delimiter. This process evaluates whether this type of attribute overloading is taking place and determines if there is a need for another data structure to represent this.

- **Floating data:** Often, for a number of reasons, values that are intended to be in one field are inadvertently shifted into another field. For example, data incorrectly extracted into a fixed-column format might move values across the intended breaks. Profiling can be used to identify common patterns when this shifting occurs to find a rule for validating that data values have not floated across column boundaries.
- **Business constraints:** Evaluating column patterns may reveal the existence of constraints related directly to business operations. Any patterns that stand out should be reviewed with a business subject matter expert.

14.5.2 Cross-Column Rule Discovery

Cross column analysis can yield rules such as these:
- **Conditional completeness:** A review of data dictionaries and table layouts may indicate that certain column values are required, although often the requirement is conditioned on some other constraint. Profiling can be used to look for dependencies embedded within the table that indicate a condition for alternate column value presence.
- **Conditional exemption:** When looking at columns, one can expose null occurrences; often the presence of nulls (as well as defaults) is triggered by conditions associated with other column values within the same instance.
- **Consistency and derivation:** Approximate dependencies that are evident in a table may indicate the existence of consistency rules with a small number of violations. When the data profiling tool supports approximate dependency analysis, then discovered dependencies are likely to represent a

consistency business rule for which subject matter expertise would provide insight.
- **Uniqueness:** Each record in the table should be unique; profiling can test for uniqueness and can also be used to determine candidate keys, which should be evaluated with a subject matter expert to determine feasibility and appropriateness.

14.5.3 Cross-Table Rule Discovery

The kinds of rules that can be derived or discovered through cross-table analysis involve expected assertions imposed on the join of two (or more) tables:
- **Implicit relationships:** Implicit relationships exist when there is connectivity between two tables even though there is no explicit documentation of the connection. For example, primary and foreign key relationships are discovered in the data but referential integrity constraints are not explicitly defined.
- **Conditional completeness:** Similar to the types of conditional completeness rules between columns, the same types of rules can be identified across joined tables.
- **Conditional exemption:** Similar to the types of conditional exemption rules between columns, the same types of rules can be identified across joined tables.
- **Conditional consistency and derivation:** Similar to the types of conditional consistency and derivation rules between columns, the same types of rules can be identified across joined tables.
- **Aggregate dependence:** These are rules that constrain values in one set when compared with the value of an aggregate function in another set.
- **Cross-table association or dependency:** Similar to the cross-column association or dependency rules, the same types of rules can be identified across joined tables.

14.6 Metadata Compliance and Data Model Integrity

Metadata compliance is a relatively straightforward concept. Every structured data set has some associated descriptive structure metadata, although in some instances the metadata are not explicitly documented. But when documentation exists, either in the form of an entity relationship diagram with a detailed physical or logical model, or in DDL, a COBOL copy book, other data model descriptions, an excel spreadsheet, or a text document, the data profiler can be used to validate the defined metadata. This structure metadata usually contains information about data tables and about the attributes within each table, including attribute name, data type, length, along with other constraints, such as whether the field may be null. In addition, often appropriate data domains are documented along with each data element.

There are typically three areas of metadata that can be reviewed for conformance using a data profiling tool:

- Type compliance, in which the data type of values are compared with the expected data types
- Domain compliance, in which the set of valid values are reviewed for compliance with documented value sets
- Constraint compliance, in which defined constraints are reviewed for compliance with documented constraints

In each of these situations, the data quality practitioner should be alerted if any discrepancies are identified.

14.6.1 Type Compliance

As discussed earlier in this chapter, a data profiling tool can scan the values in each column and propose the data type and length of the values in the column. These proposed data types and lengths for each column can be compared with documented column metadata.

14.6.2 Domain Compliance

Because profiling provides information about the sets of values that appear within a column, it can be used to compare to any lists of valid values. In this situation, the profiler can use cross-table analysis (actually, the need is for comparing two column sets) to verify that the set of values used in the column are a subset of the values in the enumerated value domain.

14.6.3 Constraint Compliance

The cross-column and cross-table analyses can be used to determine when known constraints are violated. This uses the data rule validation capabilities of the profiler.

14.6.4 Data Model Integrity

A data model contains inherent specifications regarding attribute-level constraints, cross-table relationships, and cardinality. For example, a data model may specify that there is a one-to-one relationship between two tables. Profiling can be used to verify that the actual data corresponds to the constraints, as well as more sophisticated approaches to automatically analyzing relational structure and creating a proposed model. This proposed model can then be compared to the actual model as a review of differences between the logical view and what actually is in the data.

In addition to the other metadata aspects discussed in prior sections, it would be worthwhile to capture the discovered data model for tracking purposes to determine if there are specific data model issues that have been highlighted as a result of profiling and whether those model issues have been addressed.

14.7 Coordinating the Participants

Is it worth reviewing the roles associated with the use of data profiling and clarifying how each of the individuals in those roles uses the profiling tools?

14.7.1 Data Quality Analyst

The data quality analyst does the profiling using the data profiling tool and collates the results for presentation to the subject matter experts. Often, a flawed bit of information identified at one point in the information production flow may have its origin in upstream processing. In these cases, it is possible that the same flaw will have affected other downstream processes as well. In this case, being able to track how flaws propagate through applications can aid evaluation of the seriousness of a problem and prioritization of problems for review.

These kinds of cascading impacts can be evaluated using data profiling when the information flow is well documented and data dependencies are made explicit. Using those tools, one may use profiling to evaluate expectations with specific business rules at different places in the information chain to locate the earliest processing stage at which a flaw is introduced. This facilitates the isolation of the location of a process problem and helps in reducing the amount of time spent in diagnosing data quality issues.

14.7.2 Data Steward

As data profiling is used in assessing the quality of information as well as metadata compliance, the analysis of data sets using data profiling tools must be coordinated with the data stewards associated with each data set. Because the data steward is accountable for the quality of the information, it is the steward's responsibility to ensure that profiling is used for its proper purposes, notably that:

- Ongoing auditing and monitoring takes place.
- The results of the profile are documented.
- Any metadata discovered is documented and compared against expectations.
- Any business rules that are discovered are documented and incorporated into the auditing process.
- Metrics measurements are captured and tracked.
- Regressions are identified and investigated.

14.7.3 Business Subject Matter Experts

The results of data profiling should be shared with a business subject matter expert. Because data quality is contextual and depends on the purposes for which the data is being used, a business subject matter expert can evaluate the business impact of unexpected data values or discovered business rules.

Together with the business expert, the data quality practitioner can use profiling to find flaws that are related to specific business problems. The costs associated with a data flaw should be assessed, as described in chapter 1. The business data consumers can then use the intelligence gathered to determine the business impacts of these flaws as well as the potential approaches for remediation.

14.7.4 Metadata Analysts

Once business rules have been identified, they must be managed in concert with the data stewards. The business rules metadata manager is tasked with maintaining the set of business rules, vetting the rules with the business client, and, if necessary, ensuring that the rules are used for ongoing monitoring

14.8 Selecting a Data Set for Analysis

In any environment there are probably numerous data sets that, when subjected to data profiling, could lead to ways of improvement. However, at different stages of developing the data quality program, the suitability of subjecting any specific set to profiling should be evaluated in terms of a number of factors. In this section we address those factors, as well as explore whether one should be satisfied with subjecting a sample to profiling instead of the entire data set.

There are at least five factors to be considered in selecting a data set for analysis:

1. Maturity of the program: In the early stages of the program there may be an opportunity to clearly establish the value of profiling, either in terms of exposing anomalies or for metadata discovery, and so a data set that is already suspected to harbor unexpected values or a data set of early vintage (e.g., file-based tables from legacy systems) whose metadata are largely unknown may make good targets. However, as the program matures, the business client may have specific requirements for scheduling regular and periodic profiling sessions for specific data sets.

2. Criticality of the data: Criticality can be evaluated in a number of ways:

   a. Necessary to effectively running the business: If the data set is one that is used to drive standard business, it increases the data set's criticality.

   b. Widespread use: If many individuals or groups use the data, it increases the data set's criticality.

   c. Heavy use: If the data set is heavily referenced, even by a single application, it increases the data set's criticality.

   d. High impact: If flawed data is known to have a significant business impact, it increases that data set's criticality.

3. Accessibility: If the data set is hard to access (e.g., it cannot be accessed natively or through standard connectors, or is not easily extractable), or if there are security or privacy concerns, this may contribute to determining the priority of profiling that data set.

4. Data set size: If resource usage is an issue, then the size of the data set may be a factor in selecting a data set, since smaller data sets are more amenable to profiling than larger sets.

5. Availability of subject matter experts: Since the profiling results should be reviewed with a subject matter expert, the availability of one becomes a factor in data set selection. In the absence of a subject matter expert, one may select data sets that do have less business process dependence than other data sets.

14.8.1 The Question of Sampling

Should the entire set be subjected to profiling, or should profiling be performed on a sample? This is a common question when considering which data set to assess. The major argument for sampling is that anything that is learned through profiling a sample will apply to the entire data set. Alternatively, though, there may be additional things that can be learned from the entire data set that may be missed in a sample. Here are some rules of thumb:

- Experiment with the profiling tool to determine a data set size that is the most reasonable in terms of analyst time and system resources, and this will become the "recommended data set size."
- If the selected data set is smaller than the recommended size, extract a sample that is of the recommended size.
- Make sure that your sample is truly random and is not subject to some predetermined set of constraints that may mask out any discoveries.

14.8.2 Combining Multiple Data Sets

One major challenge is the need to profile more than one data set at a time, especially when there is a need to validate data across systems or identify business rules that span multiple data sets or different systems. Some profiling products are better than others in including data from different sources for analysis at the same time, and this capability may be a valuable differentiator when it comes to selecting vendor products.

14.9 Summary

In this chapter we have looked at the ways that data profiling tools are engineered, and a number of different ways that the tools support aspects of the data quality program. When evaluating data profiling products, it is valuable to first assess the business needs for a data profiling tool (as a by-product of the data requirements analysis process and determination of remediation as described in chapters 9 and 12). In general, when evaluating data profiling tools, consider these capabilities, as discussed in this chapter:

- Column profiling
- Cross-column (dependency)
- Cross-table (redundancy)
- Structure analysis
- Business rules discovery
- Business rules management
- Metadata management
- Historical tracking
- Proactive auditing
- Business rule importing
- Business rule exporting
- Metadata importing
- Metadata exporting

PARSING AND STANDARDIZATION

As discussed in chapter 13, proactive data quality management concentrates on inspection, monitoring, and ultimately prevention. Instituting inspection and monitoring for potential anomalies is a way of flagging issues when they occur, identifying the source of error introduction, and facilitating the elimination of the root cause. However, there are certain situations in which individuals within the organization are, to some extent, prevented from being able to exercise immediate control over flawed data. A frequent example is when business applications rely on data that originates from external providers, such as:

- Data acquired from third-party data aggregators,
- Data entered by external parties, and
- Data automatically created and provisioned via straight-through processing.

Though in these cases it may be possible to identify a potential error, it is difficult if not impossible to prevent them from entering the environment. Yet if there is a need for the data values to conform to specific internal expectations, some action must be taken to bring the data into alignment with the organizational standards. To maintain high quality data, the data management practitioner may need to resort to *cleansing the data* – in other words, transforming what is recognized as non-standard data values into ones that meet expectations.

In this chapter we look at parsing and standardization, which together are a combination of techniques used to scan data values and compare them to known value domains, formats, and patterns to:

- Map values to standard formats,
- Identify errors,
- Potentially correct recognized errors,
- Standardize value representations, and
- Normalize data values.

Applying these corrective measures adjusts the data values so that they can be more effectively used within business processes. To understand how these value domains, mapping, formats, patterns, and business rules are defined, we first look at common data error paradigms – descriptions, examples, and ways that data set quality is impacted by these common root causes for introducing errors. We then consider aspects of data standards and metadata management (as discussed in chapter 10) that help to limit the scope of introduced errors, and then how that meta-data is used by parsing and standardization utilities to normalize data.

The use of parsing and standardization is by no means limited to ex post facto cleansing, and it is reasonable for the practitioner to consider how these techniques can be designed and integrated into the application framework to help identify potential errors as data enters the environment. Even when the data comes from beyond the organization's administrative control, being able to present recognized anomalies to the originating source can help block data errors as a "data quality firewall" and prevent those errors from impeding the information production flow.

15.1 Data Error Paradigms

The need for "cleansing" data is rooted in flawed processes that allow for different types of errors to be introduced into the information flow. The methods employed to fix unexpected values are refined in relation to the ways that the errors are introduced in the first place. That being said, many types of what might be considered random flaws are attributable to relatively common error paradigms (some are shown in Table 15.1) related to specific root causes. These error paradigms provide some

Table 15.1 Common Data Error Paradigms

Error Paradigm	Description	Example	Potential Impacts
Attribute granularity	The data model is not configured to correctly incorporate the value granularity necessary to convey the managed information	A *customer name* field, which incorporates first, middle, and last names all in the same data element; if the user wants to have each name separated, it would be better to use three fields: last name, first name, middle name	Natural variations in the ways that person names are presented will lead to duplicated records
Overly strict format	The model is constrained and does not enable the representation of each of the complete set of values	Managing a customer name using a *first name*, *middle initial*, and *last name* date elements	For anglicized names, there may be individuals who prefer to be called by their middle names, which cannot be accommodated Given names and surnames for nonanglicized names might not conform to the strict format Customer is liable to be addressed in a manner that is not according to their preference
Use of semistructured forms	Somewhere between normalized structured representations and unstructured data, semistructured data maps to a heuristically determinable format	Variations in parts descriptions such as "sheet metal screw" vs. "thread cutting screw" vs. "Sht metal screw" vs. "S MT screw"	Variations and localized inconsistency of format in the context of an imposed structure
Finger flubs	Common typing and documentation errors such as transposed letters inside words, misspelled words, mis-keyed letters	The numeral "7" appearing when it should be the symbol "&" due to a sticky shift key	Variation and duplication or entities in the data set
Transcription errors	Mistakes in copying data between mediums	A customer service representative incorrectly transcribes a name provided during a telephone call	Variation and duplication or entities in the data set

(Continued)

Table 15.1 Common Data Error Paradigms—*Cont'd*

Error Paradigm	Description	Example	Potential Impacts
Transformation errors	Errors that are introduced when applications extract from one source and transform it before depositing it into the target data set	Automated expansion of abbreviations incorrectly applied when abbreviations are embedded in other strings	If the transformation rules are not completely correct, or if there is a flaw in the transformation application, errors will be created where none originally existed
Misfielded data	Values stored in the wrong data element	In older screen-based data entry systems, when values exceeded the size of the field, the cursor automatically tabbed over to the next field, allowing data to "overflow" into incorrect fields	Correct data values in the incorrect data elements
Overloaded attributes (version 1)	Either a reflection of poor data modeling or due to changing business concerns, an overloaded attribute is one that is used to carry more than one conceptual data element	A *foreign country* field that contains email addresses because there is no defined data element to store email addresses and the foreign country field is usually null	Confusion in downstream use of available data attributes
Overloaded attributes (version 2)	A data element that holds more than one data value	Customer account records containing "account names" with multiple entities such as "John and Mary Smith"	Difficulty in managing one-to-one relationships with each individual customer

insight into how different types of rules for parsing, standardization, and transformations can be used to remediate data errors – via both corrective and preventative measures.

15.2 The Role of Metadata

The data error paradigms described in Table 15.1 share a common feature: users are more likely to introduce errors in the absence of tight controls over the types of values that populate data elements. Of course, there are some contexts that it would be not only difficult to assert tight control, it would even stymie the business process (entering company names is a prime example). However, well-defined reference data domains, common value patterns, and domain membership rules contribute to more effective ways to differentiate between valid values and ones that are potentially flawed.

Adhering to good practices in defining and managing reference metadata associated with each data element will enable better control, especially with respect to these specific metadata concepts, some of which were discussed in chapter 10:

- **Conceptual domains** are sets of value meanings (presented using a list of concepts or a description of the members of the set) and are used to describe the set of concepts that can be represented within a data element. An example is "States of the United States," which describes the set of concepts (the geopolitical units comprising the United States) but does not specify their values.
- **Value domains** provide the representations of values that can be assigned to a data element. An example is an enumeration of the two-character abbreviations of each of the states in the United States.
- **Mappings** either map concepts in a conceptual domain to a specific value in a value domain or can be used to map equivalent values across value domains. An example of the former maps the United State Postal Service (USPS) two-character string value "CA" to the concept "California," whereas an example of the latter maps the USPS two-character string "CA" to the two-digit Federal Information Processing Standard (FIPS) code "06" (which both map to the concept "California").
- **Format patterns** describe the syntactic constraints for value sets. For example, a ZIP + 4 code must be represented as five digits followed by a hyphen, followed by another four digits ("99999-9999").
- **Business rules** applied to data elements specify constraints such as domain membership rules (e.g., the *state* field must take its value from the USPS two-character state codes value domain), specifications of dependencies between data elements characterized as observing a mapping between value domains, nullness constraints, and conformance to defined format patterns.

To effectively employ parsing and standardization methods for data cleansing, the practitioner will require access to a metadata repository managing just the right amount of metadata. Controlled management of data domains, data element definitions, and additional constraints as metadata supports the data cleansing process and helps the practitioners employ cleansing techniques to reduce the introduction of errors into the environment in the first place.

15.3 Tokens: Units of Meaning

Data values stored within data elements carry meaning in the context of the business process and the underlying data model. In addressing any of the error paradigms, the first step is identifying distinct meaningful concepts embedded in data values. When the conceptual and value domains associated with each data element are strictly controlled, the potential variability of the data values is likewise restricted. This concept is often manifested by imposing restrictions on the data producers. For example, a company's web site may only allow a customer to select one of a list of valid values (such as "country" or "state"), and refuse to allow free-text typing. Another example is limiting the responses allowed within an interactive voice recognition inbound call system ("Press or say one for account balances").

However, at the same time, tight restrictions on data entry pose challenges to the people performing data entry, especially when one of those restrictions prevents a person from being able to complete a task. For example, if a data entry screen for new customer data requires that the user enter a "State" value from a drop-down list of the 50 U.S. states, the interface forces that user to enter incorrect data if the customer lives outside the United States.

This leads to two different conclusions – either the data entry process must be carefully reviewed to ensure that the application's controls cover all of the potential cases, or (more likely) the controls will end up being loosened, allowing for more freedom, and consequently, more variance. And since data sets are often used for purposes for which they were not originally intended to be used, data values may sufficiently meet business needs in one context, but not meet the needs of any new contexts. In both of these cases, a combination of inspection and data cleansing techniques will institute some degree of control over the data acquisition process.

15.3.1 Mapping "Data" to "Information"

In either of these situations, there is a challenge in mapping the actual values within data elements to their underlying *meanings* within each business context for which the data set is used. As value length increases, the constraints on structure diminish, with more information being crammed into the data element, and the precision with which one can define a conceptual/value domain are also diminished. And with the more complex data values, each "chunk" of data that is inserted into the data field may (or may not) carry information. The objective of the parsing and standardization process, then, is straightforward:

1. Scan the data value and break out the individual information chunks.
2. Determine which chunks carry the information.
3. Rearrange the identified chunks into a standard representation.
4. Normalize the chunks into an agreed-to format to reduce variability across the data set.

15.3.2 What Is a Token?

What the first step, breaking out the information chunks, really means is that the parts of a data value that carry the meaning should be identified. Each of those pieces of information is called a *token*. A token is representative of all of the character strings used for a particular purpose.

For example, free-formed character strings that appear in a *name* data element actually may carry multiple pieces of information, such as "first name," "middle name," "title," "generational suffix," among others. Those tokens can be configured into one out of many recognizable patterns. If we are able to differentiate between the different token types – last names, first names, initials, punctuation, and so on – we can define different patterns for recognizing an individual's name:

- first_name first_name last_name ("Howard David Loshin")
- first_name initial last_name ("Howard D Loshin")
- initial first_name last_name ("H David Loshin")
- last_name, first_name ("Loshin, David")
- last_name, first_name first_name ("Loshin, Howard David")
- last_name, first_name initial ("Loshin, Howard D")

As is seen in these examples, individual characters, strings, and punctuation may be represented as tokens. And these are just a few of the hundreds, if not thousands of different patterns that can be configured based on a relatively small collection of token types. Although not all names will conform to these patterns, a large number will.

Token types can be further refined based on the value domain. For example, if we can distinguish male first name tokens from female first name tokens, we can use the tokens to infer gender assignment. This distinction and recognition process starts by *parsing* the tokens and then rearranging the strings that mapped to those tokens through a process called *standardization*.

15.4 Parsing

The goal of parsing is to scan the value(s) that are stored in a data element to identify those that map to which defined token types. In order to do this, we need these pieces:

1. Token types, definitions, and the types of the tokens expected to be found in the data attributes (for person names, this might include title, first_name, last_name, generational_ indicator, and suffix)
2. Value domains, or the set of valid values for each data component type (such as enumerated lists of valid first names or valid titles)
3. Formats and patterns for collections of tokens that must be recognized together
4. Acceptable forms that the data may take (such as "mixed case," or "without punctuation")
5. A parser, which is the tool used to recognize when data values match defined patterns
6. Methods for arbitrating situations where character strings map to more than one token or pattern
7. Error handling, or a means for tagging records that have unidentified data components

15.4.1 Types of Tools

Tools that perform parsing combine different algorithms for pattern recognition and value validation. Some tools perform pattern recognition with regular expressions and context-free grammars. Others will include a knowledge base containing reference value domains, and may take into account the vendor's experience working with specific data domains (such as customer names, product names, or location descriptions) and allow the tool to rely on predetermined rules as well as inferred data domains. Pattern-based tools can be made even more flexible in concert with data profiling tools, in that they can first analyze the user's data set to identify common patterns that can be presented back to the user for review. Selected patterns will be integrated back into the parsing methodology for identifying distinct tokens in the data. Consider the example of USPS state abbreviations, which is a token set defined using a pattern ("a character string of length 2 in which both characters are upper case") and an enumerated value domain, which lists the valid values.

15.4.2 Formats, Patterns, Value Domains

Metadata is used for parsing rules. Data element types that correspond to the token types must be defined, such as names, street names, city names, and telephone numbers. For each data element type, we define a value domain for the valid values. This allows the parser to test to see if any particular data element is recognized as belonging to a specific domain. In turn, the actual parsing algorithms are implemented within an application that, given a character string value will output a sequence of individual tokens. These tokens are then analyzed to determine their element types.

Format specifications for matching distinct patterns are also employed to evaluate the degree of similarity of values to known data element structure. Comparing data fields that are expected to have a pattern, such as telephone numbers, addresses, and identification numbers, enables a measurement of conformance to defined structure patterns.

Extracted tokens are evaluated for pattern matching. If the token does not match a particular pattern, then we will see if that value exists in one of the predefined data domains associated with the parsing metadata. Note that a token may appear in more than one data domain, for which the algorithm might require an attempt at determination based on probability assignation.

Whenever a token value is recognized as belonging to more than one data domain, the algorithm will also assign some probability that the token belongs to each recognized domain. We can do this based on some heuristic rules, which may depend on the context from which the data value was originally taken. For example, it is more likely that the token "HOWARD" is a first name than a city name, if the token was taken from the *name* field. However, it may be equally likely that the token "HOWARD" is a *first name* or a *last name*, and therefore some arbitration must be performed based on context – where the token appeared, whether it appeared next to other known tokens, and so on.

15.4.3 Error Tokens

Knowing that there are going to be character strings that are recognized as not belonging to a known token type is of value, since it suggests the possibility that the parser can be used to determine that invalid values have been assigned to a data element. The simplest form of error handling involves creating a "catchall" token type for unrecognized tokens, coupled with a simple error logging and reporting scheme. A more sophisticated approach anticipates the kinds of errors that might be introduced (recall our error paradigms in section 15.1?) and defining value domains, patterns, and formats to attempt to catch (and therefore possibly correct) different types of known errors.

15.5 Standardization

Although parsing identifies recognizable as well as unrecognizable tokens belonging to a specific element type, standardization attempts to map both the valid and invalid tokens to their semantic meanings, to review the relationship between the values in the original representation, and to suggest options for transformation into a standard form. There are two basic tasks:
1. Rearrange recognized token sets into a standard format
2. Identify known errors and correct them

15.5.1 Standardized Formats

Some examples of the first task include:
- Stripping extraneous punctuation from a character string
- Rearranging different name tokens into a standard "last name, first name" format
- Reordering the location components within a street address

There are many different data element types for which there are context- and content-related standardization rules, such as mapping nicknames to standard names. Given names in many cultures may have variant forms that relate one or more names to at least one standard form. For example, "Bob," "Rob," "Bobby," and "Robbie" are all used for individuals named "Robert," whereas "Liz," "Lizzie," and "Beth," may all be forms of the name "Elizabeth."

This suggests that sets of standardization rules can be embodied as (many-to-one) mappings from one value domain to another value domain. And although the actual individuals represented in the data may not go by the formal name, mapping nicknames to standard names will reduce variation for subsequent data cleansing methods (such as identity resolution, as described in chapter 16). This holds true for other kinds of data as well: last names, business words, addresses, industry jargon, and transaction types are just a few element types where this technique can be used.

In other words, it may not matter if the standard form is applied in a manner inconsistent with real life. For example, "Beth Smith" might not be named "Elizabeth," but we can assign the standard "Elizabeth" to the records anyway, and that will help for subsequent determination of potentially duplicated data. In this context, standardization is being used purely as a means to a different end: enhancement and linkage.

15.5.2 Error Correction

The second task, which presumes knowledge of potential errors, applies rules to correct data. A review of one of the common error paradigms in section 15.1, finger flubs, describes the fact that inadvertent typing errors lead to transposed or replaced letters. By enumerating common character strings for which there is a tendency for finger flubbing along with a set of potential misspellings for each of those words, the parser can seek out those error words, then the application can consult a standardization rule for the corrected version.

Consider the samples in Table 15.2. Commonly misspelled business words can be mapped to their misspellings. In the simplest approach, the misspelled forms can be characterized as "error tokens," recognized, and then standardized to the correct format.

More complex approaches involve heuristic methods such as mapping unknown values to similar valid values, mapping known shortened values (such as nicknames) or aliases (such as vanity location names) to appropriate valid values, or expanding abbreviations or acronyms to fully conformed values. These are reviewed in greater detail in section 15.6.

Table 15.2 Some Examples of Finger Flubs

Target word	Misspellings
their	*ther, thier, thire*
international	*Internatoinal, interational, intrenational*
client	*clinet*

15.6 Defining Rules and Recommending Transformations

Ultimately, data transformations are based on a decision process involving selected application of business rules. After profiling the data for the purposes of data quality assessment (as is described in chapters 11 and 14), many of the discovered anomalies can be adapted into rules for validation, parsing, and standardization.

15.6.1 Defining Rules

Parsing rules can essentially be broken down into the following categories:

- Token description, which is a description of the types of tokens that can appear within a specific data element, along with their format or value domain
- A pattern, which is a format context describing the ways that tokens can be assembled into a recognized value string
- Error tokens that are to be identified for potential transformation
- Error patterns, which are similar to correct patterns except that they incorporate known error tokens to be identified for potential transformation

Token descriptions can take on the form of a specified data range ("integer values between 0 and 100"), a described format or pattern (such as "length two character string in which both characters are upper case"), or a value selected from an enumerated value domain (such as {"AL," "AK," "AS," "AZ," "AR," "CA," "CO," "CT," "DE," "DC," "FM," "FL," "GA," "GU," "HI," "ID," "IL," "IN," "IA," "KS," "KY," "LA," "ME," "MH," "MD," "MA," "MI," "MN," "MS," "MO," "MT," "NE," "NV," "NH," "NJ," "NM," "NY," "NC," "ND," "MP," "OH," "OK," "OR," "PW," "PA," "PR," "RI," "SC," "SD," "TN," "TX," "UT," "VT," "VA," "VI," "WA," "WV," "WI," "WY," "AE," "AP," "AA"}).

Profiling can reveal the collection of patterns associated with the data values in a data element, and in some cases these patterns can be put to use for parsing purposes. For example, profiling the values in a PHONE data element may reveal these patterns (among others), in which the character "9" is used to represent a digit:

- (999) 999-9999
- 999 999-9999
- 999 9999999
- 999 999.9999

- (999) 9999999
- 999-999-9999
- 999.999.9999
- 999,999,9999
- 9-999-999-9999
- 9 (999) 999-9999
- 9-(999) 999-9999

This set of patterns can be adapted as a set of valid telephone number formats.

For error correction purposes, sets of error tokens can be defined as those character strings likely to appear misspelled within the data element. Often theses sets also include common abbreviations or acronyms that are to be expanded. In turn the error patterns describe where those error tokens are likely to appear within the value string.

15.6.2 Transformations

Once a set of patterns for parsing has been defined, the next step is to specify how (if at all) the token values within a known pattern are to be transformed and reorganized. Some specific transformations commonly performed by parsing and stan-dardization tools include:

- Abbreviation expansion, which is a rule-oriented process that maps shortened forms to expanded forms. There are different kinds of abbreviations; one type shortens each word in a set to a smaller form, where the abbreviation consists of a prefix of the original data value. Examples include "INC" for incorporated, "CORP" for corporation, "ST" for street. Other abbreviations contract the word by eliminating vowels or by contracting the letters to phonetics, such as "INTL" or "INTRNTL" for international, "PRGRM" for program, and "MGR" for manager. Another alternate form is the acronym, in which multiple words typically seen together are reduced into a single string, such as "RFP" for "request for proposal." Abbreviation expansion employs data value mappings from the abbreviated form to the full form.
- Differentiation, which is a process that determines that an attribute's value contains more than one value, extracts the values, and presents them back to the user, such as "Mr. and Mrs. Paul Johnson: transformed into "Mr. Paul Johnson" and "Mrs. Paul Johnson."
- Data enhancement, which is a collection of techniques for appending additional data to a record that increases the value

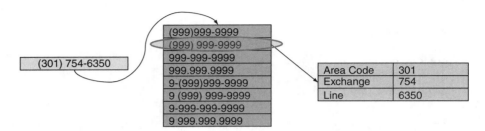

Figure 15.1 Example of parsing, standardization, and normalization.

of the data. Enrichment intelligently merges data from different data sources, adding linkage and table lookups to incorporate new information with the existing record.

Lastly, normalization is the phase that ensures that the resulting standardized formats meet the desired business expectations. For example, parsing the different tokens in the different North American Numbering Plan telephone number patterns will pull out the area code, exchange number, and the line number tokens, while standardization rules will strip out the punctuation. Normalization will assign the tokenized values parsed out of the single character string into three distinct data elements for the area code, exchange, and line numbers, as seen in Figure 15.1.

15.6.3 Automation and Knowledge Bases

Like parsing, these transformations rely on an accumulated knowledge base to help automate the transformation of data into a standardized format, although overreliance on a knowledge base may have some drawbacks:

- Knowledge acquired over a long period of time may lead to an explosion of rules, some of which may conflict with others, leading to a dependency on the order of rule evaluation.
- Rule sets derived from specific types of data may be biased based on the applications from which the data originated.
- Every organization's data is somehow different than any other organization's data, as are the business rules that govern the use of that data.
- Data can only be perceived to be incorrect when there are rules indicating correctness. Relying on one set of correctness rules allows other errors in the data that might have satisfied the provided correctness tests.

Reliance on external rules provides a great starting point, and the process needs continual observation and refinement in order to get the most appropriate automation to meet each situation's business needs.

15.7 The Proactive versus Reactive Paradox

The approaches advocated throughout different chapters of this book for maintaining the necessary levels of data quality are focused on reducing or eliminating the root causes of the introduction of errors. Chapter 9 looked at soliciting, documenting, and operationalizing data quality requirements, chapter 11 looked at data quality assessment to identify potential anomalies and prioritize data issues, and chapter 13 looked at the creation of a data quality service level agreement and the need for continuous inspection and monitoring. Presuming so much effort is spent on attempting to prevent errors, it seems paradoxical that we still must expend resources to *correct* errors!

The paradox stems from three factors associated with the creation, sharing, and consumption of information as a reusable resource:

1. Unguided data reuse: Data sets are typically created for the purposes of facilitating the completion of specific tasks (such as processing transactions or operational activities), but once created, available data sets are freely used for multiple purposes for which they were not originally intended. Reuse almost always relies on reinterpretation, and overloaded data element uses complicate things even more, and when combined with the varying degrees of priority assigned by operational processes to different data elements, what passed as suitable for one purpose is disastrous for other purposes.

2. Opaqueness of latent issues: Even in the best of circumstances, in which an enterprise-wide data quality requirements analysis is performed and organizational expectations have been accumulated, organized, and normalized into an ordered set of continuously monitored data quality assertions, we are still limited in our ability to only anticipate the issues that we know about while blindly ignoring those latent issues that are yet to be revealed.

3. Practical needs: When push comes to shove, it is unreasonable to stand on ceremony when business processes are impeded as a result of low-quality data, and so if there is no way to prevent data errors, there will still be a business requirement to correct those errors.

Table 15.3 Benefits and Drawbacks for Automated Cleansing

Benefits	Drawbacks
Data is brought into conformance with expectations.	Transformations are limited to the body of well-defined patterns, formats, and business rules.
Nonstandard data can be aligned to normalized representations.	With respect to periodic data exchanges, it is likely that the same errors will be repeatedly corrected.
Reference data (in the form of conceptual domains and their associated value domains) can be consolidated and managed as enterprise information assets.	If rules are not managed centrally, they may be applied inconsistently by different data consumers.
The process of defining business rules for standardization helps to resolve semantic differences.	As the size of the set of rules grows, so does the chance that some of the rules will conflict with each other.
Data cleansing rules can be shared with external data providers.	Modifying the order of execution of the standardization rules may lead to different (or unexpected) results.

15.7.1 Benefits and Drawbacks

That being said, it is worth considering some of the benefits and drawbacks of cleansing data with parsing and standardization; some examples are shown in Table 15.3.

15.7.2 Data Supplier Management

In situations where automated cleansing is introduced because shared data originating outside your administrative control does not meet defined standards, there may be an opportunity for a process improvement that can benefit multiple parties, and that lies in exposing the data failures to the data supplier along with the set of parsing and transformation rules identified for cleansing. Practically, an argument may be made that if the data does not meet your needs, the errors may also impact the data supplier in some way as well. Sharing what you have learned with the supplier can be used as leverage to recommend that the supplier consider the risk of introducing errors within their processes and how those errors impact their own business success.

The supplier can use the shared rules to correct their data before publication to downstream consumers, or (better) may perform their own root cause analysis to determine the source of the introduction. If that is not sufficient motivation, in cases where the data supplier is compensated for their data, that supplier may be coerced to agree to a service level agreement in which the quality of the data is measured and its score is used to verify quality as a prerequisite for receiving the compensation.

15.8 Integrating Data Transformations into the Application Framework

Traditionally, parsing and standardization tools have been relegated to the back end of the information production chain and firmly dropped in the lap of the information management engineers. However, as we have seen, the ability to control the data entry and acquisition processes can help in reducing data errors that lead to serious business impacts. Just as these methods are used to recognize data flaws at the end of the business process, it is reasonable to consider using parsing and standardization techniques for data quality management at the *front end* and *throughout* the information production flow.

By integrating parsing and standardization (as well as other data cleansing) services into appropriate locations in the information production flow as value-added services, potential errors at the data value level can be captured at the point of creation or at the point of entry into the environment. In the case of data creation, if the provided values do not meet expectations, they can be presented back to the user, perhaps with suggestions for adjusting the value to one that is acceptable.

In the case of supplied data, records whose values do not pass the parsing validation can be culled for manual review and modification. And even if corrective measures are taken, fixing those errors once at the beginning of the information flow is preferable to fixing multiple times (and possibly inconsistently) downstream. By incorporating parsing and standardization in these ways, data quality and governance can be manifested through continuous inspection, validation, and perhaps even correction at any point that data values are created or updated across the enterprise.

15.9 Summary

This chapter considered aspects of data cleansing – the process of evaluating, validating, and correcting incorrect data – through the use of parsing and standardization techniques.

We looked at some common error paradigms, such as attribute granularity and format conformance, and we discussed other common errors like finger flubs, transcription errors, and transformation errors. When these errors are considered along with the problems associated with information appearing in the wrong context, we hope it will stimulate thought processes for identifying where data errors can be flagged and potentially corrected automatically. Approaches to automation enable data cleansing applications, including data correction, data standardization, expansion of abbreviations, and the application of business rules.

Obviously, data cleansing is an important part of information management, although we would hope that a good data quality program could finesse the need for ongoing data cleansing. Providing parsing and standardization services that can be shared across the enterprise and are invoked early in the information production flow can help in identifying and possibly correcting errors before they can be propagated downstream.

ENTITY IDENTITY RESOLUTION

Both the data quality assessment process and analyses driven by the desire for unifying and consolidating multiple sources of data are likely to expose many situations in which there is duplication of records referring to unique entities. Customer data integration projects, "householding," master product catalogs, security master projects, and enterprise master patient indexes are all examples of technology-driven projects intended to resolve multiple data sets containing similar information into a single view, all with the hope that a unified data asset will lead to better quality data and improved business processes. This is particularly true when the (inadvertently approximate) duplication of data suggests a need to correct sets of records with similar data into a single record of reference.

This drive for "entity unity" creates many opportunities for data consolidation as part of any data integration process, either in the guise of a master data consolidation or as a data cleansing project. And the success of this entity integration process hinges upon the ability to determine when different data instances in the same (or other) data sets refer to the same real-world entity. Searching through data sets for matching records that represent the same party or product is the key to the data consolidation process, whether it is for a data cleansing effort, a householding exercise for a marketing program, or for an enterprise initiative such as master data management.

Identity resolution is a collection of algorithms used to parse, standardize, normalize, and then compare data values to establish that two records refer to the same entity or to determine that they don't. Feeding sets of records into an identity resolution process allows the practitioner to determine which if any of a set records contain references that resolve to a unique entity. Not only that, the data culled from all of the records can be used to materialize a high quality representation of each entity type. This process is used to resolve different entity representations and determine that they all refer to the same real world entity. The techniques used in this process are critical for any business applications that rely on customer or product data integration as part of a data quality assurance, data cleansing, master data management, or enterprise information management initiative. In this chapter we examine the root cause of the "dual challenge" of identity resolution, look at how parsing and standardization contribute to the process, review different ways that similarity scoring and approximate matching algorithms can help determine and resolve identical entities despite variant representations, examine issues regarding errors in record linkage, and determine what data values survive the resolution process.

16.1 The Lure of Data Correction

Because of the perception that inconsistent records represent critical flaws that must be immediately corrected, from a simplistic point of view the value (that is presumably) provided by identity resolution forms the basis for a data correction process. Many environments employ identity resolution as a crutch, applied late in the information production process as a corrective measure. The result of this type of application is a somewhat incremental improvement, but it is neither efficient nor sustainable.

Both issues emerge when data is modified (or as some like to think, "corrected") late in the information stream. An example is correcting customer names after the data has been loaded into a data warehouse in preparation for downstream reporting and analytics. Yet since the records need to be corrected every time the data is loaded into the warehouse, it is likely that the same source records are being corrected repeatedly. And despite the perception that the cleansed records lead to better reporting, the fact that records have changed from the original source means that there are bound to be inconsistencies between what is in the data warehouse and those original sources. A dichotomy between the operational systems and the reporting systems leads to increased manual reconciliation and will not be able to track with a growing demand for reporting and analytics.

Essentially, the practitioner needs to advocate for a different deployment of identity resolution, specifically one that is used to identify potential duplicate records before they are committed into the environment, instead of a long time after the fact. Recommending these approaches to process improvement is supported with a better understanding of what we can call the "dual challenge of unique identity."

16.2 The Dual Challenge of Unique Identity

Identity resolution is intended to address two interesting data integration challenges that are basically two sides of the same coin. One aspect of the challenge is being able to determine when two records refer to the same real-world object, whereas the other aspect is being able to accurately determine when two records *do not* refer to the same real world object. Without being able to make that clear connection or distinction, it would be difficult if not impossible to identify potential duplicate records within and across data sets.

16.2.1 Root Causes of Duplicates

There is an expectation of uniqueness of entities within a data set. This means that for any real-world object to be represented in the data set, there should be only one record. There are a number of potential root causes for the existence of duplicated data about unique entities. Some examples include:

- An environment with an organically developed application infrastructure is likely to have multiple touch points in different business applications that request the same information, and because the applications were developed in essentially their own vacuums, there is little horizontal awareness that the same data is being modeled, requested, stored, and/or used.
- Many organizations grow through acquisition, and each acquired organization has its own sets of products, customer, parts, and so on, that will, at some point, need to be merged.

- Minimal controls supporting a search of existing data sets for a matching record mean that a data entry person who cannot find a record will create a new one.
- Self-service environments (such as web-based applications) easily allow individuals to create multiple records.
- Data sets sourced from multiple vendors are not examined for overlapping records, allowing duplicates to be incorporated multiple times.
- The protocol for use of punctuation when searching for or entering data is only loosely governed.

16.2.2 Using Identity Resolution Services to Prevent Duplicates

Usually a combination of these causes leads to the introduction of duplicated records. By developing services for identity resolution as part of the data creation or integration process early in the information production flow, potential duplicates can be identified before they are absorbed into one of the many organizational data stores. The identity resolution service can be consulted when any new record is to be inserted into a data set. If it turns out that similar record(s) exist, the issue can be addressed once before a duplicate is created or integrated.

16.3 What Is an Entity?

Unique entity identification is a common theme across any data integration effort, but what is meant by *entity*, and how does that notion relate to the data integration process? For the purposes of identity resolution, an entity is an instance of a core data concept that is used in either (or both) transactional/operational and analytic applications; typical examples include "party," "customer," "product," and "part." That core data concept is usually represented using various data models intended to capture that concept's core characteristics. In a perfect world, each entity instance appears only once, is unique within the data set, and can be differentiated from any other instance stored within the data set.

The proliferation of databases and applications, though, creates the opportunity for redundancy and variation:

- Similar structures: Often the same underlying concepts interact in different roles, such as individuals who are manifested as employees, customers, or beneficiaries. In this case, different relational structures may be used to represent the concept of an individual in any of the roles, and each model may carry different data attributes, or even the same attributes but with different data element names and data types.

- Similar content: Data values are subject to variation, especially in semistructured attributes such as individual names or product names. In this situation, different values may be used in different records, even if they represent the same real-world entity.

One common aspect of any entity instance is its name. People, products, documents, and any real-world object all have some kind of handle used for reference. Yet what is the difference between an entity and the names that are used to refer to that entity? An object's name is just an arbitrary collection of character symbols, usually assigned by other individuals, and used as a tag to refer to that object. There is nothing intrinsically definite about an individual's name or a product's name, nor is it particularly unique or distinguishing. In fact, one person might be known by a number of names, each meaningful within a specific context.

As an example, consider the names used to refer to baseball legend Ty Cobb; aside from his given name, he was also referred to by his nickname, "The Georgia Peach." On the other hand, that same name might be used to refer to a completely different entity in some different context as well; continuing our example, the name "Georgia Peach" can also be used to refer to a variety of peach that grows in the state of Georgia. In some cases, the data values are not particularly useful when it comes to differentiation. A quick scan of an online phone directory will yield hundreds, if not thousands of individuals sharing the name "John Smith." Yet even individuals with uncommon names such as "David Loshin" still might not be distinguishable – a search at an online bookstore will show that there are *two authors* with that name!

These examples highlight the fact that despite the arbitrariness of an object's name, it often carries additional descriptive content that could be used to describe more than one single entity, either in different conceptual domains or even (in some instances) within the same domain. But if different objects have the same or similar characteristics, how does one differentiate between them? More to the point: what are the characteristics of any entity set that can be used for unique identification, and consequently record matching and consolidation?

16.4 Identifying Attributes

The need for unique identification is inextricably linked to the success of any data consolidation project, but automating the matching process remains a bit murky, especially in the presence of semistructured or unstructured data values, data errors, misspellings, or words that are out of order. The existence of variable meanings of values appearing in free-formed text attributes also raises the question as to how automated algorithms can parse and organize values and determine which entities are represented, how many times and different ways, and how their identities can be distinguished or resolved. Therefore, automated identity resolution requires techniques for approximate matching that compare a variety of entity characteristics in a search for similarity.

16.4.1 Intrinsic versus Assigned Attributes

Unique identification relies on comparing a combination of intrinsic attribute values (such as a person's eye color) and assigned attribute values (such as a name) to distinguish one entity from another. Name alone may not be enough, nor name plus other intrinsic attributes, but there is a set of "identifying attributes" whose combined values uniquely define an entity. For any collection of entity records, there should be *some* set of data attributes that can be used for unique identification; otherwise, there is the chance that there are exact duplicates in the data set, which would violate the expectation that each entity is represented only once in the data set!

Determining those data elements that can be used as identifying attributes becomes a critical task, whether the objective is for data cleansing, master data management, or other data consolidation needs. There are a variety of ways that these attributes can be included within an entity model, with various data attribute names, data types, sizes, and structures. Sometimes many data attributes are collected into a very wide table, whereas other (perhaps more normalized) models have a relational structure allowing for a more flexible connectivity with different types of characteristics.

16.4.2 Characteristics of Identifying Attributes

Candidate attributes should be evaluated based on how well their constituent semantics and values contribute to addressing both aspects of the dual challenge: enough information to distinguish two records representing different entities and enough to link two records representing the same entity. Some qualitative dimensions for evaluation include:

- Inherence – the degree to which the attribute is intrinsic to the entity. Examples include engineering specifications of a product, such as the "head diameter," "shank diameter," or "threading type" of a screw.

- Structure stability – the degree to which the attribute's structure is subject to variance. Attributes relying on a well-defined value domain have a high degree of structural stability; attributes like dates, telephone numbers, and individual names can appear in a variety of patterns or formats, and have a medium degree of structural stability; free-formed text values have a low degree of structural stability.
- Value stability – the degree to which the attribute's value ever changes, and if so, how frequently. An example of an attribute with a stable value is an individual's eye color.
- Domain cardinality – the size of the domain that the value can take. Attributes that use a domain with many values are more likely to be used for differentiation than those using a domain with a small number of values. For example, a birth date domain may have a limited set of 366 values.
- Completeness – attributes that are missing data are less likely to contribute significantly to differentiation.
- Accuracy – attributes with a high degree of trust may be more reliable for similarity comparisons.

Even though the criteria may be different depending on the entity type as well as the quality of the data, establishing an evaluation process based on reviewing criteria such as these should not only simplify the selection of identifying attributes, but should also lead to more effective choices in supporting the automated record matching and similarity scoring that makes identity resolution possible.

16.5 Similarity Analysis and the Matching Process

When you think about it, automated identity resolution for record linkage is purely based on the fact that errors creep into the data set and prevent straightforward matching algorithms from working. Therefore, we use a more complex means for determining when there are enough *similar* data values shared between two records so that the practitioner can reasonably presume that the records refer to the same entity.

The approximate matching process employs a number of strategies for similarity scoring, which is intended to measure the conceptual distance between two sets of values. The closer the distance between two sets of values, the more similar those two records are to each other. For each data type or data domain, we assign a similarity function. For each set of data attributes, one may also provide a weight to be factored in when computing an overall similarity or difference score.

For example, given a set of data records with name, address, telephone number, and birth date, we can configure a similarity function that is the composition of the weighted similarity functions associated with each of those identifying attributes. Since the name may contribute more to unique identification than the birth date, we would assign a higher weight to the name. High quality telephone numbers may contribute even more to unique identity, suggesting that telephone number be weighted even higher than name! Each data attribute's weight is often based on the measures associated with the criteria used to select the identifying attributes in the first place.

Each data type is subjected to its own similarity scoring method. Integer values may be scored based on a simple distance function – the closer the values are, the higher the score. Although scoring the distance between two numbers is straightforward, a comparison of string-based attributes (such as names, street addresses, descriptions, or dates) is a bit more complex, requiring qualitative measures for "distance." This is a sampling of some of the techniques; these and other algorithms can be adjusted and improved through the incorporation of business rules, statistical analysis, and predictive assessments that can more accurately (and potentially dynamically) adjust weighting factors to provide an accurate and trustworthy similarity score.

16.6 Matching Algorithms

These measures often look at perceived similarity between the character strings and rely on different approximate matching techniques, such as the following:

- Parsing and standardization
- Abbreviation expansion
- Edit distance
- Phonetic comparison
- N-gramming

16.6.1 Parsing and Standardization

As opposed to their use for cleansing, parsing and standardization can be employed as a means of reducing the search space when looking to link entities together. For example, standardization rules can be used to manage a mapping from known names to a normal form that can then be used for similarity analysis. This is not limited to names, but can be used for other kinds of data as well: product types, business words, addresses, industry jargon, and transaction types are just a few element types where this technique can be used.

16.6.2 Abbreviation Expansion

Similar to standardization, abbreviation expansion is a rule-oriented process that maps shortened forms to expanded forms to support the similarity analysis process. Abbreviations come in different flavors. One type of abbreviation shortens each word in a set to a smaller form, where the abbreviation consists of a prefix of the original data value. Examples include "INC" for incorporated, "CORP" for corporation, "ST" for street. Other abbreviations shorten the word by eliminating vowels or by contracting the letters to phonetics, such as "INTL," or "INTRNTL" for international, "PRGRM" for program, "MGR" for manager, etc. Also included are acronyms (such as RFP for "request for proposal") that are formed from the initial letter of each word.

16.6.3 Edit Distance

Comparing character strings for an exact match is straightforward. However, when there are simple errors due to finger flubs or incorrect transcriptions, a human can still intuitively see the similarity. For example, "David Loshin" is sometimes misspelled as "David Loshion," yet in that case one can see that the two names exhibit similarity.

One way to measure similarity between two character strings is to measure what is called the *edit distance* between those strings. The edit distance between two strings is the minimum number of basic edit operations required to transform one string to the other. There are three edit operations: insertion (where an extra character is inserted into the string), deletion (where a character has been removed from the string), and transposition (in which two characters are reversed in their sequence).

As another example, the edit distance between the strings "INTERMURAL" and "INTRAMURAL" is 3, since to change the first string to the second, we would transpose the "ER" into "RE," then delete the "E" and insert an "A." Some people include substitution as a basic edit operation, which is basically a deletion followed by an insertion. Strings that compare with small edit distances are likely to be similar, whereas value pairs with large edit distances are likely to be less similar or not similar at all.

The algorithm for calculating edit distance is implemented using an iterative dynamic programming method.

16.6.4 Phonetic Comparison

There are many situations where data values sound similar even if they are not spelled correctly. Foreign names are often anglicized in different ways, and there are varying transliterations in effect over different time periods (consider Peking vs. Peiping vs. Beijing). Alternatively, "noisy" signals contribute to transcription errors, where similar sounds are inadvertently introduced, leading to misspellings.

To address this challenge, it is necessary to compare character strings based on what they sound like, as well as how the values are spelled, and phonetic comparison processes consider how similar two strings sound. Some of the algorithms sport names such as Soundex, NYSIIS, and Metaphone; all of these encode character strings based on mapping sets of similar sounding consonants and/or vowels into a standard format. As an example, Soundex groups sounds that share characteristics together, and those similar phonetic sounds are represented using the same code.

The first character of the name string is retained, and then codes are assigned to characters using the assignment shown in Table 16.1. Each character string is essentially compressed into a much smaller string, and these compressed strings can be compared for exact equality, or they can be compared for approximate similarity using the other algorithms as well!

Table 16.1 Soundex Code Mappings

Soundex Code	Letter Group
1	B, P, F, V
2	C, S, K, G, J, Q, X, Z
3	D, T
4	L
5	M, N
6	R

16.6.5 N-Gramming

Finger flubs and transpositions are relatively common, but a few transpositions will increase the edit distance between two similar strings. N-gramming is a process that attempts to account for that by looking at any string as a composition of its substrings, grouped consecutively in discretely sized chunks moving from left to right. Each string is broken up into its set of chunks of size n by sliding a window of size n across the word, and grabbing the n-sized string chunk at each step. The chunk size is determined by the "n" in the n-gram; in other words, if we look at substrings of size 3, we are 3-gramming. For example, when bi-gramming, the name "DAVID" is broken up into the four two-character strings "DA," "AV," "VI," and "ID." If two strings match exactly, they will share all the same n-grams, but if two strings are only slightly different, they will still share a large number of the same n-grams. This similarity measure between two strings compares the number of n-grams the two strings share.

16.6.6 Alternate Similarity Methods for Defined Value Domains

Any finite value set that can be described or defined as a data domain should also have a defined similarity methods specific to that data domain. For example, if we have a data domain for geographic regions, we could define a new similarity measure between values from that domain that is based on the "as the crow flies" distance instead of lexicographic distance. As another example, values within a color attribute might be scored for similarity based on closeness within their composite Red/Blue/Green values. For similarity functions within enumerated domains, we can define a mapping between a composed pair of domain values mapped to a similarity score.

16.7 False Positives, False Negatives, and Thresholding

These techniques all contribute to a numeric score of distance between two values, and those scores are optionally scaled and weighted to provide a single similarity score. The similarity score is used within the identity resolution to determine whether two records match. If there is a high degree of similarity, there is a greater likelihood that the records refer to the same entity. If there is a low degree of similarity, there is greater likelihood that the records refer to different entities.

16.7.1 Match/No-Match Thresholding

The perception of "high" and "low" translate into a defined threshold for matching, and conceptually any score above that threshold indicates a match, and otherwise is not a match. Yet recalling our dual challenge of identity resolution, we must beware of the possibilities of two types of failures:

1. Type I errors, or a false positive, in which two records that do not represent the same entity are determined to be a match, and

2. Type II errors, or false negatives, in which two records that do represent the same entity are not matched.

False positives occur when the *match* threshold is set too low, whereas false negatives happen when the *match* threshold is set too high. Practically, therefore, a more effective approach is to provide two thresholds: a *match* threshold and a *no match* threshold. When the similarity score is above the *match* threshold, the process automatically deems the records to represent the same entity, and when the similarity score is below the *no match* threshold, the records are deemed to represent different entities.

Scores that fall between the two thresholds require special attention for two reasons. First, because the identity resolution process was unable to discretely provide an answer, there is a need for human intervention for clerical review. In this situation, a subject matter expert will look at the two records and decide whether they match or not. The second reason involves evaluating any patterns or commonalities in those record pairs selected for clerical review that can help in tweaking the similarity scoring algorithms to improve the precision of the similarity scoring and consequently, improve the matching. Iterative refinement of the similarity scoring algorithms will ultimately help to reduce the area between the *match* and the *no match* thresholds. This in turn will reduce the number of questionable records pairs and the need for manual intervention!

16.7.2 Scoring Precision

When determining the thresholds for matching/not matching, it is important to consider that the scoring precision and criteria are factors of the application context, and that the thresholds may drastically change depending on the business need for searching and matching. On the one hand, direct marketing campaigns are tolerant to some amount of duplicate entities; if a pair of duplicates is not caught, the worst that can happen is that some household might get some extra unwanted mail. In this case, we might prefer that any borderline matches be assumed to be mismatches, so that our coverage is greater. On the other hand, airport screening processes may want to err on the side of caution when filtering out potential terrorists. Visitors whose names match one of the names on the list of known terrorists may be detained, and further investigation is performed to determine if the visitor should not be allowed through security. In this instance, where safety and security are concerned, the worst that can happen if there is a missed match is that a dangerous person is allowed to enter the country, possibly to wreak havoc. In this case, we might prefer that the match threshold be lowered, and that any borderline matches be brought to the attention of the examiners, so as to avoid missing any potential matches.

16.8 Survivorship

Based on the discussion in this chapter, when two records have been determined to refer to the same real-world entity, it means that for some reason a duplicate version of what should be a unique record has been introduced. Whether it is due to a merging of data sets from different sources or the absence of controls to prevent duplicates from being entered is irrelevant if the business objective is to resolve multiple records into a single representation. The challenge is that when faced with two (or possibly) more versions of information supposedly representing the same entity, how do you determine which values from which records will be copied over into the unified record?

The answer to this question reflects a philosophical standpoint regarding the question of "correcting bad data," namely whether one should ever delete or overwrite values assumed to be incorrect. From one perspective, inconsistent data will have impacts to the business users downstream, and reducing or eliminating inconsistency leads to improved business processes. From the other perspective, any piece of information is valuable, and deleting one version of a person's name or a product description because they don't match another version means the deleted version will be lost. Therefore, in some situations, a "best" record can be created that is used to update all identified duplicates, whereas in other situations, all the values are maintained and the "best" version can be materialized on demand when requested. This process of determining the "best" values is called *survivorship*. Of course, if all the values are the same, survivorship is not questioned. But when there are variant data values, survivorship decisions must be related to additional measures of quality. These quality measures are a function of three contextual factors: the quality of the data source from which the record comes, the measure of quality of the record (i.e., based on defined dimensions), and the quality of the specific values.

16.8.1 Quality of the Sources

Different data sources exhibit different characteristics in terms of their conformance to business expectations defined using the types of data quality dimensions described in chapter 8. In general, if a data set is subjected to an assessment and is assigned a quality score, those relative scores become one data point. In other words, given a record from a data set with a high quality score matched with a record from a data set with a lower quality score, it would be reasonable to select values from the first record over the second when they vary.

16.8.2 Quality of the Records

Similarly, each record can be viewed within its own context. Data quality rules can be measured at the record level of granularity (such as completeness of the data elements, consistency across data values, conformance to domain validation constraints, or other reasonableness directives), and these measures can provide a relative assessment of the quality of one record over the other. So when there is variation between the two records and the sources are of equal quality, assess the quality of the records, and that will provide the next level of guidance.

16.8.3 Quality of the Values

If the sources are of equal quality and the records are of equal quality, the next level of precision involves the values themselves. Referring again to the dimensions of data quality discussed in chapter 8, there are some intrinsic dimensions associated with the values themselves, such as syntactic consistency, semantic consistency, and domain validity. Here are some additional suggestions for comparing the values pulled from the set of matched records:

- Value currency: Objectively, more recent values can be presumed to be better.
- Content "density": Value strings containing more information might be considered to be better. A fully spelled-out first name contains more information than just an initial, and that can be presumed to be a better value.

- Value frequency: When multiple records are flagged as potential duplicates, values that appear with higher frequency may be considered more reliable than those that do not.

Of course, these suggestions are still relatively subjective, and in fact may even conflict with each other in practice, so it is wise to integrate your decision process with the results of a data quality assessment (as described in chapter 11).

16.9 Monitoring Linkage and Survivorship

The linkage process and the survivorship process are both amenable to automation, especially if the qualification rules are well defined and can be applied without manual intervention. However, there are always going to be situations in which the value that was automatically selected is not the best choice. Therefore, it is reasonable for the practitioner to institute a monitoring process for review and, if necessary, roll back selections that are not correct.

Manual observations are going to be necessary, and those inspections will require both the original versions of the data that are to be modified along with the proposed modifications. Although manual inspection may be suitable for smaller applications, there is a challenge when the scale of the data exceeds the staff hours available for reviewing the results of the matching and linkage processes. In this case, one approach is to determine a reasonable sample size, take a random sample, and manually inspect the records from the sample.

16.10 Entity Search and Match and Computational Complexity

The basic identity resolution service is searching for a named entity from among records in a known pool. The identifying attributes of what can be referred to as the "search record" are extracted and compared against the identifying attributes of the records that are in the known pool.

To provide this type of service, there must be some method of simplifying the searching process based on the size of the known pool. This is because the computational complexity of searching is based on the number of records in the pool that require comparison. In other words, if there are ten million records in the pool, a naïve approach will compare the search record against the ten million records, which is clearly going to be inefficient.

Some methods must be used to reduce the search time, and most identity resolution techniques will employ a collection of approaches to increase the speed of searching and comparison, such as the following:

- Blocking algorithms: One or more of the identifying attributes are used to restrict the set of records to those that have a higher expectation of matching. For example, one selects out only those records that share all the digits of the search record's ZIP code.
- Tiered block searching: A hierarchy of records is searched. An example is first selecting the records that share the first three digits of the ZIP code, then identifying subsets within those records that match other blocking attributes (such as the first letter of a person's last name, or the area code of the telephone number).
- Parallel execution: This approach allows for exhaustive search by employing many processing units to stream through comparisons of the entire known pool.

16.11 Applications of Identity Resolution

In the past, identity resolution has been used after the fact as a data cleansing activity, to identify errors and attempt to correct them. As organizations become more mature, and as their focus leads toward enterprise entity data management strategies for key data concepts and corresponding entities (such as master data management), identity resolution will be used proactively as a data governance process to reduce the introduction of duplicate or inconsistent entity information.

In addition, identity resolution processes provide added value in particular analytic applications. Any business environment that relies on the ability to identify and match unique entities from a pool of candidate entities will benefit from the use of identity resolution.

16.11.1 Duplicate Reduction and Elimination

Duplicate elimination is a process of finding multiple representations of the same entity within the data set and eliminating all but one of those representations. In some instances, such as with a primary key in a relational database table, duplicates are not allowed, and so it is important to find duplicate records and reduce them to a single entity. When duplicates are exact matches, they can be discovered through the simple process of sorting the records based on the data attributes under investigation. When duplicates exist because of erroneous values, we use identity resolution for finding and eliminating duplicates. Duplicate elimination is essentially a process of clustering similar records together, then using the threshold ranges to guide the determination process.

16.11.2 Merge/Purge

Merge/purge is a similar operation to duplicate elimination, except that while duplicate elimination is associated with removing doubles from a single data set, merge/purge involves the aggregation of multiple data sets followed by elimination of duplicates. Data from different sources will tend to have inconsistencies and inaccuracies when consolidated, and therefore simple matching is insufficient during an aggregation phase. Identity resolution can be used to cluster similar records, which again, depending on the application, can either have a reduction phase automated or passed through human review.

16.11.3 Householding

Householding is a process of resolving a common set of characteristics associated with sets of records that map to a higher order entity. The name is derived from the application of the process to identify a set of individuals living at the same location, or in the same "household." A household could be defined as a single residence, and the householding process is used to determine which individuals live within the same residence. Householding is more than just finding all people with the same last name living at the same address. Associated with householding is a more advanced set of knowledge, such as marital status, family structure, and residence type (single vs. multi-family home vs. apartment).

The business application defines the business objectives of the householding process. For example, a mail-order catalog company might want to ensure that only one catalog was being sent to each residence. In that case, the householding process is meant to aggregate records around a particular delivery address, attempting to recognize all names that belong to the same address, whether or not they belong to the same family. Alternatively, an application that is targeting only the teenagers in a household would want to identify all members of the same family as well as each family member's role. A third application might be to find unmarried couples living together. In each of these applications, the process is similar, but the details of which attributes are used in the process may differ.

16.12 Evaluating Business Needs

Another aspect of attribute similarity scoring incorporates statistics as input to the determination of the weighting factors. Whereas a deterministic approach relies on defined business rules that determine when a pair of records will match, a probabilistic approach incorporates some percentage likelihood that two records will match. Informally, probabilistic algorithms consider both frequency analysis of value sets associated with the identifying attributes and dependent variables that might impact the precision of the scoring.

Resuming an earlier example, the fact that "John Smith" is a very common name means that it is less likely that two records associated with the name "John Smith" are going to be a match. On the other hand, two records associated with the same very uncommon name have a much higher probability of referring to the same individual.

The question often arises: which approach is better? Fortunately, this question is a bit of a red herring; it suggests that one approach is objectively better than the other. But in reality, the effectiveness of an algorithmic approach must be measured within the context of how well it helps achieve the intended business objectives. The following are some factors to consider:

- Number of records
- Required matching precision
- Number of identifying attributes
- Variation in identifying attribute values
- Risk tolerance/business impacts of false positives
- Risk tolerance/business impacts of false negatives
- Performance
- Traceability
- Adaptability to changes over time

Ultimately, deciding which approach is better depends on whether one choice significantly impacts the way identity resolution meets defined business requirements. However, for many business applications, either approach is more than sufficient to satisfy the business needs.

16.13 Summary

The need to link and consolidate entity information with a high level of confidence depends on meeting the challenge of comparing identifying data within a pair of records to determine similarity between that pair or to distinguish the entities represented in those records. Identity resolution employs techniques for measuring the degree of similarity between any two records, often based on weighted approximate matching between a set of attribute values in the two records.

The selection of an identity resolution tool must be accompanied by a process to analyze the suitability of entity data elements as candidate-identifying attributes. This assessment must consider a number of factors, especially when observing how well that attribute selection helps meet the dual challenge associated with unique identification, entity differentiation, and record matching.

By applying approximate matching techniques to sets of those identifying attributes, identity resolution can be used to recognize when slight variations suggest that different records are connected, where values may be cleansed, or where enough differences between the data suggest that the two records truly represent distinct entities. Identity resolution is a critical component of most data quality, master data management, and business intelligence applications. The desire for customer centricity or a comprehensive product catalog is predicated on the capabilities provided by identity resolution to find all records that carry information about each unique entity and resolve them into a unified view.

INSPECTION, MONITORING, AUDITING, AND TRACKING

CHAPTER OUTLINE

Chapter 13 discussed the data quality service level agreement (DQ SLA) and introduced the concepts of instituting metrics and associated measurements for monitoring conformance to the data quality expectations of all data consumers, published via a data quality scorecard. These are the fundamental facets of data quality control and management, and while chapter 13 provided a high-level overview of the processes, this chapter will consider the technical requirements to enable the inspection, monitoring, and auditing conformance to expectations as well as reporting and tracking data quality issues.

We have considered the need for evaluating and reporting compliance of a data set with data quality rules that correspond to defined data consumer expectations and suggested two approaches: auditing and monitoring. Auditing is performed on complete data sets, isolated from other processing activities, outside of any information processing flow. Monitoring identifies rule noncompliance in process, as part of the operational system. The essential difference is that auditing reports noncompliance over a static data set, whereas monitoring reports instance noncompliance in real time, on a periodic basis. Changes can be detected and reported and can be used by the business as feedback to business processes.

In essence, both auditing and monitoring are indications of a more sophisticated information quality program, because both processes are proactive in early detection of potential flaws. And in both cases, there is a need for techniques for defining data quality rules, either as a result of the data quality requirements analysis (as described in chapter 9) or the data quality assessment (as described in chapter 11). In turn, tools are employed to validate the data values against these defined rules and notify the appropriate stakeholders when an exception has been identified.

In addition, once it is has been determined that data values do not conform to the defined expectations, either because of an inspection that has failed, or any new issues that emerge, there must be tools in place for reporting issues and managing them as they are analyzed through the triage processes described in chapter 12. This chapter will review the concept of the data quality service level agreement and then consider the technologies used for deployment.

17.1 The Data Quality Service Level Agreement Revisited

By reviewing the components of the DQ SLA, we can identify the component technologies necessary for instituting inspection, monitoring, auditing, operational data quality control, and data governance. As described in chapter 13, for each data handoff between processes within an information processing stream, we can define a DQ SLA incorporating a number of items. Table 17.1 reviews some of the components of the DQ SLA described in chapter 13, with corresponding operational requirements necessary for execution.

17.2 Instituting Inspection and Monitoring: Technology and Process

Looking at the operational technology requirements, a combination of methods, tools, and techniques is used as part of the process for instituting the inspection and monitoring necessary for observing the SLA:

- IP-MAPs: as described in chapter 12, an information production map describes how information flows from the initial introduction points to the ultimate data consumers

Table 17.1 Dissecting the DQ SLA

SLA Component	Operational Technology Requirements
The location in the processing stream that is covered by the SLA	Refine the information production flow map (IP-MAP) as described in chapter 12
The data elements covered by the agreement	Metadata management and data standards, as described in chapter 10
The data quality dimensions associated with each data element and the expectations for quality for each data element for each of the identified dimensions	Dimensions of data quality, as described in chapter 8, and data quality business rules
The methods for measuring against those expectations and reporting conformance	Inspection using data profiling, business intelligence tools for monitoring and reporting results
The acceptability threshold for each measurement	Data profiling and metadata management for data quality rules
The individual to be notified in case the acceptability threshold is not met; the times for expected resolution or remediation of the issue; the escalation strategy when the resolution times are not met	Incident reporting and tracking

- Metadata management: as discussed in chapter 10, capturing information about data elements and their use
- Data quality business rules using dimensions of data quality, as described in chapter 8
- Data profiling, as presented in chapter 14
- Business intelligence tools as a way of reporting data issues within a prioritization scheme
- Incident management (incident reporting and tracking)

17.2.1 Defining Controls

Once data quality expectations have been reviewed and finalized, the next step in instituting inspection and monitoring is to engineer the inspections framework. This includes identifying the best points in the data flow process to inspect the data, deciding which tools and system platforms will be used, designing the inspection and tracking reports, and specifying the actions to be taken when conformance to data quality thresholds and metrics is exceeded. This can be summarized using these steps:

- **Review data quality expectations:** Look at the expectations associated with the consumers of each information product at the point where the information is used. This will be the starting point for specifying data controls; the data quality practitioner will work *backwards* from the points of data consumption. At each processing stage, data values can be created, modified, or not touched, and the expectations can be validated at the end of the processing stage.
- **Identify critical data elements:** Identify those data elements that are associated with each of the data quality expectations. These will be the subject of any defined controls.
- **Refine the IP-MAP:** The information production flow can be refined at a higher level of granularity to identify each of the specific processing stages. At each stage, specify the inputs and outputs for each of the critical data elements that are the subject of one or more data quality expectations. At each input location and output location, specify whether the level of granularity of data exchange is a collection of data sets, one data set, records, or data values.
- **Identify inspection points:** In conjunction with reviewing the refined information flow diagrams, partnering with the database development and administration teams can provide considerable input in identifying the appropriate processing points where quality inspection procedures can be executed. This is driven by many production factors that must be considered with business needs and best practices. As a general rule, data quality issues should be identified and corrected as early in the data flow process as possible. However, scope of authority, limits to remediation opportunities, and other system limitations constrain the optimal inspection points.
- **Identification of controls:** At the point of data exchange, determine whether controls are required for any levels of granularity associated with any of the data quality expectations. Review the metadata entry to determine if required controls already exist for the data under inspection.
- **Specify rules:** Specify a business rule for the control, specified using a standard representation.
- **Measurement processes:** Provide a measurement process, an acceptability threshold, and variance for the control.
- **Notifications:** List the individuals to be notified when the control fails. This list will include the data stewards associated with the data quality expectations; it may include the business data consumer, as well as other data consumers with a vested interest in the quality of data elements associated with the expectations and rules.

Data Inspection Item Reference Name	Granularity	Criteria	Metric	Conformance Threshold	Sample	Audited Measure	Variance
An identifier used to uniquely reference the inspected data	*Data value, data element, record, column, data set, collection of data sets*	*Description of what is being measured*	*Business measure and scoring*	*The minimum metric score for acceptability*	*The sample size and rules for extraction*	*Measured value*	*Percent variance between threshold and audited measure*

The metadata repository must be updated each time a data control is associated with a data element to indicate:

- The creation and the creator of the data control,
- Where the control is located in the information flow map,
- The business rules associated with the control, and
- The names of the data stewards and the business data consumers to be notified.

By reviewing the metadata entry for the data items to be inspected, the data quality practitioner can determine the list of stakeholders associated with that data element. In addition, if the same controls have already been created for that data element, this can be determined and the business data consumer can be added to the notification list without duplicating the inspection.

17.2.2 Data Quality Inspection Points

Reviewing the information flow diagrams is intended to find the most appropriate locations within the business processes to insert controls for inspection. The most common inspection points include:

- **Data inputs:** Source system input data is an optimal inspection point. The first time data enters the environment is the best location to identify quality issues. When this is not feasible, the information flow diagram can be traced from the source of introduction to identify the next earliest opportunity for inspection.
- **Data outputs:** Data outputs along the information flow can serve two purposes for inspection. The first is to identify

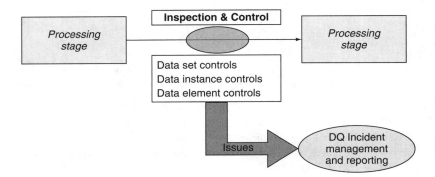

Figure 17.1 Inspection for monitoring data quality controls.

alternative locations for inspection when constraints within the system architecture or the business processes prevent inspection at input points. Second, instituting the same controls before and after a processing stage helps to verify that inputs and outputs are consistent and as expected.

- **Data transformations:** As part of validating that inputs and outputs are consistent, inspection allows for validation of data transformations performed at various points in the process.

The transformation algorithms provide guidance for the relevant quality dimensions to test, although when defining data controls for transformed data, the control must take into account what specific transformations were performed and adjust the control accordingly. For example, consider a transformation of a numeric date code (representing a day offset from a defined start date such as January 1, 1900) into a text string representing a specific version of a Gregorian calendar date. In this case, the control for validating the formatted date string will be different than the control validating the numeric offset, even if both controls verify the same reasonableness constraint.

Figure 17.1 shows how inspection for data controls at different levels of granularity can be located at the handoff points in a business process flow.

17.3 Data Quality Business Rules

Data quality business rules are materialized as a by-product of two processes. The first is the data requirements analysis process (as described in chapter 9), in which the business data consumers are interviewed to identify how downstream applications depend on high quality data, and clarifying what is meant by "high quality." The data requirements analysis process will result in a set of data quality assertions associated with dimensions of data quality. The second process providing data quality rules is the data quality assessment (chapter 11), in which empirical analyses using tools such as data profiling are used to identify potential anomalies that can be transformed into directed business rules for validation.

Either way, the intention is to use the business rules discovered to measure compliance. This implies that we have some reasonable capability to manage business rules metadata and have those rules be actionable in a proactive manner. Most data profiling tools provide a capability to document and manage business rules that can be directly incorporated into later profiling sessions, or even as invoked services to validate specific data values, records, or data sets on demand.

On the other hand, if there is no data profiling tool for managing data quality rules, there remain approaches for representing and managing data quality rules using logical expressions. Recall that chapter 9 reviewed the definition of different types of data rules reflecting these dimensions:

- **Accuracy,** which refers to the degree with which data values correctly reflect attributes of the "real-life" entities they are intended to model
- **Completeness,** which indicates that certain attributes should be assigned values in a data set
- **Currency,** which refers to the degree to which information is up-to-date with the corresponding real-world entities
- **Consistency/reasonability,** including assertions associated with expectations of consistency or reasonability of values, either in the context of existing data or over a time series
- **Structural consistency,** which refers to the consistency in the representation of similar attribute values, both within the same data set and across the data models associated with related tables
- **Identifiability,** which refers to the unique naming and representation of core conceptual objects and the ability to link data instances containing entity data together based on identifying attribute values
- **Transformation,** which describes how data values are modified for downstream use

As is shown in Table 17.2, in general, almost every high-level rule can be expressed as a condition and a consequent:

If (condition) then (consequent)

Violators are expressed as those records where the condition is true and the consequent is false:

If (condition) and not (consequent)

Table 17.2 Example Data Quality Business Rules

Dimension	Rule type	Example Representation	Pseudo-SQL
Accuracy	Domain membership rules specify that an attribute's value must be taken from a defined value domain (or reference table)	*Table.Data_element* taken from *named domain*	Select * from *table* where *data_element* not in *domain*
Completeness	A data element may not be missing a value	*Table.Data_element* not null	Select * from *table* where *data_element* is null
Currency	The data element's value has been refreshed within the specified time period	*Table.Data_element* must be refreshed at least once every *time_period*	Select * from *table* where TIMESTAMP(*data_element*) within *time_period* Note that this will require timestamps as well as a coded method for accessing and verifying the time period duration
Structural consistency	The data attribute's value must conform to a specific data type, length, and pattern	*Table.Data_element* must conform to *pattern*	Select * from *table* where *data_element* not in_pattern (*pattern*) Note that this will require a coded method for parsing and verifying that the value matches the pattern
Identifiability	A set of attribute values can be used to uniquely identify any entity within the data set	(*Table.data_element1, Table.data_element2, Table.data_element3, Table.data_element4*) form a unique identifier	Join the table against itself with a join condition setting each of the set of attributes equal to itself; the result set will show records in which those attributes' values are duplicated
Reasonableness	The data element's value must conform to reasonable expectations	*Table.data_element* must conform to *expression*	Select * from *table* where NOT *expression*
Transformation	The data element's value is modified based on a defined function	*Table.data_element* derived from *expression*	Select * from *table* where *data_element* <> *expression*

Therefore, as long as the rule can be reduced into the if–then format, it can be expressed in any number of coded representations. For example, here is the transformation into SQL as a select:

Select * from table where (condition) and not (consequent)

For more information on the representation of data quality business rules, consider reading one of my previous books, "Enterprise Knowledge Management – The Data Quality Approach," published by Morgan Kaufmann in 2000.

17.4 Automating Inspection and Monitoring

Relying on manual reviews of the validity of data at any (if not all) of the control points in the information flow will prove to be an overwhelming task. Automating the inspection will simplify the role of the data stewards, allowing them to prioritize issues as they emerge and concentrate on remediating the most critical ones.

In general, controls for inspecting the quality of data values, data elements, and data instances can be integrated directly into the business processes themselves. Controls for collections of data instances or one or more data sets require the availability of the data to be reviewed and, without the ability to manage persistent state, would only allow the inspection to be performed when all the data items are available, such as when there is a bulk exchange between processing stages.

17.4.1 Inspection Services

The DQ SLAs and data quality scorecard become the focal point for the inspection services that monitor the controls and provide metrics demonstrating that defined expectations are being met. An inspection service encapsulates the methods for evaluating conformance with data quality business rules. We have already discussed two approaches for automation methods for encapsulation:

- Data profiling: Data profiling tools can be configured with rules that can be invoked directly to return the validity result. In addition, data sets can be passed to a profiler, which can execute a prearranged set of rules, returning scores corresponding to each validation. This provides the ability to measure compliance with data rules directly within the business process or at specific handoff points.
- SQL queries: For persistent data sets stored in databases, query and reporting tools can be invoked at handoff points to provide counts and result sets, but this approach is not as adaptable to in-process inspection.

Nor are we limited to these approaches; rule engines, rule-based programming languages, and even well-architected object-oriented frameworks can be used for programming and then encapsulating both in-process and handoff inspections.

17.4.2 Auditing

An audit is a review of a whole data set to evaluate compliance with a set of business rules that can be applied regarding relationships across a collection of data items at discrete periods. For example, an organization might arrange for a weekly audit of corporate data sets, with the result forwarded to data stewards and their management hierarchy as a way of observing governance performance.

When a data profiling tool provides auditing capability using managed business rules, the tool can be used to audit the data. If the tool does not provide auditing capability, the auditing process should be coupled with a profiling session that reports on the relevant metrics, or query/reporting tools can be employed. The result of an audit is a report that details each business rule that is being reviewed, the way that rule is measured, the expectation, any desired goals, and the actual measurement.

17.4.3 Monitoring

Monitoring is more of a business rule conformance process to be integrated into a business process along with a method for notification when a violation is detected. For example, a business rule might assert that a new customer record is incomplete if the telephone number is not supplied. For business rule monitoring, each rule must be accompanied by an action to take if the rule is violated. Typically this is either a rejection of the data instance with some explanation of the violated rule, or some message sent to notify a third party that a violation has occurred. Continuing the same example, when an incomplete customer record is identified, the individual entering the data is notified that part of the record is missing and is prompted to supply the missing values.

For the most part, because this monitoring is intended for in-process inspection, the business rules that may be used in monitoring may be limited to those that apply at the attribute and record level. Rules that apply across all elements in a data set may not be completely testable when the data set is not complete, and in an application where new records are being processed in a stream, the complete set will not be available.

In that situation, the monitoring must wait until a point in the information flow in which the necessary data sets are all available for review, and at that point the inspection service can be invoked.

17.5 Incident Reporting, Notifications, and Issue Management

Growing awareness in the organization that data quality is managed proactively will also lead to modified expectations associated with identified errors. In organizations with a low level of data quality maturity, individuals might not be able to differentiate between a system error that resulted in incorrect business process results (like those associated with programming errors) as opposed to data errors (such as inconsistencies with data inputs). It is the data quality practitioner's role to educate the staff in this distinction, as well as transitioning the organization to properly respond to both emergent errors and remediation (as described in chapter 12).

Conveniently, many organizations already have some framework in place for incident reporting, tracking, and management, so the transition to instituting data quality issues tracking focuses less on tool acquisition, and more on integrating the concepts around the "families" of data issues into the incident hierarchies and training staff to recognize when data issues appear and how they are to be classified, logged, and tracked. The steps in this transition involve addressing some or all of these directives:

- Standardize data quality issues and activities, which may be organized around the identified dimensions of data quality.
- Provide an assignment process for data issues, which will be based on the data governance framework from the organizational standpoint, and on the DQ SLAs from an operational standpoint.
- Manage issue escalation procedures, which should be explicit in the DQ SLAs.
- Document accountability for data quality issues, in relation to the data stewards assigned to the flawed data sets.
- Manage data quality resolution, also part of operational data governance.
- Capture data quality performance metrics.

This last bullet item is of particular interest, because aside from improving the data quality management process, issue and incident reporting and management can also provide performance reporting, including mean-time-to-resolve issues, frequency of occurrence of issues, types of issues, sources of issues, and common approaches for correcting or eliminating problems. A good issues tracking system will eventually become a reference source of current and historic issues, their statuses, and any factors that may need the actions of others not directly involved in the resolution of the issue.

17.5.1 Incident Reporting

There are essentially two paths for reporting data quality incidents. The first takes place when an automated inspection of a defined data quality control fails. Alerts are generated when inspection shows that control indicates missed objectives. The second occurs when an individual recognizes that unexpected error has impacted one or more business processes and will manually report the incident. In either case, reporting the incident triggers a process to log the event and capture characteristic information about the incident, including:

- A description of the error,
- Where and how it manifested itself,
- The name of the individual or automated process reporting the incident,
- The measure or data quality rule that failed as well as associated scores,
- The type of error (e.g., data quality dimension),
- The list of stakeholders notified,
- The time the incident was reported,
- The resolution time as specified in the data quality service level agreement, and
- The name of the data steward with initial responsibility for remediation.

At some point, the data steward will start the remediation process, initially assessing impact and assigning a priority.

17.5.2 Notification and Escalation

The DQ SLA will enumerate the list of individuals to be notified for each data quality rule and each type of violation. Once an incident is reported, the DQ SLA will indicate the expectations regarding resolution of the issue in terms of completeness and in terms of the time frame in which the issues is to be resolved. The resolution process may involve multiple steps, and each time one of the associated tasks is completed,

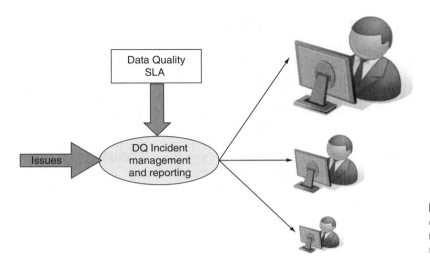

Figure 17.2 Progressive escalation to more senior managers as issues remain unresolved.

the record in the incident management systems needs to be updated to reflect the changed status.

If one of those steps does not occur within the defined time frame, it suggests that the data steward may require additional assistance (or perhaps "motivation") from superiors in that steward's management chain. An escalation strategy (as depicted in Figure 17.2) provides a sequential list of more senior managers within an organization notified when the level of service defined in the DQ SLA is not met.

Of course, both the level of attention and tolerance decrease as one marches up the management chain, so it is in the best interests of the data governance team to resolve critical issues within the directed time frames.

17.5.3 Tracking

One last aspect of the incident management process is to maintain tabs on the status of outstanding data quality issues. In chapter 12 we reviewed a process for determining criticality of data quality issues. Tracking allows for the data governance team to review issues that have not yet been resolved, ordered by their prioritized level of criticality. This provides an opportunity to review the assignment of priority, decide to either increase or decrease the dedicated resources assigned to each issue, and perhaps change the assigned priority.

17.6 Putting It Together

Data quality incident management combines different technologies to enable proactive management of existing, known data quality rules derived from both the data requirements analysis and the data quality assessment processes, including data profiling, metadata management, and rule validation. The introduction of an incident management system provides a forum for collecting knowledge about emergent and outstanding data quality issues and can guide the governance activities to ensure that data errors are prioritized, the right individuals are notified, and that the actions taken are aligned with the expectations set out in the data quality service level agreement.

DATA ENHANCEMENT

The rates at which data volumes are growing continue to increase, encompassing both structured and unstructured data. Making sense out of the massive data archives (as more information is being pumped into the system) is enough of a challenge, as is capturing and communicating those critical pieces of information to data consumers. Data enhancement is a process of increasing the value of a data instance (or data set) by appending additional value-added knowledge. Typically, enhancement is performed by mapping one data set to other data sets and pooling information taken from multiple sources. The goal of enhancement is to identify actionable knowledge from collections of data that are used to improve consuming business processes. In essence, enhancement can be used to learn more about entities using data taken from a set of databases, and potentially increase the quality of a given data set.

One example of enhancement is to improve the precision of targeted marketing while reducing credit risk. An enhancement process would combine records in the customer database, geographic characteristics of each customer's home location, and credit scores. The resulting customer records can be ordered in terms of the biggest predisposition to purchasing certain products while using the credit score to minimize exposure to default on payments. In turn, that enhanced data can be used to make special offers to these preferred customers.

Another example involves enabling efficient financial transaction interchange. In the financial world, different companies have different representations for securities trades, but there are unique identifiers for each stock, option, bond, and so on. Through combining incoming transaction messages with internal data tables, we can enhance financial electronic data interchange messages to enable automated straight through processing.

In any case, data quality is critical to successful enhancement, and enhancement is often intended to improve data quality. In this chapter, we look at the data enhancement process and its dependence on parsing, data standardization, identity resolution and matching, and how they are used as part of the enhancement process.

18.1 The Value of Enhancement

The value of data instances collected purely for supporting transactional systems are limited to the operational aspects of successfully completing the transaction. Once the transaction has completed, the data's original purpose has been fulfilled. The inclination to collect data from multiple transaction systems for analytic purposes is intended to drive business process improvements by leveraging the combination of different pieces of data to expose some piece of actionable knowledge.

As a straightforward example, sales representatives are provided with lead lists – the contact information (name, telephone number, address, etc.) for a set of prospective customers. For any individual prospect on the lead list, there is some chance that the sales representative might close a sale, but it would be anybody's guess as to which lead is more likely to convert to being a customer than any other. In the absence of any additional knowledge, there is no particular benefit to selecting any one lead over another, with an expectation that some minimum amount of time must be spent with *all* of the prospects in order to reach the sales volume quota.

To optimize the sales process, the account managers would like to prioritize the leads and contact those prospects who are most likely to buy a product; in turn, even those high-probability leads might be ordered based on the projected sales volume. None of this can be done without any insight about the prospects. Additional data can be added to each lead on the list, such as demographic data detailing the lead's household income, or even analytic information derived from sales histories to help predict the probability of that lead's inclination to purchase your product. In this case, the value of the original list has been improved by adding the extra demographic or predictive information.

The value of an organization's data can be greatly increased when that information is enhanced. Data enhancement is a method to add value to information by accumulating additional information about a base set of entities and then merging all the sets of information to provide a focused view of the data.

18.2 Approaches to Data Enhancement

Traditionally, many opportunities for enhancement took place at some unspecified time and place downstream from the creation or integration of the records being enhanced. Increasingly, the need for integrating real-time analytics and predictive analysis within business presents opportunities for introducing enhancements directly in the information production streams. This suggests two approaches to data enhancement that can support either enhancement requirement – enhancing data in batch, and enhancing data within the structure of an operational business process.

18.2.1 Batch Enhancement

One approach is batch enhancement, where data collections are extracted and subjected to parsing, standardization, consolidation, and aggregation. In this approach the methods are applied to link records across a collection of data sets. These may all be internal data sets, or some internal data sets linked with reference data sets or externally sourced data sets. Algorithms can then be applied to append the enhancements to the selected records.

18.2.2 Inlined Enhancement

The other approach will focus on incrementally improving data instances by inlined linkage with other data sources, adding information to records at particular locations within the business process flow. Incremental enhancements are useful as a component of a later analysis stage, such as sequence pattern analysis and behavior modeling. In this approach, there is a need for inlined searching and matching, typically implemented using parsing, standardization, and identity resolution for the linkage. Once the data instances to be used for enhancement are located, the methods can be applied to append value-added attribute information to the data instance under scrutiny.

18.3 Examples of Data Enhancement

The objective of data enhancement is to append information to a target data set and increase its ability to improve or optimize a business process. In essence, the added information addresses improvement in achieving one or more of the business impacts or value drivers introduced in chapter 1. The example provided in section 18.1 shows how demographic data improves the sales process, thereby improving revenue generation as well as productivity. Other examples include:

- Real-time traffic and weather data used to enhance supply chain decisions for truck routing
- Drug effectiveness data used to enhance patient health records to assist in suggesting treatment options
- Part commodity prices and availability used for enhancing product data to inform just-in-time manufacturing processes
- Customer data enhanced with product preferences used to organize ad placement on web sites

In each of these examples, the desired outcome is improved as a result of appending the appropriate piece of information at the right time. The "right time" is triggered by some expectation on behalf of the business process and incorporates the different ways employed for enhancing data. Some of these enhancements are derived enhancements, whereas others are based on incorporation of different data sets. This section reviews alternate types of enhancements, such as the ones suggested in Table 18.1.

18.3.1 Audit Data

In business processes that require some degree of tracing capability (such as supply chain processing), a frequent data enhancement is the addition of auditing data. Creating a tracking system associated with a sequence of related events provides a framework for evaluating efficiency within a business process. For example, in a customer support database, each time a customer has a discussion with a customer support representative, both the conversation and the name of the representative the customer spoke to are noted, along with a timestamp.

18.3.2 Temporal Data

Historical data provides critical insight to a business intelligence program. Although in some cases the history is embedded in the collected data, other instances require that activity (i.e., events or transactions) be enhanced by incrementally adding

Table 18.1 Types of Enhancements

Enhancement Type	Sample Business Context	Enhancement Example
Audit	Maintain a history of events or interactions	Patient profile is enhanced with types of drug samples provided
Temporal	Maintain a history of events or interactions	Customer profile is enhanced with the date and time that the customer called customer support
Context	Specific information about the business context	Customer emailed using PDA
Geographic	Information about location of a business transaction	Encompassing county data used to calculate tax rates
Demographic	Clustering and classification	Customer age, sex, income
Psychographic	Clustering and classification	Customer preference data
Inference	Derive conclusions based on activity	Web site advertisement placement
Role	Inference regarding the entity in relation to other entities	Characterization of individual's level and sphere of influence within a social network.

timestamps noting the time at which some event occurred. With data, this can refer to the time at which a transaction took place, the time at which a message was sent or received, the time at which a customer requested information, and so on.

18.3.3 Context Data

Sometimes it is not the time that is interesting, but rather the place where some action was performed that is critical. The place, or context, of data manipulation is an enhancement as well. A physical location, a path of access, and the login account through which a series of transactions were performed are examples of context that can augment data. Examples include:

- Logging the IP address from which a user's account is accessed,
- Tracking the stores in which credit cards are used,
- Keeping track of the companies from which specific products are purchased, and
- Identifying and logging the locations from which calling-card calls are made.

Contextual enhancement also includes tagging data records in a way to be correlated with other pieces of data. An interesting example can be seen on a number of retail web sites, where source location information regarding sales popularity of particular products is displayed under the heading "This item is popular with these groups." In terms of personal marketing, using contextual popularity provides both an internal direct marketing directive ("if the user's domain is one of the popularity groups, then display the product on the home page") as well as an information-driven influence technique ("be like the others in your peer group and buy this product").

18.3.4 Geographic Data

Data enhanced with geographic information allows for analysis based on regional clustering, as well as data inference based on predefined geodemographics. The first kind of geographic enhancement is the process of address standardization, where addresses are cleansed and then modified to fit a predefined postal standard, such as the U.S. Postal Service standard. Once the addresses have been standardized, other geographic information can be added, such as locality coding, neighborhood mapping, latitude/longitude pairs, or other kinds of regional codes.

18.3.5 Demographic Data

Demographics describe the similarities that exist within an entity cluster, such as customer age, marital status, gender, income, and ethnic coding. For business entities, demographics can include annual revenues, number of employees, size of occupied space, number of parking spaces, and years in business. Demographic enhancements can be added as a by-product of geographic enhancements or through direct information merging.

18.3.6 Psychographic Data

Psychographics describe what distinguishes individual entities within a cluster. For example, psychographic information can be used to segment the population by component lifestyles based on individual behavior. This includes product and brand use, product and brand preferences, organization memberships, leisure activities, vacation preferences, commuting transportation style, shopping time preferences, and so on. Psychographic information is frequently collected via surveys, contest forms, customer service activity, registration cards, and specialized lists. The trick to using psychographic data is in being able to perform the linkage between the entity within the organization database and the supplied psychographic data set.

18.3.7 Inferred Enhancements

Analysts are constantly asked to draw conclusions from supplied data, and in fact a large component of business intelligence (BI) process is interpreting the patterns that emerge through analysis and applying some business value to that interpretation. Information inference is a BI technique that allows the user to draw conclusions about the examined entity based on supporting evidence and business rules. Inferred knowledge can be used to augment data to reflect what we have learned, and this in turn provides greater insight into solving the business problem at hand.

18.4 Enhancement through Standardization

Chapter 10 discussed data standards, and chapter 15 discussed standardization, and we can broadly summarize standardization as ensuring that a data instance conforms to a predefined structural format. That format may be defined by an organization with some official authority (such as the government), through some recognized authoritative board (such as a standards committee), through a negotiated agreement (such as XML schemas used for data interchange agreements), or by generally accepted convention (such as the use of hyphens to separate the parts of a U.S. telephone number).

Converting data to a standardized format is an extremely powerful enhancement. Because a standard is a distinct model to which all items in a set must conform, there is usually a well-defined rule set describing both how to determine if an item conforms to the standard, and what actions to take in order to bring the offending item into conformance. A significant value proposition for standardization is that since it relies on predefined structures and formats, it can be largely automated. A good example is ensuring that a U.S. street address has been assigned the correct ZIP code, and inserting the correct ZIP code when it is missing.

Automated standardization is not always simple; there are some situations that are relatively complex, such as standardizing person names, or differentiating person names from business names. But when the standard can be directed using defined parsing and transformation rules, the process is more likely to be automated. Continuing our example, one can standardize the ZIP code portion of a U.S. street address through a process that is determined based on the ways that ZIP codes are assigned. The U.S. is divided into geographic regions designated by a 5-digit ZIP code. Each region includes a number of the streets within a political geography, and the U.S. Postal Service maintains a database that maps street addresses to ZIP code regions. Given a street address within a named city and state, the determination of the correctness of the ZIP code is the same as the process for standardizing the address by adding a ZIP code:

1. Determine if the city is a valid city name within the state. This corresponds to a query in a city–state mapping table.
2. If so, determine if the street name is a valid street name within that city. Again, this corresponds to a query in a database mapping between streets and cities.
3. If the street is valid, check to see if the address (the street number) is in a range that is valid for that street. Another mapping lookup, and this mapping, should also reflect the ZIP code mapping as well. A test will compare the found ZIP code, and an assignment will just use that found ZIP code.

If the search fails, the default next step would be to resolve the ZIP code to the closest level in the geographic hierarchy. For example, if the street is valid, but the number is not, then assign the ZIP code for the street. If the street does not exist within the city, assign a default ZIP code for that city. Though the result is not always correct, it may still be in standard form.

18.5 Enhancement through Context

There is an ever-increasing number of touch points associated with the entities represented within our business applications. Explosive growth in electronic commerce via the Internet not only augments the traditional brick and mortar world, but with additional media channels (such as mobile communications), subchannels throughout the World Wide Web, as well as social media networks, there is a wealth of context information that potentially adds value to operational business processes.

In other words, data can be enhanced with context information. This kind of information includes the virtual location from which the activity takes place (e.g., visiting a particular web domain name), a physical location (e.g., from a home computer versus an office computer), process or data lineage, type of event or activity, and other data that can be collected directly during the business process.

This type of enhancement provides substantial marketing benefits, because context information can be fed into behavior analytics for reporting on the behavior of users, based on their locations or times of activity. These analyses can be quite revealing and the results themselves become pieces of actionable information that can enhance other data sets. As an example, a web-based business can determine that many of its customers browse through catalog entries during the daytime while at work, but peruse the content for a subselection of entries at home in the evening. The business can retool the web site to provide different kinds of presentations during work hours or leisure hours that will encourage users to purchase products.

18.5.1 Lineage

An interesting enhancement is the operation of associating lineage with a data instance, which would consist of a source code and a timestamp (i.e., marking the time at which the data was updated). Lineage enhancements can be as simple as a single string data field describing the source, or as complex as a separate table containing a timestamp and a source code each time the record is updated, related through a foreign key. Because there is a complete audit trail for all tagged data records, this second approach allows for a more complete history to be compiled.

One interesting benefit is that later analysis can show the value of different sources of data, as well as different pathways or traces of modifications to data. For example, if it can be shown that one particular original data source consistently provides information that is never updated, it can be inferred that that provider's information is more reliable than that of a provider whose records are consistently updated. Another example might allow for measures of volatility with respect to information acquired through different tracks.

18.5.2 Audit Trails

The more advanced form of this enhancement allows for not just a source of a creation of, or an update to a data set, but also additional activity fields. When we combine source, time, and activity information into a record, we can trace back all occasions at which a piece of information was touched, giving us the opportunity to truly understand how activities cause data to flow through a system.

18.6 Enhancement through Data Merging

As one might surmise, the key to enhancement is linkage – the ability to connect records from disparate data sets based on a common theme (more specifically represented as some set of attribute values) and derive some information that adds value to one or more of the connected records. These kinds of operations are performed all the time, most commonly as database joins. Other situations, in which a database join cannot effectively identify the proper precision for connectivity, other techniques are employed, especially parsing, standardization, and identity resolution.

How is data linkage and merging done? It is basically a matching operation: select a number of attributes that can be used to uniquely identify the entity or its characteristics (we'll call them the identifying attributes), and then search for all records that have the same attributes. Those records form a candidate set for enhancement, and all of those records may contribute data to a new enhanced piece of information. This process works well when merging new records into an already existing data set, but may be less effective when applied directly to different data sets. Strategic value can be attained through combining data sets, especially when the analyst performing the linkage and merging employs a combination of technical savvy and qualitative assessment regarding the information that needs to be combined and how additional knowledge can be derived.

18.6.1 Examples

Some examples of processes that benefit from data enhancement through merging include:

- **Householding:** A process called householding attempts to consolidate a set of entities to a single grouping unit based on the database record attribution. A household consists of all people living as an entity within the same residence. The simplest example is that of consolidating husband and wife records to a single residential household. Households can be differentiated by demographic data as well as geographic data. In a residential household there may be different subsidiary roles, such as primary earner and primary decision maker (these two may be different individuals). More complex examples include identifying dependents, categorizing dependents by class, and separating out boarders or transient residents. Householding can be used to improve demographic analysis and marketing optimization, and target particular defined roles in the household. Alternatively, there are other household concepts that benefit from this process, such as corporate hierarchies and organizational structures.
- **Affinity and collaborative marketing:** Affinity programs, which manage interactions with customers based on a preexisting affiliation with an organization, such as frequent

traveler programs or vanity credit cards. Affinity programs are often coupled with both internal and collaborative marketing efforts, such as health and life insurance tie-ins, product discounts, and service discounts. In each of these cases, there is some aspect of data merging. To exploit potential synergies among partners, many companies will embark on collaborative marketing campaigns. While some organizations may try to build cooperative marketing programs using "brute force" techniques, a more refined method to create a more effective marketing campaign combines data enhancement as a by-product of database merging to provide the desired narrowed focus for marketing.

- **Corporate mergers:** When two companies merge, they will eventually need to merge their customer databases, employee databases, and their base reference data. Consolidating customer records prevents potentially embarrassing situations, such as multiple sales agents contacting the same customer, or attempting to market products the customer already has. However, because each organization will have a different perspective for managing customer data, the merging process will yield enhancements as the records are combined.

- **Data cleansing:** Because customers move, get married or divorced, change their name, and so on, very often, large customer databases tend toward entropy in turns of accuracy. This temporal entropy coupled with the potential for introduced errors through manual entry lead to frequent duplication for all types of data entities. Linking the duplicate records together is a way to cleanse the database and eliminate these duplicates.

- **Health information management:** Many countries already mandate the creation and use of electronic medical records. However, patients are able to see many different practitioners, which presents the opportunity for variation in entity representation. In addition, many privacy regulations limit the ability to share identifying data. These two issues mean that effective data enhancement is necessary for managing master patient indexes (sometimes referred to as EMPI, or enterprise master patient index). More interesting from an enhancement perspective, professional medical cooperatives may pool their individual patient information (most likely having been made anonymous first) as a means for building up a knowledge base about diagnostic methods and treatments. The information, which consists of a patient's history, diagnosis, and treatment history, must be enhanced to fit into the collaborative data model.

- **Fraud detection:** Data enhancement can be used as a way to both identify fraudulent behavior patterns and use those patterns to look for fraud. Opportunities exist for fraud in all kinds of businesses, such as transaction-based services (e.g., telephone and mobile phone service), claim-based services (all kinds of insurance), or monetary transaction–based services (where there are opportunities for embezzlement, for example). In fact, there are many areas of crime that call out for data matching and merging: money laundering, illegal asset transfer, drug enforcement. This is referred to as POI (person of interest) analysis.

18.6.2 The Data Merging Process

One might say that data enhancement is essentially the "business end" of a number of data quality and data cleansing techniques. At the most basic level, enhancement is performed by selecting the identifying attributes for connectivity, then joining two data sets and looking at the records that intersected. Those records are candidates for linkage, and the other attributes are examined to determine the closeness of a match. In this case, linkage is established only when the chosen attributes match exactly. But simple record linkage is limited when the data sources are in different formats, when critical data values are missing, when the data sets are not current, or if the attribute values used for linking have slight variations. These are the situations that rely on our data quality techniques:

- Profiling for assessing the suitability (i.e., identifiability) of the attributes for linkage
- Parsing and standardization for determining a normalized representation for linkage
- Identity resolution to accommodate variation and missing data

18.7 Summary: Qualifying Data Sources for Enhancement

The results of enhancement can only be trusted under the presumption that the source data sets are of sufficient quality to meet business objectives. In some instances, there is a predisposition to consolidate data from multiple sources without assessing their quality first, and this typically leads to questionable results. Yet this process cannot be performed effectively without qualifying the expectations as well as the source data.

Before implementing the matching and linkage, it is worth reviewing these aspects of the process:

1. How do business processes benefit from enhancement?
2. What data characteristics are to be improved as a result of enhancement?
3. What business questions are answered as a result of enhancement?
4. What decisions are enabled as a result of enhancement?
5. What source data attribute values are required to satisfy the business process requirements?
6. What source data attributes are required for matching and linkage?
7. Do the source data attributes meet the business expectations?

Fortunately, the process for answering these questions relies on those same data quality principles and processes presented in this book: data quality assessment, profiling, and the components of data validation and cleansing.

MASTER DATA MANAGEMENT AND DATA QUALITY

An unintended consequence of the history of technology development is that organizational resources (including staffing, hardware, and software) end up being aligned to accommodate the needs of business applications for different lines of business. Application architectures designed to support the operational aspects of each line of business have required their own information technology support, and all its accoutrements – data definitions, data dictionaries, table structures, application functionality, and so on, all defined from the aspect of that business application.

The result is that what we refer to as the "enterprise" is often composed of many applications referring to multiple, sometimes disparate sets of data that are intended to represent the same or similar business concepts. Previous chapters have already dealt with the issue of variant definitions and semantics, as well as the way that identity resolution is used to search for and merge similar data instances. But there is a growing desire to consolidate common data concepts from multiple sources, analyze that data, and ultimately turn it into actionable knowledge for the common good.

To exploit consolidated information for both operational and analytic processes, an organization must be able to clearly determine what those commonly used business concepts are, identify the different ways those concepts are represented, collect and integrate that data, and then make that data available across the organization. Organizing, integrating, and sharing enterprise information is intended to create a truly integrated enterprise, and this is the challenge of what is known as master data management (MDM): integrating tools, people, and practices to organize an enterprise view of the organization's key business information objects, and to govern their quality, use, and synchronization and use that unified view of the information to achieve the organization's business objectives.

Master data management covers many topics that go beyond the scope of this book, and the excitement about ways to resolve variances that have evolved over many years leads to relatively high expectations for what can be accomplished using MDM. And though some of the expectations for MDM may exceed what is generally achievable, MDM does provide a laboratory example of the implementation of data quality techniques and practices for managing a high quality data resource. Therefore, it is important to review the basics of MDM and examine its relationship to the data quality management program. This chapter will look at some approaches to master data management, and consider how MDM can be utilized as yet another tool to help maintain the quality of enterprise information.

19.1 What Is Master Data?

In any organization, there are going to be commonly recognized concepts that are the focus of transactional/operational systems and reporting/analytics systems. Enterprise information architects will consider ways that enterprise integration projects are driven by expectations for a unified view of data, especially for customer relationship management (CRM), master product catalogs, as well as the ever-elusive (conceptual) "360° view of the customer." In each of these programs, the underlying objective is to create a synchronized, consistent view of an organization's core business entities. That unified view of each of the common data themes that exist across the business, along with their corresponding metadata and characteristics, compose what is called "master data." In this unified view, common reference data as well as the dimensional data associated with the data warehouse are all managed in concert with that data's use in the operational applications.

Terms such as "critical business objects," "business concepts," or "business entities" are frequently used when referring to the common data themes and corresponding representations that exist across any business. But what are the characteristics defining master data? From an abstract perspective, master data objects are those core business objects that are used by and shared among the different applications across the organization, along with their associated metadata, attributes, definitions, roles, connections, and taxonomies. Master data objects are those key "things" that we value the most – the things that are logged in our transaction systems, measured and reported on in our reporting systems, and analyzed in our analytical systems. Common examples of master data include customers, employees, vendors, suppliers, parts, products, locations, contact mechanisms, profiles, accounting items, contracts, and policies.

Master data tends to exist in more than one business area within the organization, so the same customer may show up in the sales system as well as the billing system. Master data is used within transactions, but the underlying object sets tend to be static in comparison to transaction systems, and do not change as frequently. Within a master data object category there may be implicit or explicit hierarchical relationships. For example, there may be individual customer contacts within each client organization, or a product may be a shrink-wrapped collection of smaller product items. Classifications and reference tables are likely to be included as well.

Although we may see one natural hierarchy across one dimension, the nested ways in which we describe, characterize, and classify business concepts (commonly referred to as "taxonomies") may actually cross multiple hierarchies in different ways. For example, when we use the concept of a "party," we may simultaneously be referring to an individual, a customer, and an employee. Alternatively, a "customer" may either be an individual party or may be an organization. In turn, the same master data categories and their related taxonomies are used for analysis and reporting. For example, the headers in a monthly sales report may be derived from the master data categories (e.g., sales by customer by region by time period). Enabling the transactional systems to refer to the same data objects as the subsequent reporting systems ensures that the analysis reports are consistent with the transaction systems.

A master data system comprising a master data set is a (potentially virtual) registry or index of uniquely identified entities with their critical data attributes synchronized from the contributing original data sources and made available for enterprise use. With the proper governance and oversight, the data in the master data system (or repository, or registry) can be qualified as a unified and coherent data asset that all applications can rely on for consistent high quality information.

19.2 What Is Master Data Management?

Master data management (MDM) is a collection of data management best practices associated with both the technical oversight and the governance requirements for facilitating the sharing of commonly used master data concepts. MDM incorporates policies and procedures to orchestrate key stakeholders, participants, and business clients in managing business applications, information management methods, and data management tools. Together, these methods and tools implement the policies, procedures, services, and infrastructure to support the capture, integration, and subsequent shared use of accurate, timely, consistent, and complete master data.

Master data management, then, is more than an application or a project. An MDM program is intended to support an organization's business needs by providing access to consistent views of the uniquely identifiable master data entities across the operational application infrastructure. Master data management governs the methods, tools, information, and services to:

- Assess the use of commonly used information objects, collections of valid data values, and explicit and implicit business rules in the range of applications across the enterprise;
- Identify core information objects relevant to business success that are used in different application data sets that would benefit from centralization;
- Instantiate a standardized model for integrating and managing those key information objects;
- Manage collected and discovered metadata as an accessible, browsable resource and use it to facilitate consolidation;
- Collect data from candidate data sources, evaluate how different data instances refer to the same real-world entities, and create a unique, consolidated view of each real-world entity;
- Provide methods for transparent access to the unified view of real-world data objects for both existing and newly developed business applications; and
- Institute the proper data stewardship and management policies and procedures at the corporate and line-of-business levels to ensure the high quality of the master data asset.

19.3 "Golden Record" or "Unified View"?

There is a general perception that by installing and populating an MDM tool, the organization immediately benefits from the consolidation of multiple representations of data into a single "golden record." Also referred to as a "single source of truth," this concept suggests that a by-product of data consolidation is the materialization of one representation whose quality and correctness exceed that of any other representation for any application purpose.

Relying on the creation of a golden record may not necessarily provide the value expected for a number of reasons, including:

- The semantics associated with a master data concept may differ among the application uses, which may lead to confusion (at the least) and incorrect operation (at the worst).
- The survivorship rules may cleanse out pieces of information that may be irrelevant in most contexts but critical in a limited number of situations.
- There is a need for clearly determining which attributes are to be incorporated into a single golden record, and consequently there may be confusion in choosing between locally managed data attributes and master data attributes.

In addition, the rules associated with managing that golden record need to accommodate the union of all the rules associated with managing the original replicas that are consolidated into that master version, as well as managing the data quality expectations associated with all downstream consumers. Not only is this an engineering challenge, it may expose situations in which those business rules conflict with each other. One must consider the extent to which the process of boiling multiple records that reflect different aspects of business interactions into a single representation satisfies the combined business needs of downstream information consumers.

In contrast to the use of master data as a single source of truth, a different yet practical approach uses the master data framework to provide an alternative to a single golden record: a unified view of entity data. This approach defers the decisions associated with consolidation and survivorship by providing access to the different representations. When there is a need to access data for a requested entity, the master data system can access the collection of records for that entity and then present that back to the information consumer, who can decide which attribute values are appropriate for the specific business application.

19.4 Master Data Management as a Tool

In a perfect environment, the organizational commitment to transitioning to a master data environment embraces the potential for strategic change, and staff members across the board are willing to participate and invest in the transition. In a greenfield environment, where the data management infrastructure can be designed and engineered from the ground up, a master data approach is quite appealing, because it takes the enterprise architecture and organization's collections of business process models into account. In this situation, the top-down view helps shape the models for a shared representation of commonly used data concepts.

On the other hand, the desire to transition to an environment that embraces MDM in an organization with an existing legacy infrastructure may mask some serious challenges that might be faced, such as:

- Breadth of information dissemination: The MDM team must pursue a survey of the entire range of existing data assets to identify the main data concepts, document the existing metadata, and analyze the quality and relevance of those data entities and associated metadata before considering master data models or instantiating a master data repository.

- Business process interdependencies: Existing information dependencies across different business processes and applications may be satisfied as a by-product of the implementation schemes and details, such as knowledge that certain batch programs will complete by a certain time, or that program A is scheduled to run before program B. In a services-oriented environment, business applications might not be able to rely on these implementation artifacts to ensure correct execution.

- Hidden assets: The ubiquitous availability of desktop productivity tools such as a spreadsheets and local databases enables almost anyone in the organization to become a data manager. In many large organizations, it is not unusual to discover critical business processes dependent on manual procedures involving data extractions, downloads into local spreadsheets, followed by different means of data sharing, ranging from emails to file copies and transfers. The data in these "hidden assets" will embody the same master data concepts as the highly managed data resources, and will need to be incorporated into the master data environment at some point.

- The prevalence of proprietary programs: Again, in any large organization it would be unusual if there were not one or more proprietary applications that have been brought in to address operational processes. These applications come with their own data silos with limited insight into their structure or direct data access routines.

- Determination of impact: One aspect of consolidating multiple data stores into a single representation is that any changes to the master version will have impact along multiple process streams. These impacts might have been localized before the transition, but in a master data environment there is a need to understand the potential impacts of any modification and addressing those impacts before moving it into production.

- Institution of services: To support application transition, introducing services to access the data needed by each application will help in migrating to the use of the master data asset, but this in itself is a substantial amount of effort.

Moreover, addressing these issues may still only provide nominal value until after the master data environment is fully in place. When considering the impact that instituting an MDM program will have in an organization, one begins to understand the complexity of the transition to a truly unified master data system, as well as the level of organizational commitment necessary.

Alternatively, instead of considering MDM as a program, one might consider MDM as a means for adding value in specific situations. A master entity index can be used to enhance an identity resolution process that helps to identify variances in entity data from different data sets. Aspects of master metadata discovery and management can expose and lead to the resolution of semantic differences across different data sets and application. Synchronizing data through a master repository can reduce data quality issues associated with currency and timeliness.

In other words, as opposed to considering MDM as a program, using it as a tool can enhance and improve the quality of enterprise data! The next sections describe architectural aspects of MDM, and it is worth thinking about how these architectural approaches can be used to improve enterprise data quality.

19.5 MDM: A High-Level Component Approach

For the purposes of data quality management, we can consider a component model view of a master data environment, then consider the architectural implementation spectrum.

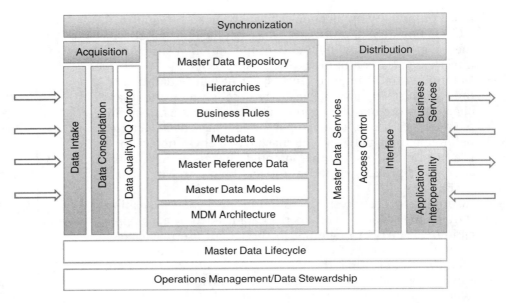

Figure 19.1 The MDM component model.

Figure 19.1 provides an overview of the component model, which essentially composes a master data repository, master data services, and the associated governance services necessary to support the master environment.

Essentially, we can divide this component model into three pieces:

1. The master data repository,
2. The collection of master data services, and
3. The data governance processes and services.

19.5.1 The Master Data Repository

The master data repository is the framework in which master data objects and entities are represented. Conceptually, this collection of components is used to manage multiple aspects of what eventually is managed as master data:

- Reference data, consisting of the enumerated data domains and associated mappings used by multiple business applications
- Metadata, including the data element definitions, semantics, and structure definitions, for the shared data models for persistent storage and for data exchange
- Master data models, for the representation of the different data entities managed as master data

- Business rules, which implement the business policies associated with the master data
- Hierarchies and relationships, used to establish connections between master data entities (such as organizational chart, financial chart of accounts, or household relationships)
- The entities themselves

All of these are accessed and managed via a set of services, subject to operational data governance processes. The data is managed using one of a variety of MDM architectures, as discussed in section 19.7.

19.5.2 Master Data Services

Managing the master data environment depends on a collection of services that enable the management of and access to the master data. For example, a master data environment could be supported using these types of services:

- Integration and consolidation, including data intake process management, master index/registry management, consolidation rules management, survivorship rules management, and source data and lineage management
- Data publication and data access, including publish, subscribe, data life-cycle services (create, read, update, retire, archive); connectors to existing data assets; connectors to existing applications; data transformations; and associated data access web services
- Data quality and cleansing, including parsing and standardization, data enrichment, data correction, identity resolution and matching, and unmerging of incorrectly consolidated records
- Access control, including management of a participant registry, participant life-cycle management (create, read, update, retire), authentication, authorization, role management, and role-based access control
- Metadata management, including master data model management, master data exchange model management, master metadata management (data element definitions, semantics, data types), reference data management, data quality rule management, business rules management, hierarchy management, relationship management, and aliasing and mapping rules management

Although this provides a high-level view of the types of services necessary for MDM, actual implementations may describe provided services with a more precise level of granularity.

19.5.3 Operational Data Governance

In support of the data governance techniques described in chapter 7 and the data inspection and monitoring described in chapter 13, a master data management environment must also provide services for operational data governance, including:

- Incident reporting and incident tracking, as discussed in chapters 13 and 17;
- Notification/alert management, so that when an issue is identified the right data steward is notified;
- Data browsing, which allows the data steward to scan through and review records as part of the issues evaluation and remediation process;
- Data profiling and assessment, as described in chapter 11;
- History/log management, which allows the data stewards to review both the automatic and manual modifications to master data;
- Privacy policy management, to review the privacy settings associated with accessing master data;
- Stewardship role management, for documenting which data stewards are responsible for which master data sets; and
- Governance policy management, for overseeing the processes of documenting enterprise data governance policies as they relate to master data, and their implementation.

19.6 Master Data Usage Scenarios

From a practical standpoint, MDM systems will focus on particular usage scenarios. Adapting MDM techniques to qualify data that is used for analytic purposes within a data warehouse or other business intelligence framework may inspire different needs than an MDM system designed to completely replace all transaction operations within the enterprise. The use of master data spans both the analytic and the operational contexts, and this is accurately reflected in the categorization of usage scenarios to which MDM is applied. Reviewing the ways that data is brought into the master environment and then how it is used downstream provides input into the selection of underlying architectures and service models.

19.6.1 Reference Information Management

In this usage scenario, the focus is on the importation of data into the master data environment and the ways that the data is enhanced and modified in support of the dependent downstream applications. The expectation is that as data is incorporated into the master environment, it is then available for "publication" to client applications, which in turn may provide feedback into the master repository.

In this scenario, data enters the master repository from multiple streams, both automated and manual, with concentration on ensuring the quality of the data on entry. Within this scenario the services must be able to support these activities:

- Creation – the direct creation of master records
- Import – preparing and migrating existing data sets, which allow the data analysts to convert existing records from suitable data sources into a table format that is acceptable for entry into the master environment
- Categorization – arranging the ways that master objects are organized
- Classification – directly specifying the class to which a master record will be assigned
- Quality validation – ensuring that the data meets defined validity constraints
- Modification – the direct adjustment of master records
- Retirement/removal – records that are no longer active may be assigned an inactive or retired status, or the record may be removed from the data set
- Synchronization – managing currency between the master environment and replicas

19.6.2 Operational Usage

In contrast to the reference information scenario, some organizations expect that eventually all application data systems will use the master environment. This means that operational systems must execute their transactions against the master data environment instead of their own data systems, and as these transactional business applications migrate to relying on the master environment as the authoritative data resource, they will consume and produce master data as a by-product of their processing streams.

For example, an organization may want to consolidate its views of all customer transactions across multiple product lines to enable real-time up-sell and cross-sell recommendations. This desire translates into a need for two aspects of master data management – managing the results of customer analytics as master profile data and real-time monitoring of all customer transactions (including purchases, returns, as well as all inbound call center activities). Each customer transaction may trigger some event that requires action within a specified time period, and all results must be logged to the master repository in case adjustments to customer profile models must be made.

Some of the activities in this usage scenario are similar to the reference usage scenario, although the operational scenario is more likely to employ automation and services for interactions between the business processes and the master repository. In this scenario, the services must be able to support the following kinds of activities:

- Creation – the direct creation of master records
- Access – the process of searching the master repository
- Quality validation – the process of ensuring data quality business rules
- Access control – monitoring individual and application access
- Publication and sharing – making the master view available to client applications
- Modification – making changes to master data
- Synchronization – managing coherence internally to the master repository
- Transactional data stewardship – direct interaction of data stewards with data issues as they occur within the operational environment

19.6.3 Analytic Usage

Analytic applications can interact with master data two ways – as the dimensional data supporting data warehousing and business intelligence, and for embedded analytics for in-line decision support. Ensuring high quality data as a result of master data management will help establish trustworthiness for downstream reporting and analysis, which suggests two expectations for MDM, which are the need to:

- Cleanse the data that is used within a data warehouse, and
- Manage any data issues resulting from the desire to maintain consistency with upstream systems.

Analytic applications will consume master data but are unlikely to create master data except for information derived as a result of analytic models. Aside from the activities mentioned in previous sections, typical activities within the analytic usage scenario include the following:

- Access – the process of searching and extracting data from the master repository
- Creation – the creation of master records, typically resulting from analytics so that the profiles and enhancements can be integrated as master data

- Notification – forwarding information to business end-clients
- Classification – applying analytics to determine the class to which a master record will be assigned
- Validation – ensuring that the data meets defined validity constraints
- Modification – the direct adjustment of master records and master reference data (e.g., customer address change, update to product characteristics)

19.7 Master Data Management Architectures

Each of these different usage scenarios demands different systems to support the business application requirements for a unified view of data, and consequently any technical approach should seek to satisfy the right set of expectations. Each of the MDM architectures reviewed here is intended to support transparent, shared access to a unique representation of master data, even in different usage scenarios. Therefore, all architecture paradigms will share the fundamental characteristics of master data access, namely, fostered via a service layer that resolves identities based on matching the core identifying data attributes that are used to distinguish one instance from all others.

Naturally, each situation carries its own unique set of requirements, ultimately depending on the data quality expectations for consistency, coherence, synchronization, timeliness, currency, and so on. Different aspects of each of these criteria are ultimately folded into the approach taken for an implementation of a master data asset. We can look at three basic architectural approaches to managing master data:

- A virtual master data index, frequently implemented using a *registry*
- A fully consolidated master data set for synchronized access, implemented as a *full repository*
- Some combination (somewhere between the previous two alternatives) of these approaches in a *hybrid* model

There may be differences between the ways that each of these architectures supports business process requirements, and that may suggest that the different architecture styles are particularly distinct in terms of design and implementation. In fact, a closer examination of the three approaches reveals that the styles represent points along a spectrum of design that ranges from thin index to fat repository. All of the approaches must maintain a registry of unique entities that is indexed and searchable by the set of identifying attributes, and each maintains a master version of master attribute values for each unique entity.

These architectural styles are aligned along a spectrum that is largely dependent on three dimensions:

- The number of attributes maintained within the master data system,
- The degree of consolidation applied as data is brought into the master repository, and
- How tightly coupled applications are to the data persisted in the master data environment.

At one end of the spectrum, the registry, which maintains only identifying attributes, is suited to those application environments that are loosely coupled and where the drivers for MDM are based more on harmonization of unique representation of master objects on demand. The transaction hub, at the other end of the spectrum, is well suited to environments requiring tight coupling of application interaction, and a high degree of data currency and synchronization. The central repository or hybrid approach can lie anywhere between these two ends, and the architecture can be adjusted in relation to the business requirements as necessary. Of course, other variables on which the styles are dependent include data element semantics, complexity of the service layer, number of proprietary applications, access mechanics, and performance.

19.7.1 Registry

In a registry style master data architecture, a thin index captures the minimal set of identifying attribute (see Figure 19.2) values. This index, in which each unique entity is "registered," maps the identifying attributes to records within the source data systems that contain information about the uniquely identified entity. Since most of the entity's data attributes are stored in the original source systems, the registry is used as a means of access to master data, which involves:

- Using an identity resolution process to search through the master registry index to find candidate matches and evaluate similarity of candidates to the sought-after record to determine a close match;
- Given a set of matches, following the pointers from the registry entries for that entity, then accessing and retrieving records for the found entity from the application data systems; and
- Returning the master data, either by provisioning the delivery of all accessed record, or optionally applying a set of survivorship rules to materialize a single consolidated master record.

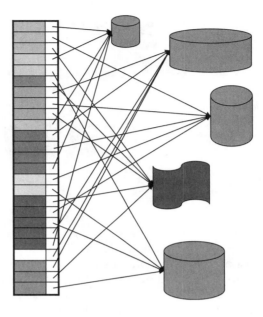

Figure 19.2 A registry maintains identifying information and maps to existing data assets.

The following are some of the assumptions regarding the registry style:

- Data attributes in the master index must be linked to existing application data silos to support existing processing streams.
- All input records are cleansed and enhanced before persistence.
- The registry contains only attributes that contain the identifying information required to disambiguate entities.
- There is a unique instance within the registry for each master entity, and only identifying information is maintained within the master record.
- The persistent copies for all attribute values are maintained in (one or more) application data systems.
- Survivorship rules on consolidation are applied at time of data access, not time of data registration.

19.7.2 Full Repository

A full master data repository, often also referred to as a transaction hub (see Figure 19.3), is a single repository in which all aspects of master data are stored and managed. Data objects are not replicated within application systems, and all access to the master repository is facilitated via the data access services in the master services layer. Though this style of master data hub functions as the only version of the data in the organization,

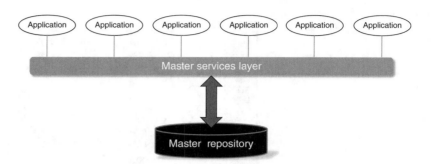

Figure 19.3 All accesses to a transaction hub are facilitated via a service layer.

the actual implementation may rely on data replication or data federation techniques.

However, within the conceptual repository-based hub, all aspects of the data instance life cycle are managed through transaction interfaces deployed within the services layer. The master hub maintains a unique record for each master entity, and data standardization and cleansing is applied to all input records. Survivorship is applied to each attribute of any newly created master record, and enhancement is only applied to surviving records whenever one or more dependent attributes change.

19.7.3 Hybrid Approach

There is a broad range between the thin master data registry and the heavy implementation of the full repository, and that void can be filled by a hybrid approach in which a master data repository holds a set of identifying attributes in addition to a set of common or shared data attributes whose centralized management benefits the business.

Two approaches can be employed for using this hybrid model. The first approach allows some degree of flexibility for the application to operate more or less independently. In this approach, the shared data attributes in the centralized master repository are published out to the applications on a periodic basis, and those applications operate directly with their own data stores. Also periodically, those master data attribute values are extracted from the application data stores and brought back to be consolidated with the centralized master. This approach builds on the registry in that the master identifying attributes are used for identity resolution, but the copies are not necessarily synchronized or coherent.

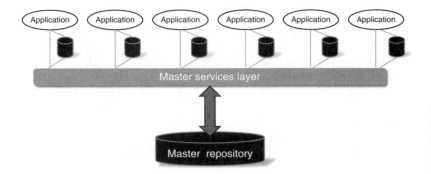

Figure 19.4 Commonly used and shared data attributes are managed centrally, but applications retain their data stores.

The second approach incrementally relegates responsibility to the central repository. In this approach, the service layer sits between the application and both the local data store and the central repository. Requests for data are split between accessing data attributes that are used only by the application invoking the request and accessing those data attributes that are shared. In this approach, there is a greater amount of synchronization and consistency.

In either approach, within each dependent system, application-specific attributes are managed locally, but are linked back to the master instance via a shared global primary key (see Figure 19.4). The integrated view of common attributes in the master repository allows commonly used data elements to be absorbed into the master from the distributed business applications' local copies. New data instances may be created at the application, and those new records will eventually be synchronized with the central system.

Since the business applications continue to operate on their own local copies of data also managed in the master, there is no assurance that the values stored in the master repository are as current as those values in application data sets. Therefore, the hybrid or centralized approach is reasonable for environments that require harmonized views of unique master objects, but do not have a requirement for a high degree of synchronization across the application architecture.

19.8 Identifying Master Data

What seems like a relatively innocuous question actually hides a surprising amount of complexity: What constitutes master data? Actually, this might be broken down into a set of questions:
- What data objects are used across multiple business processes?
- What are the data elements associated with each of the master data objects?

- What data sets comprise the organization's master data?
- How do we resolve semantic differences among the various data definitions?
- What reference data sets are shared among multiple business processes?
- How can we employ approaches for metadata and data standards for collecting and managing master metadata?
- How do we locate and isolate master data objects that exist within the enterprise?
- How do we assess the variances between the different representations before resolution?

The evolution of different application data architectures will lead to many versions of the same core master concepts, as well as the metadata and reference data. Master data concepts will share some similar characteristics, such as:

- Real-world objects that are modeled within the environment as master data objects will be used by more than one business processes.
- Master data objects are referenced in both transaction and analytic systems.
- Master data objects may be classified within a semantic hierarchy, with different levels of classification, attribution, and specialization applied depending on the application
- Master data objects are likely to be modeled differently in multiple applications, possibly embedded in legacy data structure models, or even largely unmodeled within flat file structures.

19.9 Master Data Services

Interactions with the master data system are facilitated via services, and Figure 19.5 shows a layered framework in which master data services, categorized in specific areas, are often built using other master data services.

These layers include:

- Metadata services that are used for creating, managing, and administering master data definitions, master data models, and master reference data
- Data instance services that support data life-cycle tasks – create, read, update, and delete instances of master data concepts
- Policy management services that are used for creating, managing, and implementing access control and business policies at the data level
- Cleansing and consolidation services that are used for adding new data instances into the master data environment while

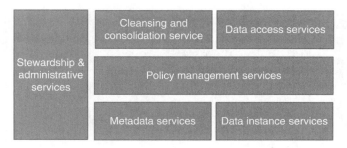

Figure 19.5 Master data services.

ensuring that there is only one data instance for any real world entity
- Data access services that provide querying requests of data
- Stewardship and administration services that are used for system configuration and operational data governance tasks and activities

Interestingly, it is at the master service layer that we see the scale of integration with data quality techniques, methods, technologies, data governance, and data stewardship. These next sections provide a glimpse of some details of master data services.

19.9.1 Metadata Services

These services manage master reference data, classification categories, groupings, and hierarchies. This category also provides administration services for master metadata such as data element definitions, data element structures, and association of data element to reference domains. Some examples are listed in Table 19.1.

19.9.2 Data Instance Management Services

These services (see examples in Table 19.2) are used to create, access, modify, or retire data instances within the master environment. Specific services can be provided for setting, reading, modifying, or deleting the values of specific data elements. These services are enabled within the constraints of access control and other business rules or policies.

19.9.3 Policy Management Services

In this context policies are used to manage a list of actors who are authorized to access data with particular access rights. They are also used to define business rules and assure compliance with those business rules (see examples in Table 19.3).

19.9.4 Data Access Services

These (see Table 19.4) include the services for requesting data from the master data asset.

Table 19.1 Metadata Services

Service Area	Example Services
Value domains	Create value domain
	Add to value domain
	Map value domains together
	Associate value domain with a data element
Data elements	Define a new data element
	Describe a data element type and size
	Modify a data element type and size
	Retire a data element
	Map data element to application use (and alias)
Modeling	Create a new entity
	Add a data element to an entity
	Remove a data element from an entity
	Create a relationship between entities
Hierarchies	Create a classification category
	Create a new hierarchy
	Access the hierarchy
	Insert a classification category into a place in a hierarchy
	Remove category from hierarchy
Exchange model	Define an exchange schema element
	Map a data element definition to an exchange schema element
	Define transformation methods between data elements and schema elements

Table 19.2 Data Instance Services

Service Area	Example Services
Data instance life cycle	Create a new data instance
	Access a data instance
	Modify/update a data instance
	Delete/retire a data instance
	Archive a data instance
Data element access	Set a data element value
	Modify a data element value
	Delete a data element value
Search	Search for a data instance in the master data set
Relationship	Add a relationship between data instances
	Remove a relationship between data instances
Groupings	Add data instance to a grouping
	Remove data instance from a grouping

Table 19.3 Policy Management Services

Service Area	Example Services
Actor	Register actor
	Access actor registry entry
	Modify actor registry entry
	Remove actor from registry
Roles	Create a new role
	Access a role
	Modify/update a role
	Delete/retire a role
	Associate a role with an actor
Rights	Create a new right
	Access a right
	Modify/update a right
	Delete/retire a right
	Apply a right to a data entity
	Apply a right to a data instance
	Apply a right to a data element
	Associate a right with a role
Access control	Authenticate an actor's role
	Authorize an actor's access rights
Business rules	Create a business rule
	Associate a business rule with a master data object
	Associate a business rule with a data instance
	Associate a business rule with a data element
	Dissociate a business rule from a master data object
	Dissociate a business rule from a data instance
	Dissociate a business rule from a data element
	Remove a business rule
Policies	Define a policy
	Associate roles/rights with policy
	Dissociate roles/rights from policy
Synchronization and serialization	Lock a data instance
	Lock an entity
	Release lock
	Serialize transactions
	Propagate changes

19.9.5 Cleansing and Consolidation Services

These (see examples in Table 19.5) services are used to parse, standardize, and cleanse data as well as validate data before entry into the master environment. Many data instances can be

Table 19.4 Data Access Services

Service Area	Example Services
Query	Request data

Table 19.5 Cleansing and Consolidation Services

Service Area	Example Services
Data quality rules	Add cleansing rule
	Modify cleansing rule
	Remove cleansing rule
	Add validation rule
	Modify validation rule
	Remove validation rule
Cleansing	Parsing
	Standardization
	Correction
	Enrichment
Consolidation	Search for an matching data instance
	Create survivorship rule
	Modify survivorship rule
	Add survivorship rule to rule base
	Remove survivorship rule from rule base
	Apply survivorship rules
	Merge matching data instances
	Unmerge

consolidated with data instances that already exist within the master environment.

19.9.6 Administration and Stewardship Services

These services (see examples in Table 19.6) are used for system adminstration and for operational governance activities performed by data stewards.

Table 19.6 Administration and Stewardship Services

Service Area	Example Services
Stewardship roles	Register data steward
	Modify data steward registry
	Remove data steward from registry
	Create stewardship role
	Add role to data steward
Incident management and stewardship	Search
	Profile data
	Add a stewardship task
	Remove a stewardship task
	Create a new incident report
	Review incident report
	Modify incident report
	Create a notification
	Alert/notify data steward
History/log management	Add lineage note
	Add timestamp
	Log event/data change
Presentation and correction	Browse data instances
	Visualize relationships and hierarchies
	Apply corrections
	Merge data instances
	Unmerge data instances
System configuration	Manage data federation
	Performance management

19.10 Summary: Approaching MDM and Data Quality

If MDM is a long-term strategic activity that involves a significant amount of work, then can the data management team institute MDM in a way that adds incremental value along the way? From the data quality perspective, the answer is an unqualified "yes." For example, consider these ideas:

- Consolidation of definitions: MDM can be used as a process for identifying and then unifying the definitions of commonly used data concepts.

- Master reference data: The prevalence and criticality of reference data (such as data domains and mappings across different data domains) cannot be understated, especially when similar reference data sets are used and are represented in different ways. MDM can be used as a tool for managing enterprise reference data.
- Matching and linkage: Identity resolution techniques are enhanced when more information is available for similarity analysis and differentiation. MDM can be used to support record linkage, searching, matching, and identity resolution.
- Policy management: As the applications are engineered around corporate policies, the organization can benefit from consolidation and standardization of the ways that these policies are deployed, and MDM can be used as a policy management system.

In each of these cases, master data management techniques are used to support business-critical activities that are reliant on high quality data and good data management practices. By employing MDM in support of data quality, immediate gains can be achieved despite the need for the long-term commitment.

BRINGING IT ALL TOGETHER

CHAPTER OUTLINE

This chapter reviews the material presented in the book and summarizes the approach to establishing the business case, developing a program blueprint, devising a road map, and implementing a proactive data quality management program that meets a targeted level of organizational maturity that best addresses the need of the collective of information consumers. The purpose of this chapter is to provide a quick guide of the high-level concepts explored in the book, with pointers for further review.

20.1 Organization and Management

The first part of the book focuses on the organizational aspects of data quality: understanding the impacts of poor data quality, aspects of a data quality program, organizational preparedness and maturity, the place of enterprise data quality among other enterprise initiatives, developing a business case, blueprint, and road map, and socializing data quality improvement as a valuable contributor to competitive advantage.

20.1.1 Developing the Data Quality Business Case

Communicating the value of data quality improvement involves characterizing the value gap attributable to variance in meeting data quality expectations. Quantifying the value gap and accompanying the descriptions with proposed alternatives for addressing those issues along with cost estimates demonstrating a positive return on investment helps to build the business case. However, this requires some exploration, including:

- Reviewing the types of risks relating to the use of information
- Considering ways to specify data quality expectations based on those risks
- Developing processes and tools for clarifying what data quality means and how it is measured
- Defining data validity rules that can be used for inspection and assessment
- Measuring data quality
- Reporting and tracking data issues
- Linking those issues directly to quantifiable business metrics

Since there are many ways in which business issues can be associated with situations where data quality is below user expectations, exploring the different categories of business impacts attributable to poor information quality and discussing ways to facilitate identification and classification of cost impacts related to poor data quality will guide the data quality practitioner to identify key data quality opportunities.

Establishing qualitative metrics for data quality as a means for establishing the value gap requires thought regarding how flawed data leads to material impact to business processes, driving a need for:

- Distinguishing high-impact from low-impact data quality issues,
- Isolating the source of the introduction of data flaws,
- Fixing broken processes,
- Correlating business value with source data quality, and
- Instituting data quality best practices to address flawed information production.

Mapping data quality expectations and business expectations involves specifying rules measuring aspects of data validity and then looking at the corresponding relationship to missed business expectations regarding productivity, efficiency, revenue generation and growth, throughput, agility, spend management, as well as other drivers of organizational value.

To determine the true value added by data quality programs, conformance to business expectations (and the corresponding business value) should be measured in relation to its component data quality rules. We do this by identifying how the business impacts of poor data quality can be measured as well as how they relate to their root causes, then assess the costs to eliminate the root causes. Characterizing both the business impacts and the data quality problems provides a framework for developing a business case.

Chapter 1 presented an approach for analyzing the degree to which poor data quality impedes business objectives that detailed business impacts, categorized those impacts, and then prioritized the issues in relation to the severity of the impacts. We reviewed a simplified approach for classifying the business impacts associated with data errors within a classification scheme. This categorization is intended to support the data quality analysis process and help in differentiating between data issues that have serious business ramifications and those that are benign. This classification taxonomy provided primary categories for evaluating either the negative impacts related to data errors, or the potential opportunities for improvement resulting from better data quality, and focused on four general areas:

- Financial impacts, such as increased operating costs, decreased revenues, missed opportunities, reduction or delays in cash flow, or increased penalties, fines, or other charges
- Confidence and satisfaction-based impacts, such as customer, employee, or supplier satisfaction, as well as general market satisfaction decreased organizational trust, low confidence in forecasting, inconsistent operational and management reporting, and delayed or improper decisions
- Productivity impacts such as increased workloads, decreased throughput, increased processing time, or decreased end-product quality.
- Risk and compliance impacts associated with credit assessment, investment risks, competitive risk, capital investment and/or development, fraud, and leakage; compliance with government regulations, industry expectations, or self-imposed policies (such as privacy policies)

The approach in chapter 1 involves defining your own classification taxonomy for business impacts, and then evaluating how known or potential data issues contribute to negative impacts. Use the approach described in chapter 1 to compartmentalize the evaluation and assessment of critical data issues and align them with data flaws. Breaking up the scope of business impacts into small analytic pieces makes building the business case for data quality a much more manageable task. In addition, the categorical hierarchy of impact areas will naturally map to our future performance reporting structure for monitoring how data quality improvement hits the bottom line.

20.1.2 Aspect of the Data Quality Program

Chapter 2 looked at the virtuous cycle executed as a by-product of instituting a data quality management program. This virtuous cycle consists of five stages:

1. Assess: Identify and measure how poor data quality impedes business objectives
2. Define: Define business-related data quality rules and performance targets
3. Design: Design quality improvement processes that remediate process flaws
4. Deploy: Implement quality improvement methods and processes
5. Monitor: Monitor data quality against defined performance targets

To implement this program and support the requirements of those stages, chapter 2 suggests considering instituting these data quality processes, which are reviewed in greater detail throughout the remainder of the book:

1. Business impact analysis: This provides the starting point for understanding how potential data-related issues lead to increased costs, increased complexity, reduced accuracy or precision in identity resolution, the introduction of inefficiencies or delays in business activities, or any other negative business impacts that are attributable to data that does not meet a specific level of acceptability.
2. Data quality requirements analysis: This is a top-down identification of data quality expectations in which data quality analysts synthesize data quality expectations for consumed data sets based on the business impact analysis, identify specific dimensions of data quality, and list specific measures that will be evaluated in relation to the business impacts.
3. Bottom-up data quality assessment: This is a bottom-up, empirical approach to identifying potential data issues using data profiling and other statistical and analysis techniques. Analysts identify potential data anomalies, which are reviewed with the business data consumers.
4. Top-down data quality assessment: This process looks at discovered anomalies, which are then reviewed with business clients within the context of the documented business impacts as a way of differentiating between relevant and irrelevant issues, prioritization, and determination of strategies for remediation.
5. Defining measures of quality: This is a process of correlating business impacts to data issues through defined business rules as a way of representing measurable aspects of data quality; these measures are used in establishing baseline levels of data quality as well as for inspection and monitoring on an ongoing basis.

6. Defining metrics: This is the process of defining specific reportable metrics that can be computed and presented to the business data stewards as part of a data quality scorecard; they also form the basis of methods used for drilling into flawed data for root cause analysis.

7. Define acceptability thresholds: Through solicitation from the business users, threshold scores are defined; scoring below the acceptability threshold indicates that the data do not meet business expectations.

8. Organizing data standards: This process describes the policies and procedures for defining rules and reaching agreement about standard data elements, within well-defined frameworks when possible.

9. Metadata management: The enterprise metadata repository effectively becomes the "control center" driving and controlling the business applications, acting as the repository for technical details and business definitions for common and shared data elements.

10. Defining data validity rules: Data validity rules are used as data controls whose implementation is incorporated directly into the application development process so that data errors can be identified and addressed as they occur.

11. Inspection and monitoring: The availability of rules for validating data against defined expectations is the basis for data quality inspection, monitoring, and notifying the appropriate people when data quality issues are identified so that any agreed-to remediation tasks can be initiated.

12. Defining a data quality service level agreement: This is an agreement that specifies data consumer expectations in terms of data validity rules and levels of acceptability, as well as reasonable expectations for response and remediation when data errors and flaws are identified.

13. Data quality incident and performance reporting: This provides a set of management processes for the reporting and tracking of data quality issues and corresponding activities, and this uses incident management systems for logging and tracking data quality issues.

14. Managing data remediation: This is the mechanism for managing the tasks performed to remedy any critical issues, including triage, classification, prioritization, and preparation for root cause analysis.

15. Root cause analysis: This process describes how data controls can be used to isolate the processing phase in which the error is introduced; it also describes ways to drill down

into the data and the associated application tasks to seek the root cause.

16. Data correction: This remediation approach is a governed process for correcting data to meet acceptability thresholds when the source of the errors cannot be fixed.

17. Process correction: This encompasses governed process for evaluating the information production flow, business process work flow, and the determination of how processes can be improved to reduce or eliminate the introduction of errors.

18. Standardization and cleansing: This process incorporates working with the data standards and metadata staff to define rules and use tools for standardizing and normalizing data values for data cleansing.

19. Identity resolution: The need to uniquely identify individual entities within and across different data sets means that the tools for entity identity resolution must be synchronized with the operational procedures for record linkage, searching and matching, batch linkage, and data consolidation.

20. Enhancement: Additional data sources can be identified that can be linked to organizational data sets to improve the utility or value of the data. This process involves identifying those data sources, engineering tasks for data integration and appending, and managing the data supplies to ensure that their data meets the organization's data quality expectations.

20.1.3 The Data Quality Scan: Assessing Organizational Maturity

Developing a data quality strategy means understanding the level of maturity needed to meet organizational needs, assessing the current level of maturity, documenting the gaps, and mapping out the high-level steps that must be taken to reach the objective. Taking on the challenge to establish the appropriate level of data quality maturity requires an understanding of the diversity of participants, regulatory bodies, policy makers, and information clients. Laying out the data quality strategy means directing the implementation of data governance, information policies, data management best practices, corresponding technology, and any other operational solutions while at the same time remaining pragmatic and practical. As discussed in chapter 3, here are some things to keep in mind:

- **The information life cycle:** When assembling a data quality strategy, it is necessary to identify the key success objectives for the program, evaluate the variables by which success is measured, establish information quality expectations, develop the governance model for overseeing success, and develop protocols for ensuring that policies and procedures for maintaining high quality data are followed by the participants across the enterprise.

- **Performance and maturity:** A data quality framework defines data quality management objectives that are consistent with the key success objectives and the enterprise expectations for quality information, either through services to be integrated across an enterprise information architecture, or through the collaborative implementation of data governance policies and procedures. Performance associated with data quality expectations can be tied to a data quality maturity model. This maturity model establishes levels of performance and specifies the fundamental best practices needed to achieve each level of performance.
- **Data governance roles and responsibilities:** Also included in your data quality framework should be a model for data governance that outlines various data quality roles for the participants in the enterprise community. This data governance model will provide an organizational structure and the policies and procedures for the data quality certification to be followed by the community to ensure high quality data. The governance model defines data ownership and stewardship, and describes accountability for the remediation of data quality issues.
- **Meeting expectations:** To achieve assurance of high quality data, the framework should provide for the identification, documentation, and validation of data quality expectations materialized as data quality rules and metrics that reflect the business impact of poor data quality.
- **Staff training and education:** Data quality requires continuous education, knowledge transfer, and training covering the appropriate topics to facilitate survival, even in the face of organizational change and employee turnover.

Chapter 3 described a model that looks at varying degrees of maturity with respect to potential end states that meet the needs of the organization without overwhelming the participants. Casting the observance of data quality expectations within the context of key business performance metrics while minimizing intrusion and extra effort enables the program to gain traction and increase participation. The chapter provided guidance for evaluating maturity and capabilities along these areas of focus:

- Defining data quality expectations
- Creating measurement using data quality dimensions
- Defining policies for measured observance of expectations

- Implementing the procedures supporting those policies
- Instituting data governance
- Agreeing to standards
- Acquiring the right technology
- Monitoring performance

20.1.4 Collaboration with Enterprise Initiatives

Enterprise data quality management cannot be divorced from any other enterprise initiatives that are under way. One must consider the context and landscape in which data quality management will be deployed when designing the data quality program. One must investigate the impact that the data quality initiative will have on other organizational initiatives and vice versa.

As organizations are gradually recognizing that the connectivity between the operational and analytic aspects of the business is driven by high quality data, there will be a recurring need to ensure that any major initiative is aligned with the data governance and data quality management processes described in this book. Chapter 4 suggested looking at planning initiatives, framework initiatives, and operational and application initiatives and their relationship with data quality management, as well as how those activities affect the scope of integrating data quality management as an enterprise program.

Although maintaining a competitive edge requires forethought by senior management, many organizations are plagued by the absence of strategic objectives that should be intended to drive innovation and excellence in the marketplace. Organizations that engage in defining a vision and planning a strategy are more likely to be focused on achieving well-defined objectives. This suggests looking at examples of planning initiatives and the interdependency with data quality management, such as performance management, Key Performance Indicators (KPIs), process improvements, organizational change, and strategic planning.

Often, the organically grown application infrastructure is perceived to have been assembled as a result of development of business applications supporting vertical lines of business. However, the perception that the organization should operate holistically in a way that optimizes general corporate benefit suggests aligning business processes along horizontal lines, and not just in silos, suggesting a review of framework initiatives such as enterprise architecture, enterprise resource planning, supply chain management, and the retirement of legacy applications.

Aside from organizational and framework initiatives, there are operational and application initiatives that impact the entire organization, especially in relation to data quality management. In this section we consider a few examples: compliance, business intelligence, and the purchase and deployment of proprietary systems.

Although the intentions of the data quality program are driven by the maturity of functional capability the scope of the data quality program is not immune to impact from other activities that are diffused across the organization. In other words, the program should be reviewed in the context of how the data quality practitioners integrate a program supporting organizational change and upheaval, new initiatives, or other broad-based organizational activities.

20.1.5 Developing the Data Quality Road Map

Given the analysis of the value gap coupled with the maturity assessment, we have the inputs that chapter 5 suggests are used to sketch the plan for implementing a data quality management program. The data quality road map combines the two by considering the level of maturity that is necessary to address identified and then prioritized issues in an order that will deliver intermediate benefits but still address the long-term program objectives.

Aspiring to reach the highest level of maturity is admirable, but not always necessary. The limits of what can be imposed on the staff are bounded by the complexity introduced by the different kinds of challenges, combined with the fact that the data quality manager is able to advise regarding change, but might not be able to mandate it. A reasonable data quality vision both supports the business objectives of the organization yet remains pragmatically achievable within the collaborative environment of the enterprise community. A practical approach is to target a level of maturity at which the necessary benefits of data quality management are achieved for the enterprise while streamlining the acceptance path for the individuals who will ultimately be contributing to the data quality effort.

Given that targeted level of maturity, the road map to attain that objective will detail phases with achievable milestones and deliverables. For example, a road map may contain five phases:
1. Establish fundamentals
2. Formalize data quality activities
3. Deploy operational aspects
4. Establish level of maturity
5. Assess and fine-tune

At the end of the final phase, there is an opportunity to review whether the stated objectives are met, and whether it is reasonable to target a higher level of maturity.

At the beginning of the program, plan to address many newly discovered issues, and over time the rate of the discovery of new issues will stabilize and then decrease, while at the same time the elimination of root causes will continue to reduce the amount of reactive work being performed. There are some lessons to be learned with respect to data quality issue analysis:

1. Subjecting a process to increased scrutiny is bound to reveal significantly more flaws than originally expected.
2. Initial resource requirements will be necessary to address most critical issues.
3. Eliminating the root causes of one problem will probably fix more than one problem, improving quality overall.
4. There is a point at which the resource requirement diminishes because the majority of the critical issues have been resolved.

Chapter 5 suggests that the life cycle for a data quality management program begins with a need for more individuals focusing a large part of their time in researching and reacting to problems, but over time there will be a greater need to have fewer people concentrate some of their time on proactively preventing issues from appearing in the first place. As data governance practices are exported to the lines of business, the time investment is diffused across the organization, which results in even further reducing the need for long-term dedicated resources. This insight helps set limits on the resource requirements over time and may reinforce the value proposition and business justification used to gain the support for establishing a data quality program.

20.2 Building the Information Quality Program

The second part of the book looks at implementing the core processes of a data quality program: metrics and data quality performance improvement, data governance, definition of data quality dimensions, data requirements analysis, data standards, metadata management, data quality assessment, remediation, and data quality service level agreements.

20.2.1 Defining Metrics

There is a difference between knee-jerk tool purchases and proactive prevention of the introduction of errors through process improvement and proactive validation, inspection, and monitoring. Using the business impact analysis as a guide, we can consider the return on the data quality investment in the context of measurably reducing the material impacts associated with data flaws as a way of establishing improvement goals. This approach is driven by performance objectives instead of remediation. If we have done our homework by identifying the critical dimensions of data quality, providing quantifiable metrics to measure conformance to expectations, and determining achievable objectives for improvement, we have the tools for determining when the organization has reached the desired maturity level.

Program and product managers often desire the ability to summarize an organization's "business productivity" for senior managers using scorecards and dashboards that present key performance indicators for periodic review. These scorecard and dashboard applications present the current state of the environment in the context of reasonable expectations, providing an overview of the "value creation" of the entire system.

In most areas of a business, the metrics that back up the key performance indicators may be relatively straightforward. Each of these metrics may be represented using various visual cues, each of which provides a warning when the performance indicator reaches some critical level. When it comes to the world of data quality, though, the analogy seems to break down, mostly because there is a difference between what can be measured and what the value of that measurement means. Knowing that poor data quality can impact the organization, the practitioners should devise a strategy for identifying and managing "business-relevant" data quality metrics as performance indicators that summarize the relationship between data that does not meet one's expectations and the organizational bottom line.

Key data quality performance indicators will measure conformance to the business representatives' data quality expectations. These KPIs reflect the key performance areas that are critical to performance management. For data quality, the number of KPIs should not exceed five of the most critical characteristics derived from the dimensions of data quality and should refer back to the desired level of the maturity model. Consider this example set of basic KPIs:

- **Trustworthiness:** Trustworthiness performance is derived from the conformance characteristics and is assessed by determining the degree to which each participant publishes their data quality statistics and the degree to which participants provide transparency into their data quality management practices. This rolls up from periodic reporting of data quality dimension metrics (at all points of data consumption or publication) and reported issues. Missing or incomplete reports from participants indicate potential underlying data quality issues.

- **Availability:** Dimensions that can be used to assess the availability performance measure include periodically examining the comprehensiveness and completeness of line-of-business data, measuring completeness of critical data elements, and assessing timeliness and response times.
- **Consistency:** Dimensions that are relevant to consistency include measurement of semantic and structural consistency, completeness of presentation, and verification that data entry and exchange edits are defined and that there is compliance with these edits.
- **Policy compliance:** Policies such as those governing privacy, security, or limitations of use are needed. Continually monitoring the different application or line-of-business groups across the enterprise to ensure compliance with these policies is equally critical.
- **Identifiability:** Identifiability, as a key performance indicator, tracks uniqueness of entity identification, uniqueness of identifier, the percentage of search and match errors, and the promulgation of corrections and updates regarding entity identification.

20.2.2 Instituting Data Governance

In chapter 7 we discussed a data governance framework for defining, agreeing to, instituting, and overseeing best practices associated with improvements in data quality. Because data quality management incorporates the participation, collaboration, and oversight throughout the organization, processes are put in place to establish data quality goals in relation to both business objectives and internal and external constraints; integrate methods for measuring, auditing, and reporting data quality metrics; and protocols for responsibility and accountability for issues resolution.

Data governance is introduced at various data touch points throughout the data life cycle to ensure consistency, conformance to the defined business rules, and to measure the degree to which line-of-business activities comply with the desired level of the data quality maturity model. Chapter 7 described a template for a data quality charter, which formalizes the organizational structure, roles and responsibilities, and workflows for oversight over data quality management. A data quality charter will include the following sections:

- **Data governance overview,** providing a high-level overview of the data governance program and how it relates to corporate and information technology governance
- **Mission and guiding principles,** which articulate the core objectives and guiding principles of the data governance program
- **Governance goals,** detailing the business goals and objectives of the data governance program
- **Work items,** providing a list of data governance activities
- **Success criteria,** describing data governance critical success factors
- **Roles and responsibilities,** summarizing the roles for the governance program (both participants and stakeholders), and the corresponding sponsor, responsibilities, and approval/authority characteristics
- **Accountability and escalation,** mapping accountability and responsibility to roles

In turn, the policies and procedures implied by the charter for data governance are proposed, agreed to, and managed by an enterprise forum that oversees the data quality community. The services provided by the forum include:

- Setting priorities and developing and maintaining standards for data quality
- Reporting relevant measurements of enterprise-wide data quality
- Providing guidance that facilitates staff involvement
- Establishing communications mechanisms for knowledge sharing
- Developing and applying certifications and compliance policies
- Monitoring and reporting on performance
- Identifying opportunities for improvements and building consensus for approval
- Resolving variations and conflicts

Data governance covers both external aspects (such as regulations, laws, industry standards, or even generally accepted practices and principles) and internal aspects of oversight as the growing needs for information utility impose rigid data quality standards. Managing policies, processes, and procedures while providing a framework for overseeing responsibility and accountability streamlines enhances collaboration and improves the utility of the organization's information asset.

20.2.3 Defining Dimensions of Data Quality

The concept of a dimension evokes thoughts of measurement, and that is exactly what is meant when the term is used in the context of data quality. A dimension of data quality describes a context and a frame of reference for measurement along with suggested units of measurement. Chapter 8 proposed a set of dimensions intended to represent different measurable aspects of data quality. The analysts can use measurements of data quality dimensions to review data quality performance at different levels of the operational hierarchy. The collected measurements can populate a dashboard indicating overall line-of-business and then rolled-up enterprise performance.

Although it is possible to describe a diverse set of measurements, the value of using metrics is being able to weigh the most critical aspects of a process that should be measured, balanced by additional qualitative assessments. Chapter 8 suggested some data quality dimensions whose simplicity enhanced their potential value in assembling a data quality scorecard:

1. **Accuracy,** which refers to the degree with which data values correctly reflect attributes of the real-life entities they are intended to model

2. **Lineage,** which measures trustworthiness by tracking the originating source and sources of modification of any new or updated data element

3. **Structural consistency,** which refers to the consistency in the representation of similar attribute values, both within the same data set and across the data models associated with related tables

4. **Semantic consistency,** which refers to consistency of definitions among attributes within a data model, as well as similarly named attributes in different enterprise data sets, and it characterizes the degree to which similar data objects share consistent names and meanings

5. **Completeness,** which indicates when attributes that should not be null are missing their values

6. **Consistency,** which compares similarity across different levels of the data hierarchy – within tables, databases, across different applications, and externally supplied data

7. **Currency,** which refers to the degree to which information is up to date with the corresponding real-world entities

8. **Timeliness,** which refers to observing the time expectation for accessibility of information

9. **Reasonableness,** which specifies statements associated with expectations of consistency or reasonability of values, either in the context of existing data or over a time series

10. **Identifiability,** which refers to the unique naming and representation of core conceptual objects as well as the ability to link data instances containing entity data together based on identifying attribute values

Chapter 8 also describes other aspects of these dimensions, and suggests that the data quality assessment helps to identify expectations that are manifested as dimensions of data quality, which are used to quantify conformance, establish performance objectives, and apply governance to ensure that the participants conform to the policies. These methods collect measurements and report the results as a way of quantifying performance-oriented data quality management as a prelude to making the changes required to meet business needs.

20.2.4 Data Requirements Analysis

Organizational data quality management almost does not make sense outside of the context of growing information reuse, alternating opinions regarding centralization/decentralization of data, or increasing scrutiny from external parties. The fact that data sets are reused for purposes that were never intended implies a greater need for identifying, clarifying, and documenting the collected data requirements from across the application landscape, as well as instituting accountability for ensuring that the quality characteristics expected by all data consumers are met.

Inconsistencies due to intermediate transformations and cleansings have plagued business reporting and analytics, requiring recurring time investments for reviews and reconciliations. However, attempting to impose restrictions upstream often are pushed back, resulting in a less than optimal situation. Data requirements analysis is a process intended to accumulate data requirements from across the spectrum of downstream data consumers. Demonstrating that all application's are accountable for making the best effort for ensuring the quality of data for all downstream purposes and that the organization benefits as a whole when ensuring that those requirements are met.

Whereas traditional requirements analysis centers on functional needs, data requirements analysis complements the functional requirements process and focuses on the information needs, providing a standard set of procedures for identifying, analyzing, and validating data requirements and quality for data-consuming applications. Data requirements analysis helps in:

- Articulating a clear understanding of data needs of all consuming business processes,
- Identifying relevant data quality dimensions associated with those data needs,

- Assessing the quality and suitability of candidate data sources,
- Aligning and standardizing the exchange of data across systems;
- Implementing production procedures for monitoring the conformance to expectations and correcting data as early as possible in the production flow, and
- Continually reviewing to identify improvement opportunities in relation to downstream data needs.

Analysis of system goals, objectives, and stakeholder desires is conducted to elicit business information characteristics that drive the definition of data and information requirements that are relevant, add value, and can be observed. The data requirements analysis process employs a top-down approach that incorporates data discovery and assessment in the context of explicitly qualified business data consumer needs. Candidate data sources are determined, assessed, and qualified within the context of the requirements, and any inherent issues that can be resolved immediately are addressed using the approaches described in chapter 12. The data requirements analysis process consists of these phases:

1. Identifying the business contexts
2. Conducting stakeholder interviews
3. Synthesizing expectations and requirements
4. Developing source-to-target mappings

Data quality rules defined as a result of the requirements analysis process can be engineered into the organization's system development life cycle (SDLC) for validation, monitoring, and observance of agreed-to data quality standards.

20.2.5 Metadata Management

Metadata and data standards usually accompany data quality and governance, relying on best practices that are often ignored. Some typical issues that drive the need for effective metadata management include absence of clarity for object semantics, ambiguity in and lack of precision in data element definition, source system variance, as well as a variety of means of data motion. It is through the metadata that business term and data element definitions (and by association, data quality rules) are aligned, and metadata can be managed through a registry that captures metadata at the data element level, documents workflow status, and provides a browsing capability that enables a greater potential for reusing business terms and definitions that already have some degree of acceptance.

Data quality management requires precision and clarity regarding data concept and data element specification and definition, yet there is often complexity and confusion when attempting to solidify or standardize data element specifications. Leveraging the data governance techniques and procedures described in chapter 7 will help address the need for coordination and oversight introduced by the organizational issues that might arise as data definitions are collected and standardized.

Providing a model, framework, and architecture that unifies semantics across business applications can enable a control mechanism, or perhaps even a "clearinghouse" for determining when data elements can be mapped to each other appropriately, and also, importantly, when they cannot. The metadata associated with an enterprise data set do more than just describe the size and types of each data element. Data integration from different sources is more reliable when it is clear that the data elements have the same meaning, that their valid data domains are consistent, that the records represent similar or the same real-world entities. Metadata management also attempts to address more complex dependencies, such as harmonization of entity types, semantic consistency, and data access control.

A conceptual view of metadata starts with basic building blocks and grows to maintain comprehensive views of the information that is used to support the achievement of business objectives. The metadata stack described in chapter 10 is driven by business objectives from the top down and from the bottom up and is intended to capture as much information as necessary to drive:

- Analysis of enterprise data for the purpose of structural and semantic discovery,
- Correspondence of semantics to data element types,
- Determination of commonly used data element types,
- Mapping of data element concepts to business applications,
- Usage and impact scenarios for data element concepts, and
- Data quality directives.

Chapter 10 then looked at different types of metadata that are of value to the data quality practitioner, starting from the bottom up:

- Business definitions, which look at the business terms used across organizations and the associated meanings
- Reference metadata, which details data domains (both conceptual domains and corresponding value domains) as well as reference data and mappings between codes and values
- Data element metadata, focusing on data element definitions, structures, nomenclature, and determination of existence along a critical path of a processing stream

- Information architecture, coagulating the representations of data elements into cohesive entity structures, and noting how those structures reflect real-world objects and how those objects interact within business processes
- Business metadata, which captures the business policies that drive application design and implementation, the corresponding information policies that drive the implementation decisions inherent in the lower levels of the stack, and the management and execution schemes for the business rules that embody both business and information policies

Data standards and metadata management provide a basis for harmonizing business rules, and consequently data quality rules from a variety of data sources. Specific metadata demands must align with enterprise activities, and the data quality team should use these requirements to identify candidate metadata management tools that support the "right amount" of metadata management.

20.2.6 Data Quality Assessment

The absence of clearly defined measurements of business impacts attributable to poor data quality prevents developing an appropriate business case for introducing data quality management improvement, and chapter 11 looked at an approach for assessment process that quickly results in a report documenting potential data quality issues. That report enumerates a prioritized list of clearly identified data quality issues, recommendations for remediation, and suggestions for instituting data quality inspection and control for data quality monitoring. It also proposes opportunities for improvement, providing an ability to provide an objective assessment of critical data and determine whether the levels of data quality are sufficient to meet business expectations, and if not, evaluate the value proposition and feasibility of data quality improvement.

This process essentially employs data profiling techniques to review data, identify potential anomalies, contribute to the specification of data quality dimensions and corresponding metrics, and recommend operational processes for data quality inspection. The process involves these five steps:

1. Planning for data quality assessment
2. Evaluating business process
3. Preparing for data profiling
4. Profiling and analyzing
5. Synthesizing results

Connecting potential data issues to business impacts and considering the scope of those relationships allow the team to prioritize discovered issues. The data quality assessment report documents the drivers, the process, the observations, and recommendations from the data profiling process, as well as recommendations relating to any discovered or verified anomalies that have critical business impact, including tasks for identifying and eliminating the root cause of the anomaly. Some suggestions might include:

- Inspection and monitoring
- Additional (deeper) review of the data
- One-time cleansing
- Review of data model
- Review of application code
- Review of operational process use of technology
- Review of business processes

The data quality assessment is the lynchpin of the data quality program, because it baselines the existing state, provides hard evidence as to the need, and suggests measures for inspecting data quality moving forward. In turn, the process can be used to evaluate whether the costs associated with data quality improvement would provide a reasonable return on the investment. Either way, this repeatable assessment provides tangible results that can either validate perceptions of poor data quality or demonstrate that the data meets business needs.

20.2.7 Remediation and Improvement Processes

The data quality assessment process will reinforce the existence of some issues, uncover some new issues, and generally add to a growing list of data issues identified and reported by data consumers as the issues manifest themselves during business operations. Although the solutions to some issues appear to be intractable, there are often some "quick wins" that address immediate issues having critical business impact, whereas other issues suggest a set of data quality assertions that require continuous monitoring and control. Either way there must be some process for the data quality practitioners to evaluate and prioritize appropriate actions to be taken.

Chapter 12 provided guidance for the triage and root cause analysis tasks performed by data quality practitioners when data issues are identified and logged in a data quality incident tracking system. Each identified data issue can be prioritized in relation to a number of variables, including severity, impact, and feasibility of resolution. The practitioner can then determine the most appropriate actions to take. This process includes these stages:

- Triage: Evaluating and assessing the issue and determining the scope and extent of the problem from both a business impact perspective and from an operational perspective
- Review of information production flow: Mapping how the data from the raw data sources is transformed into the customer information product
- Root cause analysis: Reviewing the information process map to determine the likely locations for the source of introduction of the problem
- Corrective measures: Determining strategies for immediately addressing critical problems
- Preventive measures: Researching strategies for eliminating the root causes
- Execution: Planning and applying operational aspects, including data correction, monitoring, and prevention

The objective of remediation and improvement planning is to evaluate the criticality of reported and logged data issues, and prioritize the most effective ways to address those errors. Formalizing the different tasks to perform when issues of different levels of criticality occur will reduce the effort for remediation while speeding the time to resolution. When a data quality issue has been identified, the triage process will take into account these aspects of the identified issue:

- **Criticality:** The degree to which the business processes are impaired by the existence of the issue
- **Frequency:** How often the issue has appeared
- **Feasibility of correction:** The likelihood of expending the effort to correct the results of the failure
- **Feasibility of prevention:** The likelihood of expending the effort to eliminate the root cause or institute continuous monitoring to detect the issues

The triage process is performed to understand these aspects in terms of the business impact, the size of the problem, as well as the number of individuals or systems affected. Triage enables the data quality practitioner to review the general characteristics of the problem and business impacts in preparation for assigning a level of severity and priority. Then, presuming one has reviewed the options to eliminate the root cause, institute inspection process, (or any other options for addressing the issue), the next step is a decision to move forward. As with all business activities, it is critical to make sure that the steps to be taken are properly planned so that progress and success can be measured in alleviating the pain introduced by the data issue.

Evaluating criticality helps in determining where to get the best bang for the data quality management buck. At the same time, picking the low-hanging fruit not only helps concentrate efforts for data quality improvement, it establishes credibility across the organization by reducing the time necessary for resolving critical issues.

20.2.8 The Data Quality Service Level Agreement

Data governance processes are operationalized as the data quality practitioners establish procedures for data quality control, which enables the identification of emerging data issues and the workflows for remediation. Operational data quality management increases trust in the data by inserting data controls across each business application, and operational data governance combines the ability to identify data errors as early as possible with the process of initiating the activities necessary to address those errors to avoid or minimize any downstream impacts. This essentially includes notifying the right individuals to address the issue and determining if the issue can be resolved appropriately within an agreed-to time frame. Data inspections measure and monitor compliance with data quality rules, whereas service level agreements specify the reasonable expectations for response and remediation.

Note that data quality inspection differs from data validation. The data validation process reviews and measures conformance of data with a set of defined business rules, whereas inspection is an ongoing process to:

- Reduce the number of errors to a reasonable and manageable level,
- Enable the identification of data flaws along with a protocol for interactively making adjustments to enable the completion of the processing stream, and
- Institute a mitigation or remediation of the root cause within an agreed-to time frame.

A key component of governing data quality control is a service level agreement (from chapter 13, a data quality service level agreement [DQ SLA]), which will guide the monitoring of data quality levels as data is passed across different stages in the information production flow. For each of these articulation points within an information processing stream, we can define a DQ SLA incorporating a number of items:

- The location in the processing stream that is covered by the SLA
- The data elements covered by the agreement

- The business impacts associated with data flaws
- The data quality dimensions associated with each data element
- The expectations for quality for each data element for each of the identified dimensions
- The methods for measuring against those expectations
- The acceptability threshold for each measurement
- The individual to be notified in case the acceptability threshold is not met
- The times for expected resolution or remediation of the issue
- The escalation strategy when the resolution times are not met

Defining a DQ SLA for operational data governance employs the methods for measuring conformance to business expectations coupled with notifications sent to the appropriate data stewards when specific data issues are identified because acceptability thresholds are not met. Business policies that constrain or manage the way that business is performed, and each business policy may loosely imply data definitions, information policies, and even data structures and formats. The DQ SLA embodies the techniques for ensuring conformance to those information policies, and in turn, the business policies from which the information policies were derived, and the operational data governance procedures provide a tangible means for validating compliance to business needs.

Reverse engineering the relationship between business impacts and the associated data rules provides data quality metrics that can be rolled up into a data quality scorecard for managing operational data governance. Chapter 13 discusses how this is effectively managed using a data quality scorecard that communicates:

- The qualified oversight of data quality along business lines,
- The degree of levels of trust in the data in use across the application infrastructure, and
- The ability for data stewards to drill down to identify the area of measurement that contributes most to missed expectations.

Processes for defining data quality service level agreements and corresponding metrics can provide a collection of statistics whose resulting scores can be communicated to the stakeholders via a dashboard or scorecard. A quick glance can either show that the business processes are in control and that the data is of a predictable level of acceptable quality or reveal that there are immediate issues to be addressed. The data quality team will work with the business users to integrate the hierarchies of data quality expectations and rules into the scorecard and enable drill-through to track down specific issues that impact organizational data. These operational workflows will then provide an auditable process for governing the quality of organizational data.

20.3 Techniques and Tools

In the third section we looked at the types of tools, techniques, algorithms, and other technologies that are employed to support the data quality processes described in part 2. This includes data profiling, parsing and standardization, identity resolution, auditing and monitoring, data enhancement, and master data management.

20.3.1 Data Profiling

Data profiling incorporates a collection of analysis and assessment algorithms that provide empirical insight about potential data issues, and has become a ubiquitous set of tools employed for data quality processes supporting numerous information management programs, including assessment, validation, metadata management, data integration processing, migrations, and modernization projects. Chapter 14 discussed analyses and algorithms profiling tools employ and how those analyses provide value in a number of application contexts. Profiling plays a part in some relatively straightforward analytic techniques that, when combined, shed light on the fundamental perspective of information utility for multiple purposes, such as:

- **Data reverse engineering:** Data reverse engineering is used to review the structure of a data set for which there is few or no existing metadata or for which the existing metadata are suspect for the purpose of discovering and documenting the actual current state of its metadata. Data profiling is used to grow a knowledge base associated with data element structure and use. Column values are analyzed to determine if there are commonly used value domains, to reveal whether those domains map to known conceptual value domains, to review the size and types of each data element, to identify any embedded pattern structures associated with any data element, and to identify keys and how those keys are used to refer to other data entities. The metadata discovered as a result of this reverse engineering process can be used facilitate dependent development activities such as business process renovation, enterprise data architecture, or data migrations.

- **Anomaly analysis:** There is often little visibility into data peculiarities in relation to existing data dependencies, especially when data sets are reused. Profiling is used to establish baseline measures of data set quality, even distinct from specific downstream application uses. Anomaly analysis is a process for empirically analyzing the values in a data set to look for unexpected behavior to provide that initial baseline review and is used to reveal potentially flawed data values, data elements, or records. Discovered flaws are typically documented and can be brought to the attention of the business clients to determine whether each flaw has any critical business impact.
- **Data quality rule discovery:** The need to observe dependencies within a data set manifests itself through the emergence (either by design or organically through use) of data quality rules. In many situations, though, there is no documentation of the rules for a number of reasons. Data profiling can be used to examine a data set to identify and extract embedded business rules, whether they are intentional but undocumented, or purely unintentional. These rules can be combined with predefined data quality expectations, as described in chapter 9, and used as the targets for data quality auditing and monitoring.
- **Metadata compliance and data model integrity:** The results of profiling can also be used as a way of determining the degree to which the data actually observes any already existent metadata, ranging from data element specifications, validity rules associated with table consistency (such as uniqueness of a primary key). The results can also be used to demonstrate that referential integrity constraints are enforced properly in the data set.

Review chapter 14 to see how data profiling tools are engineered and how they support aspects of the data quality program. When evaluating data profiling products, it is valuable to first assess the business needs for a data profiling tools (as a by-product of the data requirements analysis process and determination of remediation as described in chapters 9 and 12). In general, when evaluating data profiling tools, consider these capabilities discussed in chapter 14:

- Column profiling
- Cross-column (dependency)
- Cross-table (redundancy)
- Structure analysis
- Business rules discovery
- Business rules management

- Metadata management
- Historical tracking
- Proactive auditing
- Business rule importing
- Business rule exporting
- Metadata importing
- Metadata exporting

20.3.2 Parsing and Standardization

Proactive data quality management concentrates on inspection, monitoring, and ultimately prevention. However, there are certain situations where individuals are prevented from exercising immediate control in order to address errors. A frequent example is when business applications rely on data that originates from external providers, such as:
- Data acquired from third-party data aggregators,
- Data entered by external parties, and
- Data automatically created and provisioned via straight-through processing.

Even if one can identify a potential error, it may be difficult to prevent those errors from being brought into the data systems. So when there is a need for the data values to conform to specific internal expectations, some action must be taken to bring the data into alignment with the organizational standards. To maintain high quality data, the data management practitioner may need to resort to data cleansing, in which nonstandard data values are changes into ones that meet expectations.

Chapter 15 discussed methods used for cleansing, particularly parsing and standardization, techniques that are combined to scan data values, compare them to known value domains, formats, and patterns to:
- Map values to standard formats,
- Identify errors,
- Potentially correct recognized errors,
- Standardize value representations, and
- Normalize data values.

Understanding the common error paradigms sheds light on how some of those errors can be identified and then corrected. This information should be incorporated as "error metadata" used to limit the scope of introduced errors; that metadata is used by parsing and standardization utilities to normalize data. Parsing and standardization are not limited to cleansing after the fact; these techniques can be designed and integrated into the application framework to help identify potential errors as data enters the environment. Even when the data comes from beyond the organization's administrative control, being able to present recognized anomalies to the originating source can help block data errors as a data quality firewall and prevent those errors from impeding the information production flow.

Although parsing identifies recognizable tokens belonging to a specific element type as well as those that are not recognized, standardization maps both the valid and invalid tokens to their semantic meanings, and when errors are found, the tools suggest options for transformation into a standard form. There are two basic tasks:

1. Rearrange recognized token sets into a standard format
2. Identify known errors and correct them

Data cleansing is an important part of information management, although we would hope that a good data quality program could finesse the need for ongoing data cleansing. Common error paradigms such as attribute granularity, format conformance, and a discussion of other common errors like finger flubs, transcription errors, transformation errors, and the problems associated with information appearing in the wrong context, motivate the discovery of approaches for recognizing and automatically correcting data errors. Approaches to automation enable data cleansing applications, including data correction, data standardization, expansion of abbreviations, and the application of business rules.

Though it is not the immediate first choice for the practitioner, data cleansing using parsing and standardization will improve data quality when the creation point is outside of the organization's administrative control. Parsing and standardization services that are shared across the enterprise can be invoked early in the information production flow and help to identify and correct errors before their impacts can be incurred at the downstream points of use.

20.3.3 Identity Resolution

Customer data integration projects, "householding," master product catalogs, security master projects, and enterprise master patient indexes are all examples of technology-driven projects intended to resolve multiple data sets containing similar information into a unified view. The desire for unifying entity data suggests that data consolidation is a common component of data integration and data cleansing projects, whose successes depend on the ability to determine when different data instances in the same (or other) data sets refer to the same real world entity.

Searching through data sets for matching records that represent the same party or product is the key to the data consolidation process, whether it is for a data cleansing effort, a householding exercise for a marketing program, or for an enterprise initiative such as master data management.

However, a natural by-product of a number of data quality processes is the exposure of unintended and undesired duplication of records referring to unique entities. At the same time, multiple data source may be combined when it is known that they share similar data about the same real-world objects. Both of these imply the need for smarter approaches for finding similar records referring to the same entity.

This is accomplished by using *identity resolution*, which is a collection of algorithms including parsing, standardization, normalization, and then similarity scoring and comparing records to determine when two (or more) records resolve to a unique entity. The techniques used in this process are critical for any business applications that rely on customer or product data integration as part of a data quality assurance, data cleansing, master data management, or enterprise information management initiative. Identity resolution actually addresses two interesting data integration challenges:

1. Determining when two records refer to the same real-world object; or
2. Accurately determining when two records *do not* refer to the same real world object.

Without being able to make that clear connection or distinction, it would be difficult if not impossible to identify potential duplicate records within and across data sets. But automating the matching process presents some challenges, especially in the presence of semistructured or unstructured data values, data errors, misspellings, or words that are out of order. The existence of variable meanings of values appearing in free-formed text attributes also raises the question as to how automated algorithms can parse and organize values and determine which entities are represented, how many times and different ways, and how their identities can be distinguished or resolved.

Automated identity resolution requires techniques for approximate matching that compare a variety of entity characteristics in a search for similarity. And knowing that automated identity resolution for record linkage is purely based on the fact that errors creep into the data set and prevent straightforward matching algorithms from working, we need more complex means for determining when there are enough *similar* data values shared between two records so that the practitioner can reasonably presume that the records refer to the same entity.

The approximate matching process employs a number of strategies for similarity scoring, which measures the conceptual distance between two sets of values. The smaller the distance between two sets, the more similar those two records are to each other. For each data type or data domain, we assign a similarity function. For each set of data attributes, one may also provide a weight to be factored in when computing an overall similarity or difference score. Chapter 16 describes a number of approaches and factors for similarity scoring and matching and how those methods are combined to automate record linkage. Ultimately, identity resolution measures the degree of similarity between any two records, often based on weighted approximate matching between a set of attribute values, and compares the score against a "match" threshold, above which a presumed match is indicated.

The selection of an identity resolution tool must be accompanied by a process to analyze the suitability of entity data elements as candidate identifying attributes. This assessment must observe how well each attribute contributes to entity differentiation and unique identification. In turn, identity resolution applies the approximate matching techniques and recognizes when different records may be connected, even in the presence of slight variations.

20.3.4 Auditing, Monitoring, and Tracking

Auditing and monitoring are two methods for evaluating and reporting compliance of a data set with data quality expectations. Auditing is performed on complete data sets, isolated from other processing activities, outside of any information processing flow. Monitoring identifies rule noncompliance in process, as part of the operational system. Both auditing and monitoring indicate a greater level of data quality maturity, because both processes are proactive in early detection of potential flaws. They depend on defined data quality rules and tools employed to validate the data values against these defined rules; they notify the appropriate stakeholders when an exception has been identified.

Looking at the operational technology requirements, a combination of methods, tools, and techniques are used as part of the process for instituting the inspection and monitoring necessary for observing the SLA:

- IP-MAPs, which are information production maps describing how information flows from the initial introduction points to the ultimate data consumers, as described in chapter 12

- Metadata management, which captures information about data elements and their use, as discussed in chapter 10
- Data quality business rules, which use dimensions of data quality, as described in chapter 8
- Data profiling, as presented in chapter 14
- Business intelligence tools, which are ways of reporting data issues within a prioritization scheme
- Incident management (incident reporting and tracking)

Chapter 17 looks at automating inspection and monitoring, because automating the inspection will simplify the role of the data stewards, allowing them to prioritize issues as they emerge and concentrate on remediating the most critical ones. Controls for inspecting data value quality can be integrated directly into the business processes. Controls for collections of data instances or one or more data sets require the availability of the data to be reviewed, and without the ability to manage persistent state, would only allow the inspection to be performed when all the data items are available, such as when there is a bulk exchange between processing stages.

Many organizations already have a framework in place for incident reporting, tracking, and management, so the transition to instituting data quality issues tracking focuses less on tool acquisition and more on integrating the concepts around the "families" of data issues into the incident hierarchies and training staff to recognize when data issues appear and how they are to be classified, logged, and tracked. The steps in this transition are:

- Standardizing data quality issues and activities;
- Providing an assignment process for data issues, which will be based on the data governance framework from the organizational standpoint, and on the data quality SLAs from an operational standpoint;
- Managing issue escalation procedures, which should be explicit in the DQ SLAs;
- Documenting accountability for data quality issues, in relation to the data stewards assigned to the flawed data sets;
- Managing data quality resolution, also part of operational data governance; and
- Capturing data quality performance metrics.

A good issues tracking system will eventually become a reference source of current and historic issues, their statuses, and any factors that may need the actions of others not directly involved in the resolution of the issue. Data quality incident management combines different technologies to enable proactive management of existing, known data quality rules derived from both the data requirements analysis and the data quality assessment processes, including data profiling, metadata management, and rule validation. Incident management enables the collection of knowledge about data quality issues and bolsters the data steward's ability to prioritize issues, notify the right stakeholders, and take the right actions to ensure that the data meet business needs.

20.3.5 Data Enhancement

Data enhancement is a process of increasing the value of a data instance (or data set) by appending additional value-added knowledge. Enhancement links multiple data sets to pool information from multiple sources, with the intention of identifying actionable knowledge from the combined data. Enhancement can be used to learn more about entities using data taken from a set of databases, and potentially increase the quality of a given data set.

Traditionally, many opportunities for enhancement took place at some unspecified time and place downstream from the creation or integration of the records being enhanced. Increasingly, the need for integrating real-time analytics and predictive analysis within business present opportunities for introducing enhancements directly into the information production streams. There are two approaches for enhancement: enhancing data in batch and enhancing data within the structure of an operational business process.

The results of enhancement can only be trusted under the presumption that the source data sets are of sufficient quality to meet business objectives. In some instances, there is a predisposition to consolidate data from multiple sources without assessing their quality first, and this typically leads to questionable results. Yet this process cannot be performed effectively without qualifying the expectations as well as the source data. Before combining data sets, consider these questions:

1. How do business processes benefit from enhancement?
2. What data characteristics are to be improved as a result of enhancement?
3. What business questions are answered as a result of enhancement?
4. What decisions are enabled as a result of enhancement?
5. What source data attribute values are required to satisfy the business process requirements?
6. What source data attributes are required for matching and linkage?
7. Do the source data attributes meet the business expectations?

Fortunately, the data quality principles and processes presented in this book (data quality assessment, profiling, as well as the components of data validation and cleansing) can be used to answer these questions.

20.3.6 Master Data Management

Application architectures designed to support the operational aspects of each line of business have required their own information technology support, and all its accoutrements – data definitions, data dictionaries, table structures, application functionality, and so on, all defined from the aspect of that business application. The result is that the "enterprise" is often a mirage, and instead is a collection of many applications referring to multiple, sometimes disparate sets of data that are intended to represent the same or similar business concepts.

There is a growing desire to consolidate common data concepts from multiple sources, analyze that data, and ultimately turn it into actionable knowledge to benefit the common good. To exploit consolidated information for both operational and analytical processes, an organization must be able to clearly determine what those commonly used business concepts are, identify the different ways those concepts are represented, collect and integrate that data, and then make that data available across the organization. Organizing, integrating, and sharing enterprise information is intended to create a truly integrated enterprise, and this is the challenge of what is known as master data management (MDM): integrating tools, people, and practices to organize an enterprise view of the organization's key business information objects, and to govern their quality, use, and synchronization and use that unified view of the information to achieve the organization's business objectives.

Master data objects are those core business objects that are used by and shared among the different applications across the organization, along with their associated metadata, attributes, definitions, roles, connections, and taxonomies. Master data objects are those key "things" that we value the most – the things that are logged in our transaction systems, measured and reported on in our reporting systems, and analyzed in our analytic systems.

A master data system comprising a master data set is a (potentially virtual) registry or index of uniquely identified entities with their critical data attributes synchronized from the contributing original data sources and made available for enterprise use. With the proper governance and oversight, the data in the master data system (or repository, or registry) can be qualified as a unified and coherent data asset that all applications can rely on for consistent high quality information.

Master data management is a collection of data management best practices associated with both the technical oversight and the governance requirements for facilitating the sharing of commonly used master data concepts. MDM incorporates policies and procedures to orchestrate key stakeholders, participants, and business clients in managing business applications, information management methods, and data management tools. Together, these methods and tools implement the policies, procedures, services, and infrastructure to support the capture, integration, and subsequent shared use of accurate, timely, consistent, and complete master data.

An MDM program is intended to support an organization's business needs by providing access to consistent views of the uniquely identifiable master data entities across the operational application infrastructure. Master data management governs the methods, tools, information, and services to:

- Assess the use of commonly used information objects, collections of valid data values, and explicit and implicit business rules in the range of applications across the enterprise;
- Identify core information objects relevant to business success that are used in different application data sets that would benefit from centralization;
- Instantiate a standardized model for integrating and managing those key information objects;
- Manage collected and discovered metadata as an accessible, browsable resource and use it to facilitate consolidation;
- Collect data from candidate data sources, evaluate how different data instances refer to the same real-world entities, and create a unique, consolidated view of each real-world entity;
- Provide methods for transparent access to the unified view of real-world data objects for both existing and newly developed business applications; and
- Institute the proper data stewardship and management policies and procedures at the corporate and line-of-business levels to ensure the high quality of the master data asset.

Master data management is occupying a growing space in the mind share for data quality and data governance, and warrants further investigation as a critical component of a data quality management program.

20.4 Summary

Data quality management has evolved from a tools-oriented set of IT activities to a managed and governed set of best practices for data management. Hopefully, this book provides a basic overview of ways to successfully identify the business value of data quality management, socialize those ideas among key stakeholders, engender support from senior sponsors, and then execute against a well-defined program plan. Following the guidance in this book should result in a democratization of data management best practices across the organization, thereby improving data quality, strengthening business processes, and naturally, giving your organization a competitive edge!

ع

INDEX

Note: Page numbers followed by *b* indicate boxes, *f* indicate figures and *t* indicate tables.

enforcing, 205–206
established, 169
in maturity model, 47
organization, 156, 355
stewards and, 123
Statement of concept, 185
Statistical analysis, 151
Statistical process control (SPC),
99–101, 109–110
Statistical variance, 202
Stewards, 28–29, 119
Data Coordination Council
and, 120
data profiling and, 256–257
nomination of, 121
role of, 122–124
Stewardship, 122–125
MDM and, 330
services, 348, 349*t*
standardized view of, 83
Storage
locations, 196
redundant, 220
Structural consistency, 132, 137,
162, 364
business rules and, 305
dimensions, 137*t*
Subjectivity, 4
Success criteria, 220–223
Survivorship, 291–293
golden record and, 331
monitoring, 293
Synonyms, 182–183, 251
Syntactics
consistency, cross-table
anomalies and, 251
embedded structure
analysis and, 249
differences, 247
System development life cycle
(SDLC), 25
Systems
building v. buying, 61–62
business intelligence, 63–64
data warehousing, 63–64
design, 169
developers, 29
development risks, 7
ERP, 61

ongoing maintenance, 170
proprietary, 64
upgrade requirements, 170

T
Tables
analysis, 200–201
code, 195–196
reference, 178, 179*t*
rules, 163, 164*t*
Target models, 159
Taxonomies, 329
Techniques, 373–382
Technology, 41
component maturity
description for, 51*t*
in maturity model, 48
requirements, 300–304
standardization, 84
Temporal data, 316–317
Third-party data aggregators,
261
Thresholds, 133, 289–291.
See also Acceptability
thresholds
acceptance, 134
conformance, 134, 135
match/no-match, 290
Timeliness, 133, 141, 364
dimensions, 143*t*
Timestamps, 156, 321
Tokens, 266–268, 376
descriptions, 272
error, 269–270, 272
name, 270
types, 267–268
Tools, 373–382
Tracing, 316
Tracking tools, 378–380
Traffic data, 316
Training, 357
materials, 57
staff, 37
Transaction hub, 340, 341–342,
342*f*
Transaction processing, 153, 220
Transactions, 1
lost, 5
systems

sales, 4
value of information in, 3
Transformations, 162, 273–274
business rules, 305
as inspection point, 304
integrating, into framework,
277
intermediate, 365
recommending, 272–275
Transpositions, 289
Triage, 207, 208–212, 370
Trustworthiness, 97, 126*t*, 361
lineage and, 135
Tuning, 83–84
Type determination, 246

U
UCL. *See* Upper control limit
Underbilling, 8–9
Unified view, 331
Unique entity identification,
282–283
Uniqueness
analysis, 251
challenge of, 281–282
column analysis and, 245
cross-column rules and, 254
need for, 283–284
Upper control limit (UCL), 105
USA PATRIOT Act, 6
Usage scenarios, 172
User community, 122

V
Validation, 40, 125–126
constraints, 2
inspections and, 205–206, 227
IP-MAP and, 213
manual, 307
ongoing, 126
points, 196
of reference data, 201
requesting, 125
rules, 23, 247–248, 355
stewards and, 41
systems, 107–108
Value gap, 69
characterizing, 351–352
estimating, 76–79